DELIBERATING GHANA

DELIBERATING GHANA

Postcolonial Rhetorics, Culture, and Democracy

Stephen Kwame Dadugblor

MICHIGAN STATE UNIVERSITY PRESS | *East Lansing*

Michigan State University Press
East Lansing, Michigan 48823-5245

Library of Congress Cataloging-in-Publication Data
Names: Dadugblor, Stephen Kwame, author.
Title: Deliberating Ghana : postcolonial rhetorics, culture, and democracy / Stephen Kwame Dadugblor.
Other titles: Rhetoric of power and protest.
Description: East Lansing : Michigan State University Press, 2025. |
Series: Rhetoric of power and protest | Includes bibliographical references and index.
Identifiers: LCCN 2024038776 | ISBN 9781611865325 (paperback) | ISBN 9781609177829 | ISBN 9781628955453
Subjects: LCSH: Rhetoric—Political aspects—Ghana. | Democracy—Ghana. |
Contested elections—Ghana. | Deliberative democracy—Ghana. | Ghana—Politics and government—2001–
Classification: LCC P301.5.P67 D33 2025 | DDC 320.01409667—dc23/eng/20240819
LC record available at https://lccn.loc.gov/2024038776

Rhetoric of Power and Protest
Series Editors: Leroy Dorsey and Shawn Parry-Giles

Cover art: A political talk program in Ghana, courtesy of Fish TV

Visit Michigan State University Press at *www.msupress.org*

For Juliana, John, Micky, Ella, and Senam

Contents

ix Acknowledgments
xiii Introduction

1 CHAPTER 1. Deliberating Speech: Colonial Legacies and the Paradoxes of Political Participation
33 CHAPTER 2. Deliberating Genre: Oral Testimonies and the Rhetorical Work of Documentary Evidence
61 CHAPTER 3. Deliberating Participation: Digital Publics and Analogue Political Realities
93 CHAPTER 4. Deliberating Memory: Contested Remembering, National Identity, and the Re/production of Postcolonial Histories

125 Conclusion
133 Appendix
139 Notes
165 Bibliography
179 Index

Acknowledgments

A book—an academic book, for that matter—is rarely the product of a single, isolated mind. This book is no different. I have benefited tremendously from the guidance, advice, and support of so many people. I would like to thank them for their continued support throughout the years. Trish Roberts-Miller, Rob Asen, Clay Spinuzzi, Jacqueline Henkel, and Rasha Diab have all contributed in myriad ways to sharpening the ideas developed in these pages. So too have JWells, Kiara Walker, Justin Hatch, Rhiannon Goad, Jeremy Smyczek, Hannah Harrison, and several others. In the book's earliest iteration and when the arguments that would be developed here were still inchoate, these mentors and colleagues helped me imagine the bigger picture and see why the work I do matters. They connected me to people and resources, made time to read drafts, helped me think through complicated ideas, and encouraged me in pursuit of my scholarship. I am grateful for their generosity of spirit and their contribution to my life as a scholar.

At MSU Press, I thank Shawn Parry-Giles and Leroy Dorsey for creating a space for this book. As series editors, Shawn and Leroy saw the potential of this book and were enthusiastic of it from the beginning. They provided prompt and valuable feedback that greatly shaped the arguments. Shawn especially shared useful tips necessary particularly for a first-time author, saving me much time and effort. I thank Catherine Cocks and Caitlin Tyler-Richards who both provided support during the acquisition stage. Elizabeth Demers offered valuable guidance through the process, and Liz Deegan was patient in answering my numerous questions. The two reviewers offered generous and supportive feedback that greatly improved the work. I am thankful to them for their labor. Others at the press, including Kristine Blakeslee, Nicole Utter, Anastasia Wraight, and other members of the production team provided crucial editing, production, and marketing support without which this book would not have been out in the world. They deserve very special thanks.

Audiences at conferences, seminars, and talks—including the Rhetoric Society of America Conference, the Conference on College Composition and Communication Annual Conventions, RhetCanada, and others—asked challenging questions that helped me refine ideas. I appreciate, in particular, participants in the RSA Summer Institute seminar on "Decolonizing Comparative Global Rhetorics" who generously shared thoughtful suggestions as I completed the manuscript.

At the University of British Columbia, several colleagues including Jackie Rea and Kamal Al-Solaylee have been supportive of my scholarship. I have also been inspired by my fantastic friends and colleagues Alexis McGee and Louis Maraj. Through our regular writing group sessions, Alexis and Lou helped create community that made my life of writing a pleasurable experience. They also gave freely of their time and resources and provided useful feedback that enhanced the manuscript. The game nights and casual conversations were truly enriching, and I am thankful for the gift of friendship and camaraderie they continue to offer beyond work.

Other friends have been with me on this journey. They have commented on drafts, helped me clarify thorny ideas knowingly and unknowingly, and acted as sounding boards for brainstorming ideas as I completed the work. In conversations on all things political, and especially on Africa's place in the world, they have shared critical insights. I am indebted to these and many other friends, including Kundai Chirindo, Elias Adanu, Selikem Gotah, Isidore Dorpenyo, Ignatius Suglo, Smith Oduro-Marfo, David Ackuaku, Christian Bruku, Hermann von Hesse, Max Bogpene, Marcel Okorie, and Atchere Asuah-Kwasi. I am grateful, as well, to Kyenkyenhene Boateng for his assistance in helping to obtain permission for this book's cover photo from Fish TV. Through its Scholarly Publication Fund, the University of British Columbia provided financial support to cover some of the costs of publishing this book. I owe special thanks to all who make this funding possible.

The support of my family has been unqualified. My parents, Juliana and John, have always believed in my capabilities and provided much needed resources to equip me. I cannot thank them enough for their sacrifices throughout the years. My siblings Micky and Ella are unwavering in cheering me on and looking out for me. Not even distance attenuates their love and presence, and for all that they do to make my life and work possible, I am eternally thankful to them. Finally, to the Keeper of the Affections, Senam Ntow, you continue to believe in my abilities and give meaning to it all. Your love has made every bit of it bearable. *Melɔ̃ wò.*

Parts of chapter 4 previously appeared as Stephen Kwame Dadugblor, "Stories and/as Civic Pedagogies: Toward Participatory Knowledge-Making in Cultural Rhetorics," *College Composition and Communication* 75, no. 1 (2023): 137–151. They are reprinted here by permission of the publisher (National Council of Teachers of English [NCTE]).

Introduction

It was December 7, 2012, when voters in Ghana went to the polls to elect presidential and parliamentary candidates for another four-year term. Like some of its continental neighbors, Ghana had experienced alternating periods of democratic and military rule since becoming politically independent of British colonialism; in 1957, it was the first country south of the Sahara to do so. Despite military interventions in politics in the succeeding decades, a new epoch of multiparty democracy heralded by national elections in 1992 proved sustainable. By 2012 national elections had been held for six successive cycles with hardly any major incidents recorded. For observers of politics within and beyond, this electoral consistency signaled Ghana's commitment to entrenching democratic rule. And for a country that proclaims itself in trailblazing terms like the "Gateway to Africa" and the "Black Star of Africa," it was unsurprising that some would expect Ghana to live up to its reputation as an exemplar, yet again, of a stable democracy to continental peers.[1]

But Election 2012 was historic for reasons other than those of continental and or global acclaim. First, only five months prior, in July, Vice President John Mahama of the National Democratic Congress party assumed office as president following the sudden death in office of the incumbent, Professor John Evans Atta Mills. When Mahama subsequently won the NDC's nomination to run for president in Mills's stead, he found himself contesting against seven other candidates, all of whom had been on the campaign trail for months. From a presidential campaign standpoint, this late-game entry would seem to pose potential challenges for Mahama.

Second, Election 2012 marked an important development in the conduct of national elections in Ghana. Although previous elections had been generally deemed free and fair by both local and international election observers, the two major political parties in Ghana—the National Democratic Congress (NDC) and the New Patriotic Party (NPP)—frequently leveled accusations of electoral malpractice, overvoting, and a bloated roster of voters. To improve upon the integrity of the electoral process, Ghana's Electoral Commission (EC) adopted the use of biometric verification devices (BVDs) for the first time in Election 2012. The EC promoted the BVDs as an effective mechanism for reducing electoral fraud, minimizing voting irregularities, and increasing the credibility of the polls.[2] But the BVDs came with their own challenges on Election Day. Provided by an Israeli company, SuperLock Technologies Limited (STL), and intended for use primarily indoors, some BVDs malfunctioned because of tropical climatic conditions when they were deployed at outdoor polling stations.[3] Other BVDs simply did not serve their intended purpose because poorly trained electoral officials could not operate them. The malfunctioning of the BVDs interfered with the voter verification process and caused delays at the polls. To avoid the risk of widespread disenfranchisement, the EC uncharacteristically extended the voting period in affected polling stations to December 8.

Against this backdrop, when the EC finally announced results of the polls on December 9, handing the presidential victory to Mahama, there were mixed reactions from citizens on either side of the political aisle. The EC declared that Mahama had won 50.7 percent of the votes against the NPP's Nana Addo Dankwa Akufo-Addo's 47.7 percent.[4] Continental bodies like the Economic Community of West African States (ECOWAS) and an election observer group, the Electoral Institute for Sustainable Democracy in Africa (EISA), declared the elections free and fair. EISA, for instance, observed that despite some challenges (such as the late delivery of voting materials to polling stations), the polls, overall, "met regional, continental and international standards for credible and transparent elections." EISA appealed to stakeholders in the electoral process to "accept the outcome of the elections and to resort to the legally provided channels in the event that they want to challenge this outcome."[5] But Akufo-Addo's NPP alleged widespread electoral malpractices and consequently rejected the election results.

On December 28, the NPP and Akufo-Addo filed a suit at the Supreme Court of Ghana challenging the results in 4,709 polling stations. The NPP claimed their analysis of "pink sheets"—the Statement of Poll and Declaration of Results form—from more than 11,000 polling stations across the country revealed electoral irregularities that, if considered, would change the total tally in their favor. For the NPP, the choice to contest the EC's decision at the Supreme Court "will either affirm the commitment of citizens to our democratic journey and bolster their confidence in democratic institutions and the rule of law or undermine their belief in the political and legal institutions of the nation."[6] Four months of legal deliberations in court on procedural aspects of the case followed; during this time the nine-member panel constituting the court settled on two key, related issues to determine: (1) "whether or not there were statutory violations, omissions, irregularities, and malpractices in the conduct of the elections held on December 7 and 8, 2012," and (2) "whether or not the said violations, omissions, irregularities and malpractices (if any) affected the results of the elections."[7] Even as they followed through with these procedures, and to forestall an interregnum, the Supreme Court judges allowed the swearing-in of John Mahama as president on January 7, 2013, pending a decision on the case.

The deliberations proper began on April 16, 2013, with court sittings spanning between four and six hours daily for four days per week. In the landmark case that the hearings turned out to be, the court broke with traditional protocol and allowed live broadcast of the proceedings on television, radio, and the internet. For the first time, anyone who was willing and able to access the broadcast could gain first-hand knowledge of how one of the most important, yet exclusive, democratic institutions of the state operated. The law indeed is the mechanism by which governance is enforced, but except for moments when citizens encounter it, legal arguments, the world of lawyers and judges, and the operation of courts, can and often do remain an exclusive and exclusionary site of democracy for citizens. The transparency afforded by the televised proceedings therefore opened this consequential institution to the view of many citizens. As citizens tuned in, legal terms and arguments took on a more social character for them. Hard-to-parse legalese such as *amicus curiae*, *deposition*, and *preponderance of evidence* all entered popular parlance. Other expressions such as "I put it to you," "You and I were not there," and "I suggest to you that" became part of regular, everyday conversations. The work of the judiciary came to be demystified, allowing citizens to follow courtroom arguments in real time, develop their own informed perspectives on the case, and discuss the merits of the deliberations with others in the public sphere.

As one of these citizens, I grew increasingly interested in the deliberations, frequently assessing the arguments and making connections between the work of the judiciary and the power of rhetoric to shape the practice of democracy in Ghana. Amid the tense atmosphere that followed its eight months of deliberations, the court handed down its verdict on August 29, 2013: the dispute case, the ruling went, had no merit. The judges held that John Mahama had been duly elected president in the elections of December 7 and 8, 2012, and that although there were instances of electoral irregularities, those were not as significant as to change the overall results. Akufo-Addo disagreed with the verdict, but peacefully accepted it and called on his party supporters to do same.[8]

The novelty of the case—this being the first time an election dispute case was to be heard and televised in Ghana—raised in this postcolonial context both old and new questions about relations between the judiciary and citizens and among citizens in their practice of democracy.[9] Specifically, what kinds of public commentary are or should be allowed on the case? Are citizens' criticisms of the judiciary or judicial decisions contemptuous? What are the limits of the constitutional freedom of speech? How did the so-called pink sheets, the rather ordinary forms used to record electoral results, become such contentious objects of debate in court, representing and functioning as claims to evidence, authenticity, and truth? How are citizens to mobilize and deploy the affordances of digital media to engage democratically in a consequential process such as this? And how—in the aftermath—did the court deliberations figure in histories and memories of democratic practice in Ghana? These questions remain significant for considering ideas about rhetorical practices; the enduring effects of colonialism in postcolonial democracies; the link among political histories, memory, and democracy; and indeed, the possibilities and limits of thinking otherwise about democracy writ large. When considered within the postcolonial African context in which they unfold, these questions potentially expand our boundaries of theorizing about familiar ideas associated with democracy.

In making a case for the importance of this kind of boundary expansion work in theorizing social processes, Jean Comaroff and John Comaroff have observed that the Global South offers "privileged insight" into contemporary social life.[10] This privileged insight stems from the fact that "the history of the present world reveals itself more starkly" in the Global South, thereby inviting analytical pursuits that confront realities in such places.[11] As a testament to the politics of location in relation to knowledge production, Comaroff and Comaroff's call is important for (re)considering knowledge production about democracy in the postcolony. This is because although the Global South is today the site of novel articulations of sociopolitical processes, it is also at these same sites, Achille Mbembe reminds us, that gaps between such processes and conceptual assessments stand in need of further theorizing.[12] The relational dynamics of the colonial encounter makes postcolonial conditions not just a concern for the previously colonized but also a moment of reflection for previously and even now colonizing societies. My goal in this book then is not simply to add another study from the Global South in a way that keeps theoretical assumptions about rhetoric, democracy, and democratic deliberation intact and undisturbed. Rather, I aim to situate the Global South, the postcolony specifically, as a viable site of articulation of politics in relation to our knowledge-making about democracy writ large.

Deliberating Ghana: Postcolonial Rhetorics, Culture, and Democracy proceeds from this vantage point. It attends to the election dispute case and its connection to rhetoric and democratic deliberation, and it is concerned with the rhetorical dimensions of the deliberations about the case in court and in the public sphere. It is also about those deliberations culturally situated within the African (and specifically postcolonial Ghanaian) context in which they take place. Using deliberations about the case, I argue that a cultural imaginaries orientation offers a viable approach to decolonizing knowledge of democratic practice anchored particularly on Western epistemologies and conceptions. A cultural imaginaries orientation hinges on citizens' deliberative practices informed by their histories, politics, and sociocultural contexts. This orientation foregrounds democratic practice on a society's own terms; builds on the messiness of its histories, traditions, politics, and values; and responds to imperatives to unbalance its power structures. In a postcolonial African context, democratic practice remains frequently entangled in a matrix of colonial institutional legacies as well as local norms, expectations, and practices of political participation.

Democracy in a postcolonial African context operates as an unresolved and unresolvable tension between Western understandings of the concept (with its borrowed institutional and operational logics, practices, and values) and African conceptions of political participation and modes of practicing rhetoric.

As democracy scholar Jeffrey Paller has observed, traditional conceptions and values surrounding authority structures continue to inform the practice of democracy in postcolonial countries like Ghana.[13] Beyond a purist's clean distinctions between local and global conceptions, democratic practice here functions in an unresolvable tension that neither absolutely rejects a Western conception nor reverts to some version of a precolonial African mode of political participation. Instead, democratic practice here accounts for the influence of colonialism, while reframing and reformulating conceptions of democratic practice anchored exclusively on the society's terms, with all its perils and possibilities. Democratic practice here also challenges and expands canonical conceptions about what democracy should look like, offering us perspectives to (re)consider ideas associated with this form of government. I suggest that in examining democratic practice through a cultural imaginaries perspective, we can transform our understanding of concepts associated with rhetoric, democracy, and deliberation cross-culturally.

I foreground the postcolony as a viable site of inquiry to invite a reconsideration of often taken-for-granted assumptions about rhetoric, democracy, and democratic deliberation proceeding particularly from Western epistemologies. The complexities of the postcolonial condition call attention to sociopolitical and historical peculiarities that define how democracy has and can be reframed, reconfigured, and negotiated in light of the colonial encounter. As Christina Keating has convincingly argued, in India's postcolonial democracy, for example, the colonial encounter led to transformations in the country's practice of democracy along the axes of gender, caste, and minority status. The encounter reconfigured how Indians continually practice democracy along the lines of what she calls the country's racial and sexual contracts.[14]

Deliberating Ghana considers how such reconfigurations shape democratic practice in Ghana. It examines the ways that the enduring effects of colonialism inflect democratic practices surrounding freedom of speech, political participation across institutional and noninstitutional spaces, memory, and practices of evidence and knowledge production rooted in genres. The book shifts analytical attention to the possibilities and limits of thinking about democratic deliberation from the vantage point of the postcolony and ultimately toward decolonial possibilities. Those possibilities would refuse metanarratives often tethered to long histories of European colonialism about the nature and practice of rhetoric, democracy, and deliberation and expand perspectives on the forms and functions of power as it affects the lives of citizens.

Cultural Imaginaries, Democracy, and Democratic Deliberation

The idea of the (social) imaginary has been applied in a variety of fields, from psychology to anthropology to media studies, to discuss meaning-making in relation to sociopolitical action within societies.[15] The social theorist and philosopher Cornelius Castoriadis defines the term as a society's "creation of figures/forms/images" about its realities.[16] These meanings crystallize into a lens through which sociopolitical action in every society is read. Charles Taylor similarly explicates the term as "what enables, through making sense of, the practices of a society."[17] Damien Smith Pfister also puts a rhetorical spin on the idea, defining it as "how a culture imagines the role, function, features, norms, and values of communication."[18] Social imaginaries are therefore understood in the vernacular, whether that be of the societies of Europe or elsewhere. In building on these ideas of the social imaginary, I aim to work against the grain of grand narratives that say in understanding the world, Europe is central and all others are peripheral. I inflect the term with the modifier "cultural" to link the experience of democracy and democratic deliberation to political modernity understood in a specific postcolonial milieu—Ghana. Here, I follow scholars from across several diverse disciplines who have emphasized the cultural dimension to the term "social imaginary" to highlight its specificity to a collective or group rather than to society writ large.[19]

The postcolonial context referred to in this book consists of the national Ghanaian context, the nation as Benedict Anderson has theorized it: "an imagined political community . . . one that is imagined as both inherently limited and sovereign." Anderson asserts that in an imagined community, members "will never know most of their fellow-members, meet them, or even hear of them, yet in the minds of each lives the image of their communion."[20] In the postcolony, this communion is reflected in the shared sense of the postcolonial condition that has produced the nation-state and its political processes, in line with what Taylor would take to be "a wider grasp of our whole predicament."[21] In the context of national transformations following colonial rule, the cultural imaginary explicated in this book vis-à-vis democracy and democratic deliberation is understood to be reflected in shared perspectives in this postcolony.

I understand the postcolony not as the temporal end of colonialism (say, 1957, when Ghana formally became politically independent of Britain) but as the entanglements of colonial processes in the aftermath of colonialism. The postcolony takes "a critical orientation to colonialism and its legacies."[22] The assumption here is that within postcolonial societies, colonial processes shaped and are still embedded in sociopolitical phenomena, including democracy and deliberations about it. Further, although they may vary and are never homogeneous, these shared perspectives signal a strong sense of commonality of experience among citizens about the postcolonial condition. Such shared perspectives would constitute their national culture, which political philosopher Kwame Gyekye defines as "a culture whose meanings have become homogenized and can, thus, be said to be generally shared by all the citizens and considered as constituting the social context within which the individual citizen perceives herself as an individual with goals, hopes, aspirations, and life projects."[23] The nation does consist of multiple cultures, with their accompanying languages and traditions. However, the sense of culture articulated here encompasses the shared postcolonial condition that transcends ethnic boundaries and encompasses the nation-state as a bounded entity. A cultural imaginaries orientation works from this premise by highlighting the rhetorical practices and traditions of this delimited cultural context, emphasizes the rhetorical traditions and histories of a people, and inserts how those histories are lived into the analysis. The idea of the cultural imaginary articulated here privileges a conception of culture that is intersubjective and in which members share a sense of tradition, history, practices, and politics.

Deliberating Ghana also draws upon scholarship in (cultural) rhetorics and studies of democracy. Scholarship in cultural rhetorics continues to emphasize the need to study rhetorics in non-Western contexts on their own terms.[24] The impetus for this shift toward non-Western rhetorics is that normative understandings of rhetorical practices ought to be reconsidered particularly in light of democratization and globalization. For example, writing about critical communication studies, Raka Shome and Radha Hedge have observed that the notion of difference—encompassed by multiculturalism, nationhood, and cultural pluralism—proves challenging to the study of communication. For Shome and Hedge, a recognition of such difference necessitates a reconceptualization of long-held notions of identity and culture as they relate to nation, the Global North and Global South, and transnationalism.[25] This observation of the connection between culture, globalization, and critical communication is relevant for grappling with the study of democratic deliberation in non-Western societies beyond the boundaries of democracy's foundational underpinnings dominant in Western contexts.

Shome and Hedge's articulation of the notion of difference seems perhaps best reflected in cultural rhetorics scholarship that situates rhetorical practices within the specific cultural locales of their emergence. Rhetorical scholars Phil Bratta and Malea Powell provide one contextualization for such cultural rhetorics work, suggesting its goals as oriented toward "emphasiz[ing] rhetorics as always-already cultural and cultures as persistently rhetorical."[26] This culture-rhetoric dynamic allows room for conceptualizing rhetorical practices in any community at all (for all rhetoric is situated within culture) and avoids the pitfall of limiting cultural rhetorics work, as rhetorical scholar Casie Cobos et al. argue, to racialized and minoritized peoples.[27]

The point here may seem obvious, that insofar as rhetoric emerges from its cultural contexts of production and interpretation, it is necessarily cultural. But as a broad spectrum of scholarship continue to demonstrate, rhetorical studies has often tended to be Eurocentric in its approaches, methodologies, and epistemologies. The increased emphasis on the cultural dimensions of rhetorical practice derives from what has, for decades, been the field's default mode of inquiry: a point of departure for rhetorical inquiry rooted in Western epistemologies, methods, and theories. A reimagining of this status quo requires "a more situated scholarly practice," one that pays attention to "the particularity of rhetorical practices within specific cultural communities." Such a reimagination unmasks the unmarked position of scholarship that takes Western rhetorical practices as a given even in the study of other cultures. For the rhetorical critic, this reimagination involves "understanding a specific culture's systems, beliefs, relationships to the past, practices of meaning-making, and practices of carrying culture forward to future generations."[28] In short, it requires attention to what counts as rhetorical on a society's own terms.

Studying rhetoric on a society's own terms requires a methodological orientation that accounts for difference and particularity without essentializing.

As Omedi Ochieng has rightly argued, this means that any quest for authenticity, whether that be of national, ethnic, or racial essences, must be discarded in favor of a structural analysis. Such an analysis would emphasize the historicity, embeddedness, and relationality of rhetorical production. It would consider not just time and space (as articulated in Mikhail Bakhtin's idea of the *chronotope*), but time, space, and agency, or what Ochieng calls *chronotopia*. Paying attention to chronotopia involves an examination of the historical, institutional, and ideological influences that have shaped rhetorical phenomena. Moreover, in terms of a critic's position(ality) vis-à-vis the subject matter, studying rhetorical phenomena on a society's own terms entails setting aside "a *transcendental* point of view" in favor of a critical approach that privileges the entanglement of rhetorical phenomena within and across local and global politics and histories.[29]

The connection *Deliberating Ghana* draws between cultural rhetorics and democratic deliberation is premised on the linkages among democracy, culture, and deliberation. If cultural rhetorics attend to rhetoric in cultural contexts, then rhetorical studies of democracy are best situated within those cultural contexts. In order to broaden the foundational premises driving research on democratic practices in Western societies, scholars in disciplines as varied as anthropology, sociology, political science, and rhetoric have interrogated the cultural underpinnings of democracy and the need to understand democracy within cultural contexts. In this spirit, anthropologist of democracy Julia Paley asserts that the multiple meanings associated with democracy in different locales suggests that the term "is not a single condition that countries do or do not have, but rather a set of processes unevenly enacted over time."[30] Ralph Cintron also argues that democracy is "a kind of container containing millions of desires" and that rather than assume some universal abstraction, application, or applicability of the term, democracy ought to be "territorialized," or "grounded by the self-serving interests of nation-states."[31] The cultural imaginaries undergirding democracy ought therefore to inform research on how the societies we study understand democracy and practice it.

Cultural imaginaries can and do affect individuals' reception of democratic institutions and practices. In his essay "On Cultures of Democracy," Dilip Gaonkar suggests that when viewed from a Euro-American standpoint, the concept of democracy may be thought to be undeveloped, subpar, or altogether nonexistent in previously colonized societies. However, understanding the character—and practices—of democracy requires insight into "people's self-understandings, beliefs, and interpretations." Because "different societies generate interestingly different clusters of practices of democracy,"[32] I suggest that examining cultural imaginaries in relation to democracy provides a way out of normative understandings of democracy. One reason a study of such democratic character is warranted, Candice Rai maintains, is so that we can apprehend what constitutes the limitations of democracy and democratic rhetorics, and how the idea of democracy functions in context.[33] Rai cautions that critics must not take democracy or its goods as givens but should consider them creations and recreations embedded in societal systems, the rhetorical uses of which vary across time and space. Following Gaonkar and Rai, in this book, I approach the subjects of democracy and democratic deliberation, then, not as unchanging concepts but as context-driven and culturally contingent practices that respond to the sociocultural needs of a people, in this case those of postcolonial Ghana.

Although eminently important, elections alone do not make a democracy. Deliberations about democratic processes such as elections animate democracy with its force. The nexus between deliberation and cultural imaginaries is manifest in the "publicly accessible meanings, symbols, and norms [that] shape the way political actors engage one another in discourse."[34] Rather than a focus on an irresolvable universal or particular paradigm of understanding deliberation, it is important, as Jensen Sass and John S. Dryzek have argued, to conceive of the act of deliberation as a universal capacity to collectively weigh competing preferences for some common good, with "the character of deliberation . . . varying considerably across time and place."[35] Deliberation is cultural and depends on the rhetorical practices of specific communities. Indeed, the idea of cultural imaginaries I advance in this book is not to be taken as a deterministic, teleological mover of political action. Instead, it must be understood as the meanings determined by actors within a certain context as valuable for the performance of political action. This sense of the term is intersubjective and encompasses "the webs of meanings, symbols, and norms in terms of which action is constituted."[36]

Moreover, my goal in this book is not to make a claim of uniqueness qua uniqueness, nor to discover a distinctly verifiable rhetorical practice(s), unchanging and unchangeable with time, to which Ghanaians in general do subscribe. Such a perspective would reinscribe the same Eurocentric notions that cultural approaches to rhetorical studies seek to undo in the first place.

Rather, I propose to follow rhetorical scholar José Cortez's admonition to (Latin American) scholars of rhetoric. Cortez maintains that scholars risk reinforcing the same hegemonic discourses they set out to displace if they assert that rhetorical practices are unique solely based on their locus of enunciation. Thus, he urges moving from a politics of identity about (comparative) rhetoric toward one of subalternity grounded in *difference as such*.[37] This means turns to the local need not be tied to authenticity, but ought to be construed in interrelated terms. That interrelatedness is evident, for the postcolonial context, in the colonial encounter. In this respect, Cortez writes, "The figuration of exceptional difference, whether it be indigenous, hybrid, or hemispheric, can no longer simply be taken as a signified, bearing its own self-evident meaning in opposition to the West, for the positive content of what is considered 'non-Western' can only bear meaning differentially—as difference from the West."[38] There is a relationality here in terms of difference, understood as that between colonizer and colonized in the postcolony. Cortez's call for attention to *difference as such* appears to be in consonance with Ochieng's argument for a chronotopic approach that works against essentialism of any kind. Contextualizing democracy, rhetoric, and deliberation in this book as *different as such* helps position them in the postcolony vis-à-vis their embeddedness in, yet coconstitution with, Western understandings of the concepts.

Marking a Deliberative Terrain

Much of the existing research on democratic deliberation has focused largely on the normative assumptions of democracy as practiced in Western societies. These assumptions, however, are limited in explicating democracy's manifestations in all societies. Thus, by maintaining them for the study of democratic practices beyond Western societies, critics risk perpetuating universalizing narratives.[39] The paradigmatic shift necessary to tackle the study of deliberations about democracy invites an integration of the cultural sensibilities of non-Western societies in rhetorical studies. When Arabella Lyon discusses the need for this shift, she attends to the study of deliberation in cross-cultural, global contexts. In *Deliberative Acts: Democracy, Rhetoric, and Rights*, Lyon asserts that because foundational principles of democracy can no longer be adequately assumed for all societies in the wake of globalization across societies, difference looms large and must be given attention.[40]

This idea of difference in understanding democracy and deliberation is accounted for in the concept of *palabre* (or palaver) in African societies. African philosopher Jean Godefroy Bidima explains that palabre as a practice of deliberation in Africa rests on public "conversation" and discussion among citizens.[41] As a "traditional mechanism for conflict resolution and public decision making," palabre aims at the maintenance of social ties even amid dissensus.[42] It is firmly rooted in African epistemologies, and its goal in conflict resolution or deliberation is "not just to compensate or to sanction, but to restore the human relationship."[43] As Bidima puts it, against Western conceptions of deliberation about justice articulated in Michel Foucault's notion of "*discipline and punish*," palabre offers "discuss and redeem."[44] Despite its utility, palabre has become limited in public deliberation in African societies as political relations gain salience largely in terms of citizens' relations with the nation-state.[45] This reduction of the realms of politics means the *form* of palabre cannot usefully be conceived in contemporary African politics as a replacement for "technical governmental institutions"; however, palabre's *spirit* as "a model of critique and public dialogue that *keeps people together* even while they disagree" remains important for understanding politics on the continent.[46]

This spirit of palabre is bolstered by African agency in deliberation. In *Deliberative Agency: A Study of Modern African Political Philosophy*, Uchenna Okeja contends that in African societies, deliberation ought to be understood "as a process that aims to guarantee the enactment of agency as a core of political life."[47] For Okeja, consensus as a product of deliberation should not be the goal in studying African politics. Instead, understanding deliberation as an exercise of agency ensures an examination of the ever-evolving realm of politics.[48] Doing so also guarantees that explanations of African politics are not tied to era-specific political epistemologies such as negritude or African socialism.[49] In Okeja's view, the problem with such era-specific and episodic interventions is that they largely emphasize a problem-solution approach to interrogating African political experience in the wake of colonialism.[50] Deliberation conceived as an exercise of agency would affirm Africans' agency regardless of historical epoch or reigning political philosophies.

Thus, *Deliberating Ghana* intervenes to broaden studies of democratic deliberation by providing a culturally inflected perspective on democratic deliberation. It uses the election dispute case to meditate on the historical, political, and social realities of postcolonial Ghanaian society. The book accomplishes this task by examining issues of freedom of speech, evidence, modes of participation, and memory. The cultural imaginaries approach adopted deepens an understanding of the enduring legacy of colonialism that appears absent from many studies of democratic deliberation that emphasizes neither the enduring power of colonialism nor the agency of Africans in the study of these issues.

This book aims to make a number of scholarly contributions to studies of rhetoric and democratic deliberation. First, even as research on cultural approaches to rhetorical study continue to gain momentum, scholarly conversations on Africa's rhetorical traditions remain scant within the larger discipline of rhetoric. Unless one accounts for African American rhetorics, Africa-centric rhetorical traditions are largely undertheorized in the discipline of rhetoric.[51] This disciplinary gap is accentuated by studies that treat Africa as though it were a country, neglecting the diversity of spatio-temporal geographies, linguistic histories, and political legacies. Recent work such as Segun Ige, Gilbert Motsaathebe, and Omedi Ochieng's *A Companion to African Rhetoric* importantly contributes to addressing this gap by centering a diversity of African rhetorical knowledge.[52] In their discussion of possibilities for the emergent subfield of African rhetoric, Nancy Henaku and Ruby Pappoe advocate for serious engagement with African philosophies and rhetorics that eschews an "uncritical use of Western terminologies and methodologies."[53] They urge a break away from the all-too-common East-West binary that shapes much theorizing about the continent in favor of an emphasis on "sociohistorical contexts."[54]

Additionally, Yunana Ahmed's work on decolonial approaches to African rhetoric invites us to ground African rhetorical studies in cultural sensibilities encompassing the colonial ideologies underlining our theories and texts.[55] As Ahmed explains, a decolonial approach to analyzing African rhetoric demands analyses that are transdisciplinary and work against universalizing perspectives that proceed from particular canonical and disciplinary centers.[56] Moreover, Erik Johnson forwards a conceptual approach to studying African political phenomena that resists binaries by examining creolized forms of thought. Among others, such forms of thought combine "vernacular African epistemologies and Western political theories."[57] Furthermore, Omedi Ochieng highlights an infraconstitutive approach to studying African rhetorics, emphasizing the "historical, political, economic, and cultural vectors" that shape rhetorics on the continent.[58] Henaku and Pappoe's foregrounding of sociohistorical contexts and Ahmed's decolonial approach are respectively akin to Johnson's understanding of rhetorical phenomenon in the postcolony as creolized and Ochieng's infraconstitutive orientation; the latter two invite us to see African rhetoric for what it is—beyond "traditional versus the modern, the domestic versus the foreign, and the fake versus the real."[59] *Deliberating Ghana* joins and expands on these perspectives by positioning itself as an epistemological and decolonial project about the idea of rhetoric, democracy, and deliberation. It accomplishes this goal by deprovincializing Africa while simultaneously provincializing Euro-America in terms of rhetoric, democracy, and deliberation.[60]

Second, this book intervenes in rhetorical scholarship by examining the intricately intertwined connections between democratic practice and law especially in the postcolony. Law exerts enormous influences on democratic practice and creates a systemic framework within which democracy operates. As rhetorical scholar Daniel Emery notes of the controversy over the US presidential election in 2000, "Debates concerning the law and its just administration can and do determine our collective democratic future."[61] Emery asserts that given this link between legal practices and democratic culture, "reconsideration of the practices of forensic rhetoric is critical to understanding the role of discourse practices in contemporary political life."[62] Communication scholar Karen Tracy coined "ordinary democracy" to describe sites where lofty democratic ideals are actualized.[63] In addition to examining deliberations on digital public spheres as an instance of ordinary democracy, I interrogate deliberations in court during the dispute case to reveal how legal and institutional practices shape democratic practice. Ghana's judicial infrastructure, like many of the country's formal institutions, has deep roots in British colonialism. Thus, the culturally inflected nature of deliberations in court enables us to uncover important connections among legal and institutional expectations, political histories, and cultural imaginaries as they unfold in the postcolony.

Third, this book contributes to a theory of public spheres through its focus on deliberation. Extant scholarship on public spheres takes as normative the Westphalian state system that developed in Europe in the seventeenth century as the grounds for citizen engagement within imagined communities of nation-states. But state formation processes that emerged in contemporary African societies in the wake of the decolonization movements of the second half of the twentieth century have proceeded differently. They emerged in the wounds of the violence of colonialism and with consequences for citizens' relationship with the state and the practice of politics.[64] As I will demonstrate at length especially in chapter 3, the nature of the publics that emerged in the aftermath of the colonial encounter resist easy fits within the Westphalian system that undergirds many Western conceptions of the notion of public spheres. In approaching the analysis, then, with a cultural imaginaries perspective that foregrounds histories, politics, memories, and the fissures of the colonial encounter, I demonstrate the cultural foundations at the core of these public sphere formations and deliberations. I also highlight their importance for reimagining more capacious notions of publics in relation to democratic deliberation.

Overview of Chapters

The arguments in *Deliberating Ghana* are developed around transcripts I generated of several video broadcasts of the dispute case from January 2013 to August 2013. The analysis also includes a dataset of several hundred tweets, in addition to opinion articles, documentaries, and the Hansard (records of parliamentary proceedings) of the Parliament of Ghana. Anchored on rhetorical and thematic analysis, the rest of the book attempts to answer questions such as the following: How do cultural imaginaries shape democratic deliberation in courtroom and digital contexts in postcolonial Ghana? Who is allowed to deliberate, when, where, and how? In deliberation, how do institutional practices of evidence rooted in the colonial order pair with noninstitutional, informal ones in legitimating knowledge in general and truth and evidence in particular? How does the postcolonial condition shape memories about rhetorics of democracy?

Chapter 1, "Deliberating Speech: Colonial Legacies and the Paradoxes of Political Participation," develops around the tensions between the Akan (but generally Ghanaian) notion of *obuo kasa* (polite speech) and Western-inspired Ghanaian constitutional values of freedom of speech. *Obuo kasa* encompasses a form of public speech assuming asymmetrical social relations characterized by deferential, courteous addressives. I argue that while freedom of speech is foundational to democratic deliberation, its local instantiation, free speech, within postcolonial Ghanaian politics remains a fraught enterprise that vacillates between Western-derived notions of freedom of speech and local norms of who can say what, about whom, where, and when. I ask what it might mean for rhetorical studies to consider this foundational democratic principle vis-à-vis cultural imaginaries in studying deliberation. By analyzing contempt of court cases on freedom of speech leveled against citizens during the election dispute proceedings, the chapter highlights the cultural imaginaries (the histories, local norms and expectations of participation, and sociopolitical contexts in which the term is embedded) of the concept of freedom of speech. I contend that whereas freedom of speech is frequently held out as a god term for democratic practice, attention to its cultural imaginaries reveals factors that shape, promote, and constrain democratic deliberation within sociocultural contexts. I further demonstrate that rather than deference to either impulse—of commitment to freedom of speech or to local communicative values with roots in traditional courts—there is a constant negotiation between them, with consequences for who gets to talk about what and where in this postcolonial democracy.

Building on the institutional context of Ghana's Supreme Court as a colonial legacy shaping democratic practice, chapter 2, "Deliberating Genre: Oral Testimonies and the Rhetorical Work of Documentary Evidence," attends to deliberations in court among witnesses, attorneys, citizens, and Supreme Court judges. I examine a crucial genre adopted by Ghanaian authorities for electoral purposes—the Statement of Poll and Declaration of Results Form, otherwise colloquially referred to as *pink sheets*. Expanding on scholarship in rhetorical genre studies, I argue that genres such as the pink sheet and other such written, documentary evidence index an ideology in postcolonial Ghana that troubles neat delineations between documentary evidence (writing and literacy practices rooted in the colonial encounter) and (oral) testimony, stemming from traditional African modes of interaction and knowledge-making. I question rhetorical studies' investments in genre as a cultural inheritance, one that bequeaths societal values, norms, and expectations to a people, and show instead how a society's prior, traditional values may interrupt the values embedded in its genres articulated in the written word. By focusing on the pink sheets as a genre and a site of deliberation, I demonstrate the utility of examining deliberation about genres in research on rhetorics of democracy. I conclude that deliberations about the pink sheet reveal the reinforcing, rather than conflicting, influences of oral testimony and documentary evidence in making judgments about appearance and reality, and truth and falsehood, in democratic practice in the postcolony.

As a counterpoint to the institutional, courtroom contexts of the first two chapters, chapter 3, "Deliberating Participation: Digital Publics and Analogue Political Realities," shifts attention to a digital public that emerged around key hashtags during the election dispute case. Based on the analysis of four hashtags that circulated on Twitter[65]—#GhanaDecides, #ElectionPetition, #TheVerdict, and #SupremeCourt—and blog posts, opinion articles, and YouTube videos, I argue that these digital public spheres constitute a paradigm of new possibilities for citizen's political participation in the postcolony. Beyond the institutional boundaries delimited by the postcolonial state, citizens have opportunities to transpose, reframe, and repurpose political realities offline in digital publics using popular cultural resources and literacies. Analyzing the hashtags using a qualitative approach involving coding of tweets and thematic analysis, the chapter maintains that these digital publics are best understood in their relationship to the postcolonial state. I assert also that connections between offline political realities and rhetorical practices in digital public spheres offer a view into the cultural imaginaries of democratic deliberation more generally, as citizens explore new spaces of community to deliberate about democratic issues.

Chapter 4 addresses the ways that the dispute case is memorialized. Entitled "Deliberating Memory: Contested Remembering, National Identity, and the Re/production of Postcolonial Histories," this chapter inserts deliberations about the case in conversations concerning the politics of remembering rhetorics of democracy. It analyzes two documentaries: *The Election Petition* (2018) and *An African Election* (2011). While *The Election Petition* was produced by a Ghana-based media company, circulated through, and deliberated about in several media outlets, *An African Election* is a multi-award-winning documentary produced by a Switzerland-based media production company and inspired by Ghana's national elections of 2008. The Ghana-based producers of *The Election Petition* assert they were inspired by the producers of *An African Election* to "spend time and effort to research, analyze, and tell Ghanaian political stories in a documentary." *An African Election*, on the other hand, has been screened periodically across Europe and North America and in several African countries especially preceding major national elections. The analysis of *The Election Petition* is set against the backdrop of *An African Election* producers' claim that their documentary chronicles the efforts of "a third world democracy struggling to legitimize itself to its first world contemporaries."[66] The chapter argues that in addressing the memory of the election dispute, *The Election Petition* serves as a form of historical production that attunes audiences to a public pedagogy of citizenship. The documentary offers audiences lessons on how to locate and understand their role as citizens within the broader story of Ghana's democratic practice, what orientation to adopt toward electoral politics, and what kinds of electoral outcomes are worthy of emulation and aspiration. The chapter concludes that exigences to deliberate about the memory of the election dispute case are both local and global, shaping narratives about democratic practice at home and reframing global perspectives abroad.

The conclusion reflects on the postcolonial context of the analyses in the preceding four chapters to explore decolonial possibilities of democratic deliberation. Rhetorical scholars have argued that a crucial goal for rhetorical scholarship with a cultural bent should be attunement to decolonial practices, those "stories from the perspective of colonized cultures and communities that are working to delink from the mechanisms of colonialism."[67] Throughout the book, I examine deliberation in both institutional and noninstitutional contexts and from the perspective of a previously colonized African context. In doing so, I approach the topic of democratic deliberation in Ghana as a phenomenon with stories that, though linked to colonialism, resist the Eurocentric foundations to which they would appear to have been tenaciously tethered. By placing the deliberations about speech, genre, participation, and memory within scholarship in rhetoric and democracy, this final chapter gestures toward conversations about efforts to decolonize understandings of rhetoric and democracy. The chapter ties together arguments in the book to show that a cultural imaginaries perspective on democratic deliberation offers scholars a way out of Western normative perspectives on the practice of democracy. Ultimately, I reflect on decolonial pathways for reconceptualizing the meaning and practice of democratic deliberation on a society's own terms and with lessons for democracies elsewhere in a constantly evolving world order.

CHAPTER 1

Deliberating Speech

Colonial Legacies and the Paradoxes of Political Participation

Like most elections in its twenty-year history of return to constitutional democracy, Ghana's Election 2012 came with considerable public engagement by citizens. For both the apathetic voter and fervent citizen, the outcome of the elections presented compelling reasons to become interested in national affairs. The election dispute case lodged by the New Patriotic Party (NPP) at the Supreme Court brought along with it a new kind of interest in the political future of the nation. Pressing concerns about that future loomed large for citizens. Many wondered what the Supreme Court judges' decision would be and upon what basis that decision would be made. The relatively novel character of the case before the court also presented anxieties for others about the kinds of precedents that the court would follow. Public commentary by citizens on these and similar concerns was heated, energetic, and widespread. On radio and on television, in homes and at workplaces, Ghanaians with interest in the country's democracy passionately debated the merits of the case. As they considered the case's novelty, they also pondered the significance of its outcome. Within months, however, the debates in the public sphere were to take a decidedly different turn. On May 6, 2013, saying that they were concerned about the public debate muddying the ongoing judicial deliberations, the Supreme Court issued a prohibitive order to the Ghanaian public. They warned especially journalists, lawyers, and political commentators that continued debate deemed to have infringed on the reputation of the court might result in commentators being held in contempt of court. But many commentators saw in this prohibition a dangerous potential for a return to what, in Ghanaian political history, has come to be referred to as "a culture of silence," a period during previous military dictatorships when speech calling for governmental accountability was prohibited, criminalized, and punished.

Three responses by citizens in light of this court warning bear a special significance. First, in apparent reaction to the judges' prohibition, newspaper editor Ken Kuranchie of the *Daily Searchlight* published an editorial in the aftermath of the warnings, in which he vigorously criticized the court's position. Kuranchie claimed contempt citations will amount to nothing more than selective punishment. The judges would be logistically constrained, he asserted, and the sheer scale of twenty-five-million-odd citizens actively debating a case decidedly defeats any planned attempts at apprehending offenders. Second, a communication officer of the National Democratic Congress (NDC), Stephen Atubiga, went a notch higher. He declared on the popular Accra-based radio station, Asempa FM, that the only outcome of the case his party would accept is one that retains John Mahama as a validly elected president. And third, Kwaku Boahen, a regional youth organizer of the NDC, was reported in the *New Statesman* newspaper as having made similar contemptuous statements to Atubiga's.

On July 2, 2013, the court summoned these three to court on charges of contempt. Three long hours of courtroom deliberation followed, during which Atubiga was handed a three-day prison sentence, Kuranchie was convicted and sentenced to prison for ten days, and Boahen was acquitted on the basis of having made his alleged contemptuous statements before the court's final warning.[1] The contempt of court hearings represent a significant moment in the election dispute case because they turn on the very question of speech, deliberations not merely on citizens' commentary on the case but more importantly on *how* they may comment. A first of its kind, the public broadcast of the election dispute case (and the televised contempt case, for that matter) revealed for citizens the ways that judicial deliberations operate. It also provided a rare insight into the never-before-seen (at least to many citizens) inner workings of the court as an important state institution that shapes democratic practice. When viewed in the larger context of citizens' deliberative practices vis-à-vis formal institutions such as the court, the contempt proceedings provide key moments to ponder questions related to the institution of the court as a colonial inheritance. The proceedings exposed the court's values and practices, and the logics that shape citizens' ways of participating democratically. For instance, the deliberations in court echoed rhetorical strategies characteristic of traditional deliberative settings in Africa. Attorneys for one contemnor (a citizen held in contempt), admitted in open court to meeting behind the scenes to plead with the judges long before the deliberations commenced. Of course, Ghanaian law does not require this intervention by the attorneys, but the rhetorical power and efficacy of such an intervention in the deliberative context of a court recalls the peculiarities of democratic practice in a postcolonial context like Ghana's. A decontextualized approach to the judges' behind-the-scenes action might easily fall into misperception or construe the practice as a violation of fair judicial processes. However, a contextual(ized) reading based on a society's cultural imaginaries surrounding speech would furnish perspectives with which to understand this society's democratic practice *on its own terms*.

Another way in which the courtroom deliberations about speech were culturally grounded concern the ways that the tenor of the interactions appears to mirror expectations of formal speech in traditional African societies. Here, the contemnors—being citizens rather than judges—employed apologetic speech forms characterized by an asymmetrical, deferential disposition in and to speech, avoided any appearance of "uncivil language," and generally articulated their sentiments in measured, nonconfrontational ways. In general, such nonconfrontational deferential dispositions may not be unexpected in court, not least in a case of contempt intended to establish the guilt or innocence of offending citizens. But that such speech forms manifested in a courtroom setting where defense, argumentation, and debate are the coin of the realm raises important questions for the ways in which we might understand culturally situated deliberative practices. In addition to considering the courtroom as a rhetorical site shaped by formalities associated with legal practice, the interactions were marked by notions of decorum, with differing consequences for contemnors in the aftermath of the deliberations. Moreover, the contemnors' set of discursive choices and deliberative norms appear to be shaped by their cultural imaginaries surrounding the place and practice of speech—free speech for that matter—in Ghana's democracy. Ultimately, these norms of deliberation serve to influence the exercise of power and citizens' participation in this postcolonial democracy.

The interactions in court afford a site to engage with a prime example of citizens' direct engagement with a formal democratic institution on a subject of political participation and its associated anxieties. As a legacy of the colonial encounter, the institution of the court, like most postcolonial institutions, is largely divorced from the everyday life of citizens. Created to advance the colonial project, such institutions have remained in the postcolony to shape *where* and *how* citizens practice politics. These varying realms of politics constitute the publics accessible to citizens. As Omedi Ochieng has posited, such publics must therefore be conceived as historically contingent.[2] For the postcolony, this implies accounting for postcolonial African citizens' publics in relation to the nation-state and its institutions in ways that highlight how the legacies of colonialism delineated the major arenas of politics.

With the foregoing in mind, this chapter develops around the resonances and tensions between citizens' cultural imaginaries and their deliberative practices regarding speech. I begin by accounting for these resonances and tensions through an adaptation of the Akan concept of *obuo kasa*, or polite speech. *Obuo kasa* involves some kind of public speech in which participants assume asymmetrical, deferential dispositions in social interactions. I examine the manifestation of this concept in the context of Western-inspired, Ghanaian constitutional values of freedom of speech. I argue that freedom of speech is foundational to democratic deliberation; however, its local instantiation, free speech, within postcolonial Ghanaian politics remains a fraught enterprise that vacillates between Western-derived notions of freedom of speech and local norms of who can say what, about whom, and when. Through a rhetorical analysis of contempt of court cases arising during the election dispute case, this chapter demonstrates that freedom of speech tends to frequently be held out as a god term for democratic practice;[3] however, attention to its cultural imaginaries—here, the histories, local norms and values, and expectations of participation—reveal how the concept is framed, reframed, and conceptualized to reflect democratic deliberation within sociocultural contexts. The notion of free speech in the postcolony enables us to examine the exercise of power as it unfolds in and outside institutions to shape democracy.

Deliberative Norms and Formal Speech

In the postcolony, citizens' status (marginalized or otherwise), the institutions in which deliberation takes place (like the court), and the kind of speech (like *obuo kasa*) they deploy are some of the vectors that facilitate democratic deliberation. In studying democratic deliberation, scholars generally tend to see rhetoric and democracy as intricately connected. Explicating this nexus, Gerard Hauser observes that the rhetoricity of democracy makes manifest "a world of individuals and groups with history, memory, customs, and values projected through the exemplars, tropes, narratives, and political styles that have currency in vernacular and formal rhetoric."[4] Hauser's observation is closely associated in part with what I have referred to in this book as cultural imaginaries, for it offers crucial perspectives for how we might consider democratic practice cross-culturally and in relation to rhetoric as it is practiced by a people. The cultural imaginaries highlight the cultural dimensions that make rhetorical practices—and their consequent democratic practice—possible at all. The cultural dimensions of rhetorical and democratic practice have found increasing purchase in cultural rhetorics scholarship. Research in this tradition favors an approach to rhetorical study that emphasizes culturally relevant ways of understanding rhetorical production and interpretation. As I argue in this chapter, keeping a finger on the pulse of the cultural dimensions of the study of rhetoric enables us to move beyond universalizing narratives—those that see absences where there may be presences, and presences for absences.

Like rhetorical practices, deliberative norms vary culturally, and citizens' rhetorical practices that depend on norms vary just as much. Rhetoric in its cultural context as a driving force behind democratic practice finds one of its forceful expressions in the practice of deliberation. But first, as rhetorical scholar Craig Rood points out, defining the nature of deliberation in terms of what it should look like, its governing norms, and its participants' ideals is a fraught enterprise.[5] This challenge notwithstanding, a viable definition is reflected in the idea of *palabre,* with its focus on "conversation" and discussion among citizens around issues of common concern.[6] The form of palabre is limited in contemporary African societies because of the dominance of the state and its institutions in matters of large-scale deliberation around issues of common concern. However, we may hold the spirit of palabre as discussion and debate constant by extending its application to encompass the oft-circumscribed sphere of citizen participation in institutional spaces like the law court. I apply the definition to the courtroom discourse analyzed in this chapter, acutely aware that not more than a few citizens were engaged in the deliberations in court, in the sense in which the concept of deliberation is generally defined to include several participants.

Moreover, the notion of varying perspectives and proposals implied by scholars of deliberation such as Robert Asen and others may thus inherently be limited in the cases examined. A defining quality of deliberations is an assumption of discursive equality by all involved and that all perspectives be accorded due recognition. But as I will argue shortly, this assumption may be limiting culturally, not least in discursive contexts that enable some degree of social stratification and power. Deliberations as unfolded in the Supreme Court of Ghana were oriented toward the resolution of a consequential issue of citizens' political participation, namely, how to strike a balance between citizens' right to democratically participate through commentary and justifiable limits that may be placed on their freedoms. The institution of the law court, then, along with its stratified discursive space of attorneys, accused persons, and judges, shapes the nature of deliberation itself.

If we accept the argument that rhetoric, deliberation, culture, and democracy are all intimately bound up, then it follows that deliberative norms may condition democratic practice differently across geopolitical domains. But as Asen reminds us, there is in deliberation itself the presence of "unstated norms and values that privilege particular norms of engagement."[7] Regardless of whether they are stated or not, the presence of such norms proves to be conditioning mechanisms for who may speak and how they may do so. Studying deliberation within culturally specific domains requires, then, an interrogation of the nature of speech, especially public speech and its characteristics and functions in ways that intersect with expectations of citizen political participation. In this respect, turning to scholarship in ethnography of communication can inform our understanding of rhetorical strategies with roots in precolonial and colonial times that still have relevance for a postcolonial context.

In his influential *Speaking for the Chief: Okyeame and the Politics of Akan Royal Oratory*, ethnography of communication scholar Kwesi Yankah discusses the nature of speech in the royal court of the Akans of Ghana.[8] Yankah argues that Akan traditional rhetorical contexts operate on a set of assumptions about the nature and characteristics of speech. The spoken word is considered powerful and delicate, and because of risks associated with communication, it is commonplace for speakers to use rhetorical strategies that serve to "obviate crises."[9] This disposition toward speech finds special significance in formal contexts of interaction, those requiring the use of speech in public and that involve formal speech. In this group of speech contexts, one may place judicial deliberations, marriage rites, divorce proceedings, litigants' statement at court, and "the gamut of verbal interaction, including greetings at all formal assemblies."[10] Here, specific expectations characterize formal speech, deviation from which can and often does lead to punitive consequences for the rhetor.

Three key features of formal speech would help situate our discussion in context. First, indirection characterizes much formal speech and manifests in modes of speaking in which little to no direct face-attack is expected or encouraged.[11] In this respect, Yankah contends that the circuit of formal speech in deliberative settings in a king's palace is not just a matter of an addresser-addressee relationship; a crucial player in the rhetorical context is the *okyeame*, a royal appointee who relays messages between the chief or king and the assembly. To avoid the risk of impropriety to the sovereign, indirection is considered a rhetorical virtue in such a context.

Second, and linked to indirection, is the characteristic of formal speech referred to as *obuo kasa* (polite speech). *Obuo kasa* entails the use of politeness strategies or courteous addressives that show deference to other speakers. It assumes some degree of discursive asymmetry especially for authority or political figures by recognizing that while personal dignity and equality of all persons are guaranteed, high social status, political power, and the asymmetry of social relations characteristic of formal speech contexts shape expectations of how individuals relate discursively to each other.[12] The goal here is pragmatic: to "mark a degree of social distance" and to avoid "any appearance of imposition."[13] Third, and related to politeness strategies, is the use in formal speech of apologetic formulae and disclaimers. Rather than mere ornamental devices, these rhetorical strategies, according to Yankah, enable speakers to minimize the appearance of offense, irreverence, or profanity. In a sense, these strategies conform with understandings of civility frequently discussed by scholars of rhetoric, with its attendant terms like etiquette and decorum that constitute a system of rules structuring and facilitating citizens' engagement in democracies.[14]

The notion of *obuo kasa* and the undercurrent of expectations of formal speech emerge from within precolonial Akan royal courts and have withstood the test of time, extending into Ghana's postcolonial present. This postcolonial present entails not a wholesale rejection of the past, but citizens' uneasy existence with ideas, logics, institutions, and practices from Ghana's own pasts and presents.[15] In Ghana, one institution with roots in colonialism with enormous administrative capacity and power to shape political outcomes is the law court. A British import, the modern legal system in Ghana came by way of colonialism in the nineteenth century, and although political independence ensured sovereignty of the Ghanaian nation-state and its institutions, the logics, practices, and subjectivities engendered by institutions like the court remain largely tethered to foundations laid during colonialism. When situated within this historical context, the important role of the court in shaping democratic practice becomes apparent. And the contempt of court case that turns on judicial understandings of the role of the court system in national political life can be more fully appreciated.

Contextualizing a Contempt Charge

Although Ghana's electoral landscape boasts a host of political parties, only the National Democratic Congress (NDC) and the New Patriotic Party (NPP) have won presidential elections since the country's return to constitutional democracy in 1992. With constitutional democracy came media pluralism, and in this diversifying media landscape, political parties gained increasingly important voices in democratic governance. Communication officers of political parties came to be at the forefront. They came to play a pivotal role in Ghanaian politics by actively representing their party on media platforms, communicating policy programs to the public, and defending party and government positions on important issues of the day. As communication officer of the incumbent NDC, Stephen Atubiga had such a media platform constantly at his disposal, and like most citizens, employed it toward his defined democratic ends.

In addition to television and newspapers, radio—both in English and Ghanaian languages—remains one important medium for reaching a large portion of the public because of its ubiquity. While the Ghanaian-language and English FM stations give voice to citizens' political participation in the democratic process, this opportunity for increased participation in Ghanaian politics has not always been the case. Independence from British rule came in 1957. By the 1960s, there was growing discontent among a section of the population against the government of Dr. Kwame Nkrumah, Ghana's first president. Bolstered by public support, the military and police toppled the government of Nkrumah in 1966. The 1970s and 1980s saw an era of immense political upheaval in Ghana, during which military rule curtailed fundamental freedoms, including those of expression. Three additional coups d'état in 1972, 1979, and 1981, respectively, upended Ghana's emerging democratic culture and instigated a culture of intimidation and suppression that created a political climate saddled with fear of retaliation from the government. In reflecting on the effects of these military interventions on the country's democratic participation and media pluralism, Baffour Ankomah notes that a prevailing sense of a "culture of silence" hindered governmental accountability, instilled fear in the populace, and inhibited open public deliberation of national issues.[16]

With Ghana's return to democratic rule in 1992, this climate of silence began to shift toward more engaged and active citizen participation. With a return to democracy came a constitution in which is enshrined, among others, the basic freedoms of political participation and expression. Specifically, Chapter Five of the Constitution of Ghana on "Fundamental Human Rights and Freedoms" guarantees freedom of speech: "All persons shall have the right to—(a) freedom of speech and expression, which shall include freedom of the press and other media; (b) freedom of thought, conscience and belief, which shall include academic freedom."[17] These constitutional provisions have significantly enhanced a deliberative environment largely free of political intimidation. Where previously there was muted participation, silence, and apathy, Ghanaians today largely participate actively in the political process by providing commentary on political issues and holding their leaders accountable. Perhaps the most significant commitment to these constitutional guarantees came in 2001, when the newly formed government of John Kufuor repealed the Criminal Libel and Seditious Laws, themselves statutory provisions with origins in British colonialism, like much of the architecture of Ghana's legal system.[18]

But while stipulations of freedom of speech and expression are one thing, their specific instantiation in the form of free speech is yet another. Here, the distinction between freedom of speech and free speech provides clarity on the recognition of a freedom (typically in legislative documents) and its instantiation (in the quotidian experiences of citizens). Freedom of speech refers to "an inviolable fundamental human right that cannot be suppressed," whereas free speech "assumes prior compliance with cultural acceptable norms."[19] This distinction implies that although freedoms (and rights) already exist and are indestructible, it is recognition by social groups that animates them. Animated in specific politico-cultural contexts, freedom of speech becomes instantiated in the form of free speech.

In the Ghanaian context, while freedom of speech subsists in the Constitution (itself a system of political organization derived partly from British and American legal practices), the specific instantiation of this freedom, as free speech, operates in accordance with specific sociocultural norms. These norms would include discourse markers and sociocultural underpinnings of speech about who speaks and how, where, and when they are to do so. For example, research on political participation in Ghana through the medium of radio suggests increasing instances of discourse marked by impoliteness and uncivil use of language.[20] In discussing impoliteness among participants in interactive Ghanaian radio programs, Rachel Thompson and Jemima Anderson, for instance, argue that interactions were frequently indexed by direct and unrestrained face-attacks, in some cases without much regard to the face needs of interlocutors. Thompson and Anderson conclude that beyond general instances of face-attack, participants in the interactions engage in face-attack of more powerful people, in some cases deploying ad hominem attacks as an effective tool for demanding accountability from their government.[21]

Free speech in Ghana has also come to be intimately bound up with the idea that in exercising this freedom, peace ought to be a central foundation for the practice of democracy. In a specific reference to peace and democracy, Samuel Marfo observes that the freedom of expression enjoyed by Ghanaian citizens has devolved into "a theater of most vitriolic insults" particularly from political parties.[22] For Marfo, such a combative stance deviates from sociocultural norms of tolerance and detracts from citizens' participation in democratic deliberation. Marfo is not alone in this observation, however. As will become evident later in the analysis of the cases in this chapter, the Supreme Court judges' intervention in citizens' freedoms and their decision to cite citizens for contempt during the election dispute depended in part on their belief in a growing culture of "loose talk" that threatened democracy in Ghana. Even as the judges' decision to cite for contempt is rooted in legal notions of the sanctity of courts to be free from interference, that decision also rests on sociocultural assumptions and on the judges' understanding of acceptable cultural norms of speech. That decision is also tied to notions of power, which are invested in the judges not just judicially, but also socially. In what is a triptych of power, poverty, and speech, it is those with power—political or otherwise—who gain access to material resources that in turn facilitate entry into domains of speech that structure governance. In this calculus, judges are among persons positioned at the apex of the political order, while speech for those with little or no material resources and limited political power tends to be circumscribed.

The historical epoch and political context mapped here situates democratic practice in Ghana within the conditions of the postcolony. This context enables us to establish a foundation from which to understand citizens' interaction with the Supreme Court judges in the courtroom as well as the instantiation of—and limitations placed on—free speech. It also ultimately helps us understand the norms and power that undergird democratic practice in an institutional deliberative context like the court in Ghana.

Apologetic Speech Forms and Peaceocracy

Deliberative norms rooted in the colonial encounter were at the core of the contempt of court cases. During the election dispute, Stephen Atubiga was one of six persons summoned to answer charges of contempt by Supreme Court judges. Atubiga was reported to have warned that the party of which he was a communication officer, the NDC, would reject the outcome of the court's decision if the petitioner, the 2012 presidential candidate of the NPP, Nana Addo Dankwa Akufo-Addo, was declared the winner of the case. Reported to have been made on an Accra-based radio station, Asempa FM, the statement was subsequently carried by the *New Statesman* newspaper. When his case was called, Atubiga's attorney began to address the court by rendering an apology on his behalf. His attorney indicated that Atubiga had fully withdrawn his words even before his appearance in court. Atubiga followed up with an apology of his own, putting in a plea even before the case had been defined. My argument is that the rhetorical strategy adopted by Atubiga in much of his interaction with the judges entails apology functioning as an alibi for a deliberative norm. His opening statements on July 2, 2013, are revelatory of the tone that would be set for the entire discussion in court: "My Lords, I apologize for my irresponsible statement. I should have been a little bit careful and chosen my words very carefully. I humbly apologize and I think it will not happen again. And just for the record, my Lords, I started apologizing way before I even got the summon. I am responsible for my actions."[23]

Atubiga appears to recognize from the outset that he faced unequal access of discursive power in court. This is not unexpected. As state institutions with immense power over the fate of citizens, courts wield power for social control that is organized around beliefs and expectations of citizens' conduct, including those of speech. Deliberations about Atubiga's contempt case commenced without a definition of the offense for which he had been summoned to answer. There is an a priori assumption of guilt, even if by Atubiga himself, that shaped the tone and nature of the deliberations. His admission of guilt and his public apology before receiving the summons bear much significance. The practice has its roots in Ghanaian cultural imaginaries surrounding speech in relation to accusation and defense in the presence of authority and power. In this respect, it is a common traditional cultural norm for accused persons to proactively render apologies either if they believe they may be guilty or in the presence of authority and power. Both Atubiga's lower social status relative to the judges' and the power wielded by the postcolonial court informed his engagement with the judges. In apologizing before being allowed to do so, Atubiga demonstrates his sociocultural awareness of the differential access to power that structures interactions in formal speech contexts like the court in Ghana.

This awareness of power differential is not unidirectional, however. Embedded in the same cultural frame of assumption from which Atubiga draws, the Supreme Court judges similarly assume this differential access to discursive power. Their opening statement to Atubiga suggests an attempt to attribute a cause to the act of contempt. Notice here the rhetorical exchange between Atubiga and a member of the nine-member panel of judges:

JUDGE: You've heard your counsel . . . I heard that nobody gave you a calabash full of pito (a local gin), so you take full responsibility for your conduct.

ATUBIGA: My Lords, respectfully, I still apologize for if I . . .

JUDGE: No, did you say that . . . [inaudible] because I heard you on the radio.

> **ATUBIGA:** My Lords, I was making a submission that I am responsible for my actions and during the time I was making those statements it was a question that was put to me by the presenter, and I said I wasn't influenced by any pito, alcohol. Those were the adjectives that I used, and if I have crossed the line, I still apologize to be forgiven, and I will pick and choose my words carefully, and I humbly plead that you temper justice with mercy. Thank you, ma'am [courtroom laughter]. My Lords, my bad [recognizing the error in addressing the judge].[24]

In defending his constitutionally guaranteed freedom of speech, Atubiga recognizes that the differential access to power, and the courtroom as a deliberative context of accusation and defense, limits his ability to fully justify his statements. The apologetic speech forms characterizing his interaction with the judges stems more from his awareness of the authority wielded by the judges than about his recognition of a contemptuous statement that brings the court into disrepute.

The judges' interaction with Atubiga involves asking questions that may seem nonvital to the case at hand. However, upon further scrutiny, such questions would be seen to have been designed to effectively assert their power. For instance, one of the judges sought to know from Atubiga whether he was "trained in the US," presumably because of his American pronunciation of certain words. Atubiga's affirmative response prompts further commentary from one of the judges, who, while chastising him for his supposedly contemptuous remark, did note that he was "particularly happy you [Atubiga] have started apologizing over the weekend, meaning that you [Atubiga] have realized the need or the realization that the statements were in bad taste." These statements by a powerful political figure such as a Supreme Court judge to a less powerful, ordinary citizen may seem uncontroversial given just how power might be expected to operate in a courtroom. But Atubiga's decision to profusely render an apology before and during the deliberations about his conduct—precisely in a rhetorical space designed for defense—is, I contend, emblematic of relations between interlocutors of varying power dynamics. This is particularly so in formal deliberative settings within postcolonial Ghana. As Nancy Henaku has argued about the dispute case, legal and political power were intertwined in the courtroom discourse and such power "framed and determined what was significant in the courtroom interactions."[25] By apologizing, Atubiga assumes and recognizes this discursive power differential, and by stating that the court's summons is not in bad taste but only intended for "sanity to prevail in the country," the judges aligned their decision to cite for contempt with the need for national peace and order. In consequence, they established their authority and legitimacy as unquestionable guardians of Ghana's democracy.

The apology dimensions of the interactions in court are not the only strategies recalling deliberative norms. The judges also privileged the need for peace and order over and above the discomforts associated with deliberations. As political scientists Gabrielle Lynch, Nic Cheeseman, and Justin Willis demonstrate, peace narratives have become a common feature of electoral democracies in Africa. In at least the first two decades of this century, elections in Nigeria, Uganda, Côte d'Ivoire, Kenya, and Ghana have frequently been characterized by peace campaigns to prevent postelection violence. But these increasing calls for peace, a phenomenon the authors call *peaceocracy*, or "a system in which an emphasis on peace is used to prioritize stability and order to the detriment of democracy," could be counterproductive to citizens' ability to freely participate in democratic activities. Lynch, Cheeseman, and Willis contend that even given its ability to contribute to lower levels of violence, increasing "peaceocracy" can "close off certain topics of debate on the grounds that they might trigger violence."[26] Such calls for peace are redolent of similar invitations for civility all too familiar to scholars of democratic deliberation.

As rhetorical scholars of civility have demonstrated, in the midst of injustice, civility and other such appeals for decorous behavior have the potential to maintain and perpetuate injustice under the guise of peace.[27] In the case of Atubiga, not only did the judges see it fit to maintain their call for peace by emphasizing the need for "sanity to prevail in the country," but because peace, order, and stability are desirable values and god terms in democratic societies, the judges' call gains legitimacy. These aspirations for peace function to maintain the social order and sustain political participation. Against this backdrop, then, Atubiga may not set himself against these values without being portrayed as violent and unconcerned for the stability of democracy. Thus, calls for peace and order function here rhetorically as norms structuring deliberation itself.

The nature of the judges' questions also shapes the deliberative encounter, establishing the expectations between the judges and the contemnors. In recalling the basis upon which the contempt case had been called, one of the judges asked Atubiga, "What exactly did you say? No, I want to find out what you said. People are here, they want to hear you." Another judge emphasized this:

"I want to hear what you said. The people out there (Ghanaians, and the world, that is) want to hear what you said." Here the judges appear to be interested in inquiring into the nature of Atubiga's supposedly contemptuous statements not just for themselves but for others concerned with democracy. On the surface, the question itself seems intended to create a discursive opportunity for Atubiga to launch a defense and offer a rationale for his perspectives on his democratic right to comment on national issues. Considering that an apology had already preceded this question, however, the spirit of the question appears to be an example of the judges' quest to cause Atubiga to avoid deliberations and admit to his guilt.

If Atubiga's response to the question is any indication, it seems reasonable to argue that admission of guilt and avoidance of deliberation seem a safer response for him in such a rhetorical context. This avoidance of deliberation is the reason some were convinced the deliberations were "just a mere formality."[28] Atubiga's interactions in court are indicative of the ways that deliberation in a formal speech context like the court is inescapably shaped by norms. Such norms themselves have roots in culture, and they frequently emphasize avoidance of face-attack rather than a robust, if also contentious, debate on the subject matter within contexts of asymmetrical discursive relations.

Such contexts of asymmetrical discursive relations further impinge on the exercise of free speech. They recall cultural expectations that shape how persons with limited discursive power may engage. Atubiga routinely admitted his guilt despite the opportunity provided occasionally for him to defend himself. For example, in response to the question seeking clarification on his commentary on the case, he merely responded thus: "My Lords, I pray to God that those words should never come out of my mouth anymore, and I humbly stand in front of you, my Lords." To this plea, one of the judges inquired, "We've heard the apology. Are you apologizing for uttering those words or you are apologizing because those words are about us?" Atubiga's response here is rhetorically significant. Perhaps recognizing that the judges might come to a decision based on the genuineness and depth of his apology, and convinced that there was no real defense he could offer for his commentary on the case, he repeated, again, what seems to have become his stock response: "My Lords, I am apologizing because I've acted irresponsibly. I'm a father and husband and I have to live an example for my kids."

At first blush, it would appear that, for Atubiga, even a justified defense of his commentary risks being construed by the judges as a challenge to their judicial authority. Indeed, as will be demonstrated in the analysis of Kuranchie, the very idea of proffering a defense in the case risked being viewed by the judges as an affront to their and the court's authority. This is despite the larger notion of freedom of speech enshrined in the Constitution, and of which the judges themselves claim to be ardent defenders. On another, deeper level, however, it is possible to consider Atubiga's inability to defend himself as more of a complex rhetorical dilemma that accounts for his own sense of expectations of formal speech in relation to freedom of speech under the Ghanaian Constitution.[29] Atubiga's freedom of expression is doubtless shaped by deliberative norms of formal speech, and rather than a spirited defense, his enduring performance of a mea culpa serves, I suggest, as a safer and surer bet to obviate the risks associated with communication in asymmetrical, formal discursive contexts.

The Constitution of Ghana guarantees freedom of speech to all persons without discrimination. Thus, Atubiga's seeming inability to put forth a defense for himself, I suggest, originates from his recognition of the uneven authority wielded by the court rather than a constraint on free speech per se. The difficulty Atubiga experiences can therefore be located in the tension between the expectations of the court (that there be limits on freedoms) and those of a traditional Ghanaian disposition (that speech be couched in inoffensive language, especially in regard to authority). That difficulty is a result of the peculiar postcolonial rhetorical context, in which the court as a relic of the colonial encounter exists always in tension with traditional expectations of who may say what, about whom, where, and how. Atubiga's manner of interaction also accords with findings from research in African sociolinguistics pointing out that polite speech is culturally prescribed. Indirectness in African political discourse remains motivated partly by the cultural practice of not openly criticizing an elder, a person of high socioeconomic status, or a person with political authority.[30]

The cultural expectation regarding speech may seem to contradict the increasing impoliteness and the use of invectives in interactive radio programs in Ghana. However, the culturally dominant value of hardly leveling open critique particularly against individuals in authority does shape much deliberation in this courtroom case. It ought to be emphasized that it is not so much the case that Ghanaians avoid critique altogether; rather, it is *how* critique is carried out, who an interlocutor may critique in what manner, and what consequences may ensue that is at issue. Because of the communicative risks associated with political discourse, indirectness operates as one key tool rhetors within Ghanaian political contexts use to communicate dispraise and negotiate conflict. That indirectness in Atubiga's case is evidenced in his profuse and constant mea culpa, which, I argue, functions rhetorically to structure the deliberation about free speech. To be sure, my argument is not that apologies may not in and of themselves operate as defenses; instead, the point is that an imbalance of power and cultural imaginaries around speech concerning what is sayable by whom, where, and how combine in this instance to structure deliberation about the concern of speech deemed by the judges as corrosive of democracy.

Another crucial dimension to the judges' relationship with Atubiga during the deliberations in court is apparent. Perhaps motivated by their perception of difference in status, the judges excoriated Atubiga for his supposedly contemptuous remarks in at least three especially noteworthy moments following his response. First, one of the judges explicitly stated, "You can't! You don't even have the guts to say that if we deliver any judgment, you will not even obey the orders." This sheer demonstration of power is indicative of the clear difference understood by the judges between their own social status and Atubiga's—one that proves consequential for the social distance expected in communication. The judges deem it appropriate to emphasize Atubiga's position vis-à-vis the authority of the institution of state they represent. In doing so, they highlight their own power and status as representatives of the state, with power and authority that they may exercise as they deem fit. Second, the judges emphasized the difference in position between them and Atubiga by pointing out *his* societal standing to assert power. One noted, "If you, if you, standing there, you, a mere you, we are out here sitting on a matter that touches on the governance of this country and a mere you, stand there, out there, and before your colleagues tell the whole world that whatever decision comes out of this court you will not obey them."[31]

What is important here is the reference to Atubiga's position as a "mere" citizen, a description that brings into clearer focus the judges' perception of their relationship with the citizenry in regard to deliberations. The responsibilities of citizenship are not understood here as subsisting in ordinary people, those whom both colonial and later postcolonial states have considered subjects rather than citizens.[32] Instead, the judge-citizen relationship evidenced here is indexed by vectors of power, wherein the judges position themselves as representatives of the state whose actions are geared toward safeguarding democracy.

As Mahmood Mamdani has convincingly demonstrated, in understanding such a relationship, one ought to consider that the African colonial state was a bifurcation between citizens (white European persons) and subjects (local black people). While civil sphere courts ruled over urban, often white European citizens based on European laws, a customary sphere of local, traditional authorities oversaw black, often rural subjects.[33] Such a bifurcation established the relationship that postcolonial states would later allow with predominantly black subjects who became citizens following political independence. Given this backdrop, whatever form the protection of democracy takes seems to be beside the point in the election dispute case. From the judges' perspective, Atubiga's actions, statements, and commentaries are private, and therefore ought to be constrained where there is a suspicion of peril to democracy. Apart from Atubiga's level of education being deemed an important indicator of his capacity to fully participate in democratic deliberation about the case, the judges' commentary about him suggests it is poor citizens like him who are most likely to destroy the public peace. In this logic, democratic safeguard lies not with ordinary citizens, but with political office holders like judges.

In addition to these first two instances, there is a third moment where the judges' clarification on Atubiga's level of education resonates with concerns of power. When asked whether or not he was a graduate, Atubiga's response, that he was "not from any fancy family and [that he] come[s] from a very poor family" is revelatory of his acute awareness of power and class distinction between him and the judges. The judges remarked that Atubiga's supposedly volatile commentary on the dispute case embodies that of the sort of person who can "easily go and burn the market" if conflict arises. This symbolism of Atubiga as an arsonist is instructive, for it recalls the actions of one whose motive for political participation is purely that of the destruction of the community. To burn down the market is not simply to commit a crime of arson, but it also more importantly typifies the destruction of a community, its peoples' livelihoods, and the shared, communal spaces within which interactions of many sorts may thrive. To burn down the market, therefore, is to end the life of a community. As a threat to peace, the arsonist destroys democracy itself because peace is conceived as a bedrock of Ghanaian democracy. The judges' perspective, then, is not without significance. It is rooted in beliefs and values about the nature of formal, especially Western, education: an educated person, in the judges' view, is unlikely to use "irresponsible words"; an uneducated person, on the other hand, most likely will. Atubiga embodies the latter. The expectation that formal, Western education—and Western education alone—is *the* only acceptable equipment for democratic deliberation is here perpetuated.

If the articulated power differential structures norms of deliberation around the election dispute case, there is an even more compelling value that competes with freedom of speech in Ghanaian democratic deliberation: the advocacy of more influential, elderly persons. In the deliberative sessions in court, three attorneys from both the petitioner and respondent sides of the case appealed on behalf of Atubiga. Pleading with the judges to temper justice with mercy, the attorneys acknowledged that Atubiga's words may be harmful to the cause of the proceedings; however, his fervent apology seems genuine enough to warrant acquittal rather than criminal conviction and punishment. It is highly significant that these attorneys for the two parties to the case could set aside their competing interests and convene with the judges to plead clemency in behalf of Atubiga before the day set aside for judgment. Their actions mirror the traditional African practice of an influential person pleading on an accused person's behalf, not least when the offense is deemed—not necessarily established—to have been committed against an elderly person. Relying both on his apology and the attorneys' plea on his behalf, the judges decided eventually to grant Atubiga pardon. The presiding judge motioned to the court clerk, saying, "I think you can find him a place to be standing there while we deal with another person." Pardon for Atubiga meant a less severe punishment: he was sentenced to three days in prison.

Given this analysis, several points about deliberative norms and democracy in this African context may be emphasized. First, the freedom to participate in deliberation is enshrined in the Ghanaian Constitution; however, there remains underlying, just as powerful, cultural imaginaries surrounding speech that structure the attainment of the goal of democratic deliberation. Education and societal standing operate as major intervening factors for citizens' abilities to participate. In the judges' estimation, Atubiga's freedom of speech could be (de) limited by his educational status. By his own admission, Atubiga is not highly educated, a fact taken by the judges to mean he is as prone to physical violence as much as the alleged verbal violence of his inflammatory language. The judges' view of both his lowly societal status and his ability to critique authority freely and openly in public, then, are deeply rooted in Ghanaian sociocultural norms of what is sayable, by whom, where, and how. Not only is speech—particularly about authority—expected to be tempered by caution, but formal education and societal standing tend to structure expectations and realities of the proclamations and practices of freedom of speech. As a consequence, in the face of authority, in the context of the institution of the court, apologetic formulae structure democratic deliberation, ultimately shaping citizen participation.

Second, and closely related to the first point, the tension between freedom of speech in the service of deliberation and the judges' desire to keep public peace and order undisturbed seem to be resolved in favor of peace and order. Peace and order gain the status of a much-desired goal, so that speech deemed corrosive of deliberation and democracy is identified and proscribed rather than encouraged and celebrated. The spirit of palabre, to discuss and redeem, is substituted for the punitive, judicial view in deliberation, to discipline and punish.[34] In this respect, democracy becomes construed in terms of civility and fragility, pitted against "irresponsible," inflammatory speech that is regarded with suspicion. When the judges asserted what they deemed to be their responsibility to protect Ghana's democracy from the perils of irresponsible speech, they were effectively privileging public peace and order over and above the discomforts of deliberation. As deliberation scholars such as Patricia Roberts-Miller have argued, although such conflict avoidance may work to protect social harmony, "it cannot accommodate people who are deeply unhappy with the system itself."[35] The shadows of electoral violence elsewhere may have hovered over the judges' call for caution; however, their desire for peace and order seems emblematic of a larger cultural imaginary related to speech and norms of deliberation. The judges seem to suggest that a peaceful, nonconfrontational approach to deliberating about public issues is more desirable than open and frank dialogue and debate that may offend certain, particularly powerful, sensibilities. Speech, then, is disciplined in the public sphere, and comes to be shaped by an interconnecting matrix of fear of violence and respect for a cultural heritage of deliberative norms and values.

A third cultural imaginary surrounding speech in deliberation is the enduring influence of social position and authority in socially asymmetrical situations. The responsibility of attorneys toward clients is a desired imperative in any legal setting. Yet the behind-the-scenes apology and pleas by the attorneys to the judges in behalf of Atubiga speaks volumes more about cultural rhetorical norms of deliberation than it does about legal procedures for the resolution of conflict. Not just Atubiga's attorney, but attorneys from both petitioner and respondent sides of the case together put in a plea of clemency for Atubiga before the deliberations on his case began in court. In terms of who may receive this kind of treatment, Atubiga is not an outlier, however. In his closing remarks in court, Tsatsu Tsikata, an attorney on the respondent side of the case, broadened the advocacy role of the attorneys to the general public. Alongside other attorneys, Tsikata warned in a press statement that no longer would they defend "irresponsible comments." Tsikata's closing speech is well worth quoting at length and is reproduced here in part. It reveals the norm of speaking for another, not as an attorney may necessarily do for a client, but in the way that an *okyeame* would when an offense against a sovereign is assumed or established.

> My Lords, I would respectfully say that we can be confident that Mr. Atubiga is going to respect what he has said before your lordships about using the platform to withdraw unconditionally this harm that he's done with those words. I'd agree with your lordships that the harm that he's done by these words are significant and therefore all I'm asking respectfully for is that as he himself has asked for, you temper justice in this case with mercy and that he be given the chance that he has asked for. I would like to add respectfully that as lead counsel for the various parties in this case, we did take it upon ourselves during the lunch break to make it quite clear publicly and I believe it will air on the public media that we are not going to be here just trying to cover up for anybody's misdeeds, and that is not why I rise up. I do not rise up to cover up any misdeeds. I just respectfully ask that this gentleman be given a second chance as he's requested and that we, I can assure your lordships, that we will not countenance this kind of behavior from anybody and we just . . . [inaudible] taking steps to ensure that the dignity of this court is respected. We ourselves are part of the same profession and therefore we know the consequences of these kinds of words. And I can say confidently that we would do all in our power also to restrain the situation that we find ourselves. We cannot accept the culture of impunity as the learned counsel for the second respondent said publicly this afternoon, and that is all I wish to say that you temper justice with mercy in this circumstance.[36]

Deliberations in another case in court provides perspectives to interrogate deliberative norms aside Atubiga's. The interaction between the judges and Ken Kuranchie, the other contemnor called before the court, is relevant here. In contrasting Kuranchie's interactions with Atubiga's case, I highlight the ways in which the norms of deliberation manifest, deviate from Atubiga's, or are accentuated. In so doing, I argue that Kuranchie's deviation from the cultural imaginaries surrounding speech in deliberation provides compelling evidence of the influence of such local, rhetorical norms of deliberation that ultimately shape discursive access in democratic deliberation more generally.

Risky Deliberations, with Ramifications?

If compliance with deliberative norms is understood to be rooted in cultural imaginaries surrounding speech, a challenge to, and deviation from, these norms entails severe consequences particularly for interlocutors with less power in formal deliberative contexts. My argument is that the judges' expectation of the courtroom interaction with Kuranchie is premised on the view that deviation from civil, polite speech threatens the political order. In contrast to Atubiga's case, the deliberations surrounding Kuranchie's accusation entail this deviation. For its centrality to the present argument, I reproduce the Supreme Court summons to Kuranchie here in full:

> Mr. Ken Kuranchie, my Lords, it having come to the notice of the court that the newspaper known as *Daily Searchlight* Volume 10, Number 111, Thursday, 27th day of June 2013, published on its front page continued on page 2 thereof, news item heading "Is There Justice in the Land?" The Loose-Talking Supreme Court Did Not See or Hear"; as well as front-page comment "Can We Comment on Decisions of the Supreme Court Hearings or Not? Their Lordships Should Come Clear and Clean" which touched and concerned this court, and which appears to be contemptuous of this court. It is thereby ordered that Ken Kuranchie, editor-in-chief of the *Daily Searchlight,* do appear before this court on the 2nd day of July 2013, at 10 o'clock in the forenoon to answer to the first utterances for a determination thereon by this court.[37]

During deliberations, the court clerk's summons was followed by the judges' deliberations about the case, including questions to Kuranchie about whether he had been served the summons and understood its contents. Kuranchie's affirmative response led to another set of questions from the judges who asked that he state his position concerning the charge. These initial steps in the proceedings help establish a point of common ground about Kuranchie's statement, determine the allegation of contempt, and set the deliberations in motion. When asked about his position concerning the content of the summons, Kuranchie responded that he did not know. His defense was then set in motion by his attorney, Samuel Atta Akyea. Atta Akyea pleaded with the judges to understand his client's case from the perspective of the novelty of the presidential election dispute itself. He suggested that citizen commentary was inevitable and could well run afoul of any discursive boundaries set by the judges.

Atta Akyea further indicated Kuranchie meant no disrespect to the court, and that the definition of contempt would be incredibly hard to determine by citizens given the tension between notions of contempt and freedom of speech. For Atta Akyea, because court proceedings were being heard "even in the bedrooms of the citizens of this country" for the first time, the judges' seeming attempt to set boundaries on speech would be an impossible task. More to the point, if "some lawyers," said Atta Akyea, "are even confused as to the distinction between reportage, factual accuracy, and commentary," it is possible for citizens to be even more baffled by the boundaries expected by the court. Based on this logic, Atta Akyea concluded that Kuranchie's publication merely asked the judges to guide just how citizens might comment on the dispute case. In Atta Akyea's view, Kuranchie's piece was therefore never meant to be construed as contemptuous of the court. Atta Akyea's defense highlights citizens' fraught relationship to the court in that the language and practice of law remains exclusionary to the practice of democracy. Not just ordinary citizens, but some lawyers may be perplexed by the exclusivity of legalese that maintains the coercive power of law over citizens' lives.

The judges' dissatisfaction with Atta Akyea's initial defense is undergirded by an understanding of this coercive power of law. In response to the judges' questions seeking an explanation to Kuranchie's writings in the *Daily Searchlight*, Atta Akyea remarked that Kuranchie's views merely meant the judges were being "overburdened by commentaries you [the judges] will never hear" and therefore the judges could not impartially call into contempt citizens' commentary on the case. The judges' riposte, asking whether Atta Akyea was "trying to justify what he [Kuranchie] said," and if "you [Atta Akyea] think we don't understand? Or things are not clear to us?," reveals their expectations of the deliberations. Atta Akyea's attempt at an explanation is construed as justification. The judges had indeed already determined the commentary an affront to the court, if not to the culturally sanctioned notion that elderly and esteemed personalities like judges of courts may not be easily slighted without consequence.

Beyond this cultural rhetorical sanction is the judges' awareness of the necessity of free speech for democratic deliberation. There is a widely shared understanding in Ghana of the centrality of free speech to democracy. Given the long period of political intimidation inaugurated by years of coups d'état, it is unsurprising that citizens place a high premium not only on freedom of speech but also on perceived threats to the political order. The judges are no doubt aware of this political history. Thus, they needed to be seen as free speech advocates, particularly when the deliberations hinge on the tensions of free speech and the charge of contempt. But free speech in the estimation of the judges was not to be without caveats. As they noted to the court,

> You see, what these paper publishers should understand is that this court will be the last court to guard free speech. *Almost* all of us here are adherents of free speech and we have done so over the years to champion free speech, and indeed it is the cornerstone of our democracy, but we must do so in a very courteous and responsible language . . . I will wish all lawyers and also the politicians and the Ghana Journalists Association to bring to the notice of all editors and media men the locus classicus decision in the *Republic v. Liberty Press.*[38]

At first blush, the judges' caution that free speech must be attended by courteous and responsible language use may seem well-intended to safeguard a democratic experiment. On another level, however, this concern points to the tensions between the notion of freedom of speech for democratic deliberation and the local, Ghanaian discursive norm of making speech more accommodating and less volatile and offensive—not an open face-attack. Also revelatory is the judges' statement ("almost all of us") that hedges a full assent to free speech. By hedging, the judges signal the limits they believe must be placed on free speech even without a constitutional provision that guarantees the exercise of that speech. The cultural rhetorical norm of disciplining speech is therefore very much a part of the judges' call.

The interactions between Kuranchie and the judges affirm that in the deliberative encounter, the judges cannot be questioned or expected to clarify their own questions. Kuranchie's first statement was to seek clarification on the nature of the summons (whether or not it was a charge sheet) and its meaning. Doing so meant putting the judges in a position to explain—or worse, defend—the contempt charge. This initial conversation unravels the judges' expectation of the courtroom discourse:

> **KURANCHIE:** Sir, I do not know how to respond to, because it sounds as if it is something I am to plead to, very respectfully. What was read by the gentleman [referring to the court clerk] . . .
>
> **JUDGE:** You've been in this court. You've seen what others have done. We are saying admitting it, but clearly, what has gone on in respect of the other two, I mean I don't see what problem you have.[39]

Recall that Atubiga was entirely apologetic about his "irresponsible language use," and his interactions with the judges reflect unique expectations within the rhetorical situation of the court: the judges were influential members of society and did not seem to countenance open critique or an assumption of discursive equality with Atubiga. However, Kuranchie stated that he was unable to articulate a defense because he could not determine whether the summons constituted a charge sheet that would require a plea. By requesting clarification, he sought to deviate from the dominant cultural imaginaries surrounding speech in deliberative contexts. Further, by stating that Kuranchie had seen "what others have done," the judges were signaling the apologetic speech forms of the prior proceedings with Atubiga. "What has gone on in respect of the other two" may be viewed in terms of the cultural rhetorical norm of apology that structured Atubiga's case.

There is a dominant strand of deviation from expected rhetorical norms in Kuranchie's interaction with the judges. While he went to great lengths to appear polite in his deliberations, including routinely prefacing his submissions with "respectfully" and honorifics like "My Lords," Kuranchie's constant lingering on the details of the summons put him on a collision course with the judges. One of the judges warned, "When I am speaking you just have to listen and answer." This remark reflected the expectation of norms of propriety in speech expected within the confines of this African courtroom. It also reveals the disjuncture between, on the one hand, cultural notions of who may speak and where, when, and how they may do so and, on the other hand, the judges' vision of the place of those norms in the courtroom deliberative context.

Furthermore, if Kuranchie's constant inquiry to the judges deviates from the deliberative norms evidenced in Atubiga's case, even more convinced were the judges that he was intentionally bent on diverting from the path of apology and openly questioning the court's decision to cite for contempt. In response to Kuranchie's question for clarification on what a charge sheet is, one of the judges remarked thus: "No, I think you are trying to take us for a ride. You want to be a hero here; you can't be a hero." The notion that Kuranchie seeks heroism stems from the judges' belief that to seek clarification diminishes the authority of the court in the eyes of the public. They believe attempts at open critique constitute an affront to authority. By reorienting Kuranchie's quest for understanding toward a less than noble desire to be heroic, the judges suggest a discursive sphere where an apologetic tone and speech constitute the predominant and cherished values of deliberation. Beyond personal gratification, the heroism Kuranchie is believed to be aspiring toward is heroism for others who also might share in his vision of political engagement, one anchored in what may be referred to as "speech-without-caveats."

The important role of the attorney in the deliberative encounter is seen in the work of Atta Akyea yet again. Attorneys mediated where competing visions of the deliberation arise between the judges and citizens. Cognizant that Kuranchie's interactions with the judges were becoming fractious, Atta Akyea pleaded with the court to allow Kuranchie to advocate for himself and explain his position on the case. The judges invoke a principle of equality before the law to legitimize their demand for Kuranchie to engage in the deliberations as Atubiga did. In response to Atta Akyea's request, one judge stated, "Equality before the law. He cannot be treated any differently. His colleagues came here and quickly understood and we moved forward. Let him just . . . He appears to understand what is going on."

When Kuranchie finally got a chance to fully articulate his argument, he claimed that the judges' order was arbitrary and that because of the ubiquity of the commentary on the case, "there are people who are going to comment using very nice language" and "there are people who are also going to comment using very unacceptable language." Kuranchie sees only one way to resolve the impasse of determining what was sayable and what wasn't: the judges would have to "accommodate the use of strong language." The point about strong language has been articulated by rhetorical scholars who have argued that the discomforts of deliberation such as the use of provocative style are a price worth paying for the outcomes of deliberation.[40] To call on the judges to allow the use of strong language was to invite them to abandon much cherished traditional values and norms that shape deliberation within Ghana's political, and particularly asymmetrical discursive contexts. Such a position was doubtless foreign to the judges' disposition in the case, however.

The judges' power to discipline words and to determine what is sayable or not shapes their rhetorical exchange with Kuranchie and the public. By restricting deliberation on proceedings in the dispute case, the judges were operating within their self-understood capacity as guardians of the Constitution. Even more pertinent to the argument about speech for democratic deliberation in the postcolony, they were elevating a cultural norm in which elderly people discipline speech perceived to be irresponsible and inflammatory. In recognizing the impasse between Kuranchie and the judges, Atta Akyea counseled Kuranchie to apologize rather than offer a defense. Kuranchie was not one to steer away from deliberation on the issue, however. In several variants of the same statement, he predicated his apology on the conditional, repeatedly stating that "if our commentary and write-up has caused any embarrassment to the members of the panel in any personal capacity, we deeply apologize." Much against the judges' insistence, and despite his attorney's encouragement to drop the *if* clause, Kuranchie remained adamant, held steadfastly to only the conditional, and, unlike Atubiga, stood resolutely against the conventional, culturally prescribed norms of disciplining one's speech. In the end, the outcome of Kuranchie's stance was a ten-day prison term. In sentencing him, the judges held his commentary—and comportment around speech in court—to be "in defiance of the authority of this court," concluding that his statements were, without any doubt, intended to "defy the authority of this court."

Contemporary Deliberative Norms in the Idiom of Traditional Deliberative Contexts

The argument thus far is that the deliberative norms that condition democratic deliberation in institutions like the court are legacies from precolonial and colonial political practices which are in tension with those of postcolonial institutions. Indirection is carried over into the contemporary context of the court, where, like the king or chief, the judges of the Supreme Court are unarguably perceived as arbiters and rulers. The judges' position is both political and judicial. Given the interactions in court, it stands to reason to argue that the judges, being culturally wired, did expect such norms to unfold in deliberation.[41] That Atubiga followed these norms (by avoiding open, direct interaction and defense) and Kuranchie ignored them (by asking questions of the judges and directly engaging in face-attack) would seem to have shaped the contrasting outcomes of the judicial deliberations.

It is possible to view the contemnors' (particularly Atubiga's) interactions with the judges as a rhetorical expectation of courtroom interaction more generally. Indeed, the power dynamics between the contemnors and the judges is explained partly by both the interactional context of the court and the contempt of court case. From a legal perspective, both contexts put the contemnors at a discursive disadvantage given the power wielded by the judges. But while these contextual factors heighten the enactment of power, they do so only within the larger context of an orientation to political discourse characteristic of postcolonial Ghanaian society. Writing about early postcolonial political discourse, sociolinguist Samuel Obeng Gyasi argues this orientation entails a "wider Ghanaian oppositional culture of giving up on words; that is, having something to say but remaining silent either out of fear of or reverence."[42]

Gyasi's point is not to be taken, however, to mean an abandonment of critique altogether. Against the challenge of giving up on words, there exists, as Yankah has discussed, room for "creatively registering dissent, protest, or displeasure," albeit within the boundaries of polite speech (*obuo kasa*).[43] Rather than the content of critique, attention shifts to the manner of critique, what Karen Tracy has pithily referred to as the *linguistic clothing* of deliberative practices.[44] Linguistic clothing functions rhetorically as a norm of deliberation, a way in which rhetors may communicate grievance, displeasure, or protest. Being thus normed, that linguistic clothing presents difficulties for expressing dissent. Perhaps it is this difficulty Atubiga could hardly surmount and for which Kuranchie was more severely punished. The power dynamics that unfolded in court may be taken, then, to be a feature of Ghanaian political discourse and deliberation more generally.

As a corollary to the point about indirection, the tradition of routing speech in royal speech contexts through the *okyeame* resonates in the contemporary courtroom context. As has already been signaled, because of the perception of volatility of formal speech, the intermediating role of the *akyeame* (plural for *okyeame*) is designed and expected to minimize the risks of face-attack associated with speech. During the proceedings, the attorneys played a role similar to that of an *okyeame* in behalf of Atubiga when they convened with the judges even before the judicial deliberations began. If the courtroom is a place of defense and plea, it would seem curious that the attorneys decided to convene with the judges to speak in behalf of Atubiga. But this strangeness is explicable within the context of traditional Ghanaian norms of judicial deliberation. As Yankah explains, "The general predilection for interveners or mouthpieces in Akan society explains the institutionalization of plea intervention within the Akan judicial system. In the absence of attorneys or judicial advocates within the judicial system, one proven guilty by a court may plead for leniency through an elder or a political functionary."[45] Whereas the intervention of the attorneys could easily be deemed influence peddling or obstruction of justice in other jurisdictions, the same action is more usefully understood in the cases analyzed as a spillover of traditional norms into the contemporary deliberative setting of the court.

Like many institutions of the modern nation-state of Ghana, the Ghanaian court system is a legacy of British colonialism. The concept and practices of democratic governance, the rules and procedures of the law court, and the subjectivities maintained in institutional contexts like the court owe their origins partly to democratic practice in England. In *In Pursuit of Civility*, the British historian Keith Thomas traces the development of manners and civility in early modern England, noting that whereas the judicial architecture of that era was embedded in "an unpropitious environment for hierarchical ritual" that encouraged judges' social inaccessibility, the twenty-first century came to be much different.[46] "British society," writes Thomas, is today "less visibly hierarchical than it was," so that where previously status symbols reigned supreme, those "symbols of deference are much less evident, and accepted styles of speech and bodily comportment are infinitely more relaxed."[47] The result is a higher premium on informality, and a discursive environment with less emphasis on decorum and civility than before. The forms of deference that operated in English courts function today as colonial legacies in places like Ghana. For instance, although the British have long abandoned the formalities of dress associated with the judiciary, leaders in Ghana's judiciary tenaciously hold on to these regalia.[48] But such legacies also work in concert with the deliberative norms that predated colonialism, those that while not the *letter* of state-mandated processes of democratic deliberation, remain its *spirit*, its guiding disposition. Alongside local traditional norms that already operate in asymmetrical speech contexts, such vestiges of the colonial order function to shape deliberative norms.

What parallels, then, might be drawn between the case of Atubiga and Kuranchie? One important reason Atubiga received a less severe sentence is his fervent apology without an attempt to offer a defense of his commentary. By taking responsibility for his utterances, without justifying his actions, and profusely apologizing for his commentary, Atubiga's nondefense was perceived as a mark of his remorse. Based on this, he was handed a comparatively easy way out of court. The norms he deployed accorded with deliberative norms expected in formal deliberative contexts and they were consonant with familiar cultural imaginaries surrounding speech. On the contrary, Kuranchie's defense consisted mainly in an attempt to offer reasons for his commentary. He deviated from culturally sanctioned modes of address, especially where elderly, more powerful personalities were involved. Additionally, he disavowed the peace desired by the judges in favor of the risks and discomforts of deliberation. His interaction with the judges revealed the ways that the constitutional guarantee of freedom of speech can run at odds with cultural rhetorical norms of deliberation within the institutional space of the court, in turn shaping citizens' deliberation.

Conclusion

The deliberations in court hold important implications for the ways that we might consider rhetoric and democratic deliberation within postcolonial contexts. In regard to cultural foundations of communication in contemporary Ghana, there are interactional frictions created by the clash of traditional African rhetorical norms and the norms of communication required in the modern nation-state. The result is that in official public contexts of speech, "custodians of the lore expect public speech style to reflect indigenous norms and aesthetics."[49] These indigenous norms entail a host of different things: deference to authority and the expectation to inflect speech with decorum; avoidance of open critique of authority; sustaining deliberation through recourse to peace rather than open confrontation intended to subvert injustices;

and generally upholding, rather than upending, traditional communication modes and conventions.

The rhetorical tensions arising from the clash of these traditional modes and borrowed practices in public deliberative forums derive from Ghana's post-colonial condition. Here, colonial legacies and institutions of state increasingly find themselves shaped by traditional norms. In an apparent reference to this unresolved tension in the case of the judges' issuance of the contempt summons, legal scholar Stephen Asare wonders "whether culturally wired illiberal justices can enforce the rights and values enshrined in a liberal constitution."[50] The roots of the nature of the judicial deliberations are to be found in the tension previously described and the need to strike a balance between the freedoms associated with the modern nation-state and the cherished values of traditional speech forms. As Asare further explains, the judges seem "more familiar with and lean towards the cultural and swifter way of addressing conflicts," a disposition in which, at many levels, "respect for hierarchy is paramount and offensive speech directed at authority figures is frowned upon and instantly, as well as severely, punished."[51] The analysis of the contempt cases corroborates this view. It offers rhetorical theorists an example of ways that rhetoric and the cultural foundations that give it birth, understood within a non-Western context through its cultural imaginaries, serve to shape democratic deliberation.

The cultural particularity observed in the analysis suggests the limits of critiques of power, such as has been advanced in concepts like Karen Tracy's "reasonable hostility." Tracy advocates this concept in defense of "emotionally marked criticism of the past or future actions of public persons."[52] She demonstrates that when purposefully deployed in deliberation, reasonable hostility can counteract the potential of civility to squelch dissent. Insights from the analysis of the court cases extend this point by revealing its limits. The cases analyzed emphasize the idea that deliberative norms are not just culturally contingent. They are also imbricated in questions of power and social position that sustains that power. In the postcolony, deliberative norms are further shaped by the legacies of colonialism, an important index that ought to be central to analyses of democratic deliberation.

Democratic deliberation in institutional spaces like the court in Ghana remain shaped by interlocking, competing notions of traditional, cherished communication values and the logics of adopted, mostly Western practices of democracy. It is important to recognize that deliberative norms in institutions like the court hold both promise and peril for public participation: a cultural frame of reference functions to sustain democratic practice even as it remains in an unresolvable tension with colonial legacies. The concept of freedom of speech is frequently held out by scholars of deliberation as a god term for democratic practice. As I have argued throughout, in attending to its cultural imaginaries—the histories, local norms and expectations of participation, and sociopolitical contexts in which the term is embedded and operates—we can better understand factors that shape, reframe, and indeed constrain democratic deliberation within postcolonial contexts as citizens work to upend power structures.

CHAPTER 2

Deliberating Genre

Oral Testimonies and the Rhetorical Work of Documentary Evidence

The primary record around which the entire deliberations surrounding the election dispute case revolved in Ghana's Supreme Court was the Statement of Poll and Declaration of Results Form for the Office of President. This two-page form, otherwise known colloquially as the *pink sheet* because of its color, served an evidentiary purpose in court and came to evince ways of knowing, being, and doing about deliberation concerning the election dispute case. The entire case would come to rely on the supposed truths that may be uncovered by careful attention to information contained in several reams of these sheets across more than twenty-six thousand polling stations in Ghana. Beyond the immediate courtroom context, the idea of the pink sheet also entered Ghanaian popular parlance and gained prominence in public discourse. For ordinary citizens interested in deliberations about the case, whatever information was contained in the pink sheet held the key to resolving the unprecedented case at the Supreme Court. The pink sheet was the evidentiary weight behind the deliberations and held the key to arguments made in the case.

A record of voting information, the pink sheet functions as a genre, a way of knowing, doing, and being in the idiom in which rhetorical genre theorists have generally conceptualized the term. It contains values, ideologies, and beliefs instantiated in arguments about it, and it reveals information about not just citizens' deliberations but the cultural foundations that drive those very deliberations. As a genre, the pink sheet contains a knowledge-making value about deliberations in relation to the dispute case. Technical communication scholars Isidore Dorpenyo and Godwin Agboka have argued that concerning election technologies and civic engagement, election technologies like "paper ballots, . . . voter education materials, . . . scanners, ballot printing materials, user manuals and other technical documents used during elections" operate to "shape the conduct and/or outcomes of elections."[1]

These technologies (some of which we may argue are genres based on their capacity to organize knowledge, action, and being) shape electoral integrity, voter confidence, and vote legitimacy. In the case of the pink sheets, the petitioners' primary argument at the Supreme Court rested on the claim that 11,138 of these filled forms contained irregularities that impacted the election results and ultimately informed the Electoral Commission's (EC) declaration of the winner of the polls. Both the petitioners and respondents framed their legal arguments in court around the primary role the genre played in the collation and declaration of the election results. Not only the court but both parties pointed to the capacity of the genre to affirm or undermine definitive claims of overvoting, voting without biometric verification, having duplicate serial numbers on pink sheets, and counting unsigned pink sheets. These were all claims based on which the petitioners had sought the annulment of close to four million votes.[2]

This chapter interrogates the pink sheet as first and foremost a genre, in the sense in which rhetorical theorist Carolyn Miller has famously defined the term as "typified rhetorical actions based in recurrent situations."[3] The pink sheet represents a recurrent record of elections within the Ghanaian context, for it responds to the recurrent situation and exigence of documenting key issues such as ballot accounting relating to the elections. As a genre, there is some regularity to its form that makes it recognizable. It is deployed for every electoral event as a response to the exigence of capturing voter information, and it serves as evidence of votes recorded. Yet far from being the only record of evidence, the pink sheet is also embedded in a network of persons and materials—polling agents, biometric verification devices (BVDs) used for the elections, and voter registration collation sheets provided by the EC. While the pink sheets became the dominant form of evidence used during the deliberations in court, a network of genres, of persons and materials, came to shape the forms of evidence the pink sheet allowed.

In examining the pink sheet genre and the arguments it spawned, I aim to expand understanding of democratic deliberation through a shift from a focus on people deliberating toward the ways that genres' characteristic of organizing knowledge, action, and being may shape deliberative activity.[4] I invoke scholarship in rhetorical genre studies to illuminate how, for scholars of democratic deliberation, attention to arguments surrounding a genre can operate as a point of departure for examining ideological impulses, values, and beliefs within a given deliberative context.[5] I argue that an analysis of the genre of the pink sheet, the cultural imaginaries that surround it, and arguments based on it as the primary form of evidence illuminates for studies of democratic deliberation "an archive of cultural imprints." Such an archive offers sources of knowledge that underscore the cultural foundations of a society's deliberative activities.[6] In the election dispute case, the archive of cultural imprints reveal why evidence in court is construed in particular ways during deliberation. In addition to evidence provided by petitioners and respondents, interrogating the pink sheet genre also expands understanding of the pivotal role genres can play in shaping knowledge about ideologies, values, and beliefs in deliberation within specific cultural contexts.

The rest of the chapter proceeds as follows. First, I build on scholarship in rhetorical genre studies in order to situate the pink sheet as a crucial genre in the matrix of a network that makes the arguments surrounding the form possible. Second, I analyze a series of arguments advanced by various parties in court based on the pink sheet. These include a transcript of evidence concerning electoral irregularities by the chair of the EC, closing arguments delivered by both petitioners and respondents on the evidentiary role of the pink sheets, and the Supreme Court's 588-page verdict on whether there were irregularities based on the pink sheet that impacted the election results. I conclude the chapter by suggesting that in this postcolonial context, the pink sheet as a genre offers a valuable portal into the nature of deliberations as a constant tension between regimes of truth that oscillate between borrowed Western rhetorical practices and African norms and expectations of legitimating truth. I build on what the historian Sean Hawkins has described as "the world of experience" and "the world on paper"—that is, the nexus of worlds wrought by colonialism in a postcolony like Ghana. Ultimately, I contend that deliberative practices concerning the processes of legitimizing evidence and truth in particular, and knowledge-making in general, need to be conceptualized not as an opposition between documentary evidence and testimony but as a continuum, even a complement, of both.

Genre, Ideologies, and Deliberation

In "Genre as Social Action," Carolyn Miller pays attention to the role of genres in social life. Defining genres as "typified rhetorical actions based in recurrent situations,"[7] Miller argues that genres ought to be understood in terms of the social actions they encode and enable us to perform, namely those actions that point to their rhetorical character. Genres mediate actions between individuals through recurrence and typification. Through both these means, they expose the sociocultural contexts from which the actions they enable emerge. They serve, Miller observes, as "an index to cultural patterns and as tools for exploring the achievements of particular speakers and writers."[8] They condition the practices by which we communicate and deliberate. They also organize knowledge, action, and being.

This conditioning capacity of genres manifests in deliberation of many kinds. In discussing deliberations about cancer care among medical experts, for example, Christa Teston demonstrates how one genre, the Standard of Care document, functions to authorize knowledge and action in medical deliberations. Teston explains that this genre operates not only as a form of evidence based on which diagnoses are made, but it also serves as an authoritative document directing medical practitioners' courses of action. It operates as "a conceptual bridge for medical professionals—a bridge between the patient's experiences and the expectations of the medical profession as a whole." In this way, the document "rhetorically excludes and includes ways of seeing and doing," immensely shaping patient diagnoses and care within the field of oncology.[9] To say a genre like this enables the performance of social actions and directs courses of actions is also to recognize its ideological character. That ideological character is exposed in the taken-for-granted perspectives, actions, and values evidenced in the actions the genre enables. The ideological character of genres reveals the ways that values and knowledges maintain societal structures. Through the recurrence and typification that characterizes the social life enabled by and in genres, ideology emerges. As genre theorist Anthony Paré puts it, "The automatic, ritual unfolding of genres makes them appear normal, even inevitable; they are simply the way things are done. And their status in historical practice within institutions or disciplines makes them appear immutable and certainly beyond the influence of the transitory individuals who participate in them, and who become implicated in the subtle ideologies they enact."[10] The conditioning capacity of genres to shape social action and establish a sense of taken-for-grantedness is what perpetuates their existence. Ideology shapes genre, and genre, in turn, conditions ideology. What is ideological about genres is their capacity to make the ideas and actions they enable seem both natural and immutable. But while, indeed, genres' ideological capacity no doubt firmly perpetuates their existence, there is also room for individual agency. In any break from tradition—digression from the expectations of a genre, subversion of genre for other-than-intended purposes, changes in institutional exigence for a genre's deployment, and axiomatic shifts in the social context of use—the supposed naturalness of genre, Paré acknowledges, is exposed.[11] By the agency they exercise within the context of genres, individuals can fashion their identity in institutional and social life, even as ideologies structure those possibilities in the first place. The ideologies embedded in genres are a product, then, of the sociocultural contexts from which genres operate, resulting in a link among ideology, genres, and culture.

This three-pronged link is evidenced in electoral practices. In terms of ideologies associated with universal adult suffrage, technical communication scholars Natasha N. Jones and Miriam F. William have argued that genres can expose ideologies of supremacy and strategies of disenfranchisement. Jones and William examined literacy tests and voter registration applications as genres concerning elections, asserting these genres as revelatory of the ways that black voters in the United States were consistently disenfranchised between the end of the Reconstruction era and the 1960s.[12] As a window into the times, genres such as the voter instruction guides and literacy test questions served to maintain ideologies of white superiority and racial violence that excluded Black people from participating in the democratic process.

In interrogating democratic deliberation about the Ghanaian electoral dispute case via the pink sheet, it is important to recognize the network within which the genre operates. Hardly understood in isolation, genres exist in intertextual relations with other genres in ways that inform analytical comprehensiveness.[13] The pink sheets at the epicenter of the dispute deliberations exist in tandem with other genres such as the Voters' Register, the Captured Voter Information Form, and the Collation Forms. All these genres indirectly, and to varying degrees, inform arguments about vote legitimacy surrounding the pink sheet. I suggest that the pink sheet genre and the arguments it informs illustrate the ways in which deliberation in postcolonial Ghana remains a constant tension between colonial regimes of legitimating truth calcified in institutional practices and vestiges of Ghanaian (and perhaps largely African) norms of legitimacy anchored in experiences outside those institutions. The pink sheet as an example of a genre provides a conduit into deliberation and extends the locus of deliberation study beyond the predominant focus on real-time interactions among interlocuters. The potential of genres to expose ideologies in deliberation can thus become apparent.

An Archive of Cultural Imprints

Available records show that as far back as Ghana's general elections of 1996, the EC has used the Statement of Poll and Declaration of Results form.[14] During Election 2012, the EC issued the form for the purpose of recording the election results. The Coat of Arms of Ghana, positioned at the top left corner of the form, lends credibility to the genre as an official document emanating from an agency of the state. Composed of two major segments, the first part of the form has four subsections on ballot information, the polling station name and code, the polling station register and proxy voters list, and total ballot counts at the beginning and end of polls. The second segment contains information on presidential candidates' names and the votes they obtained (written in both words and figures). This is followed by a section requiring the signature of the presiding officer of the respective polling station and that of each political party's polling agent endorsing the election results. Alongside the signature is a declaration by the polling agents that reads "We, the undersigned, do hereby declare that the results shown above are a true and accurate account of the ballots in this polling station." This declaration signifies an endorsement of the ballot count, but it makes room also for polling agents to register disagreement if they choose to decline signing the form.

The content of the pink sheet indicates its evidentiary purpose as a genre intended for ballot accounting and the primary document for the record of polling station activities on Election Day. However, the pink sheet serves also as an archive for the collation and subsequent declaration of results of the presidential elections. Although other genres such as the Voters' Register, the Proxy List, and ballot papers were used during the election, these feature in our analysis here only insofar as they inform an understanding of the pink sheet. The pink sheet assumes primacy as the chief nonhuman witness to the election, and despite the presence of polling agents and presiding officers for each polling station, it came to function in the dispute case as *the* credible, incontrovertible record of the election. It possessed an allure of objectivity. Its role is akin to the action-authorizing and regulative function of such genres as the Standard of Care document earlier referenced. It directs deliberative attention toward certain versions of reality and shapes interlocutors' arguments.

If, from its form and content, the pink sheet could be considered a rather simple genre of ballot counts of the polls, how did it come to assume such centrality in arguments by the Electoral Commissioner, the petitioners and respondents who relied on it in court, and the judges who used arguments based on it to arrive at a verdict? Like the hanging chads at the center of the U.S. presidential election in 2000,[15] pink sheets became controversial in the aftermath of Election 2012 in Ghana because the New Patriotic Party (NPP) alleged there were irregularities at polling stations. The NPP alleged unsigned pink sheets, duplicate serial numbers on pink sheets, and errors in ballot accounting on pink sheets dented the credibility of the election results. In resolving these allegations in court, the pink sheet became the primary evidentiary document based on which arguments were articulated. To understand those arguments beyond a focus on interactions between interlocutors, one needs to examine the values and beliefs instantiated in the genre while considering the cultural imaginaries surrounding ideologies embedded in the genre.

The deliberations analyzed here emerge from transcripts I generated from the Supreme Court deliberations for six key days, namely June 6, June 10, June 24, June 30, August 7, and August 29, 2013. The last of these was the day the Supreme Court delivered its verdict. Deliberations on these days capture key arguments surrounding the pink sheet delivered by the petitioners, respondents, and chair of the EC, as well as the Supreme Court judges' verdict. On the first three dates, the chair, Dr. Kwadwo Afari-Djan, provided in-depth information on the country's election architecture from voter registration to declaration of election results. Those first four dates also involved attorneys of the petitioners and respondents cross-examining Dr. Afari-Djan and the court clarifying questions and answers from him. On August 7, the attorneys for both petitioner and respondent presented closing arguments summarizing their key positions. These arguments offer key insights into the connections between cultural imaginaries, genre, and deliberation.

The Electoral Commission, Pink Sheets, and the Rhetorical Construction of Evidence

Controversy over the pink sheet resulted in part from what I contend is an ambivalent cultural attitude toward documentary evidence in sections of Ghanaian society. That attitude is magnified by a history of oral testimony in tension with the demands of writing inaugurated by the colonial encounter.[16] This tension shapes the status of the pink sheet as a record and the claims and evidence it affords. In order to assess the information contained on the pink sheet, it is important first to consider both the historical milieu and the technologies and genre system within which the pink sheet is imbricated. The two-week-long testimony by Dr. Kwadwo Afari-Djan reveals the historical context of the pink sheet's emergence. Ghana adopted BVDs in 2012 to enhance the integrity of its electoral processes. The details of this verification are captured on the Voters' Register. In a June 24, 2013, deliberation in court, Afari-Djan explains that the EC deployed the BVDs to "directly capture the ten fingerprints of the applicant if they were available and to capture the photograph of the person." The use of the devices enabled both speed and accuracy, the latter particularly necessary in an electoral environment with a history of allegations of double registration and registration by minors.

However, the devices also came with major challenges, among them equipment failure, human error, and the effect of climatic conditions.[17] For example, although SuperLock Technologies Limited (STL), the Israeli company that provided the device to the EC, recommended the device be used within enclosed areas,[18] exposure to climatic conditions caused several devices to malfunction on Election Day. Consequently, the accessibility concerns that might lead to a disenfranchisement of citizens with visible disabilities on Election Day compelled the EC to implement a two-system classification of verification—fingerprint verification and face-only verification. Face-only verification was meant particularly for registrants whose fingerprints could not be detected by the BVDs. Although Afari-Djan contends that the classification of such registrants under face-only was aimed at inclusivity of all voters, this decision would come to shape the questions asked on the pink sheet, with profound consequences for connections between the pink sheet, the BVDs, and evidence.

Questions on the pink sheet establish a link among votes, verification, and evidence. On the pink sheet, one of the key questions regarding ballot accounting reads "What is the number of ballots issued to voters verified by the use of Form 1C (but not by the use of BVD)?" (Form 1C was the Captured Voter Information Form). This question intersects with the EC's decision about face-only verification, forcing a recognition of the interconnection between the BVD, the pink sheet, and other genres like Form 1C. Thus, the information contained on the pink sheet genre is understood primarily, and perhaps only, in relation to the BVD and these other related genres. Importantly, the question exposes how the BVD enables a framing of arguments about the pink sheet genre concerning evidence. For Afari-Djan, a technological glitch during the voter registration process caused the loss of voter data and the omission of some registered voters from the Voters' Register. Because these were voters with Voter ID cards, and in order to correct the anomaly, the EC re-registered the potentially disenfranchised voters and included question C3 on voters registered without the use of Form 1C. Notice here Afari-Djan's explanation, given May 30, 2013, of the origin of the question on the pink sheet:

> My Lords, it's important to relate this [point about C3] because this is the origin of the question C3 on the pink sheet. This is the reason why question C3 was put on the pink sheet and C3 asks the question, "How many people have been verified other than by the use of the biometric verification machine?" C3 was put there in an attempt to take care of those people who through no fault of theirs would have valid voter ID cards in their possession, but whose names will not appear on the register and therefore could not vote.[19]

The question addressed a technological hitch that would otherwise have disenfranchised voters. Afari-Djan proceeds to emphasize the crucial role of presiding officers trained and stationed at every polling station to verify voters other than by the use of the BVDs. It is possible to see why the inclusion of question C3 became such a focal point of controversy. Whereas the primary means of verification was by the BVD, the EC made room for verification by another means. In doing so, the EC was cognizant of striking a balance between its policy of No Verification, No Vote and the possibility of disenfranchising voters because of the failure of the technology. The risks of abuse involved in the policy then led to legitimate suspicions that fueled arguments about the role not only of the question, but of the genre itself in determining the winner of the elections.

The human element integral to determining and recording verification by face-only fueled suspicions about what may count as legitimate evidence. Errors and abuse could and did occur through the verification process. Although the genre of the pink sheet serves a consequential evidentiary role, its sufficiency as documentary evidence was called into question precisely because of the possibility of human errors. As the Ghanaian Supreme Court Justice Julius Ansah sums it up in his opinion on the case, "The pink sheet is a very vital document to consider when determining several issues in this matter [of the election dispute case], like the issue as to whether or not there was over voting at a polling station."[20] Lending credence to the pink sheet's importance, Afari-Djan similarly explained during deliberations that the process of declaration of the election results involves a transfer of figures from the pink sheets onto another genre, the Collation Form, at every constituency or electoral district across Ghana.[21] Transposition errors could occur during this transfer, which would necessitate a recollation of results at a constituency's Collation Center. When asked whether disputed results from the pink sheets rendered on the Collation Form needed to be recollated, Afari-Djan's response pointed to the limits of the evidence from the pink sheet: "To use the popular phrase, 'You and I were not there,' so we are not able to give a faithful account of what actually happened, but I supposed this is what happened, that during the collation somebody said, 'No, I'm not satisfied with the collated results,' then you'll have to go and collate and so on. First of all, you make sure that there's no transposition error. So, I suppose that is what happened."[22]

For the chair of the EC, trustworthy evidence from an individual's physical presence at a polling station may be both necessary and sufficient conditions to fully recount the events of Election Day. This is because although the pink sheet, Collation Forms, and other genres were intended as records of electoral activities, they may be insufficient, and even falsifiable. Afari-Djan emphasized the limits of absolute reliance on the pink sheet as the exclusive arbiter of truth. This emphasis suggests both a firm faith in the necessity of physical presence of the body as a form of evidence, and a suspicion of the sufficiency of documentary evidence of the pink sheet genre or other genres. What obtains in his line of reasoning is a quest for a balance between the force of a history and legacy of orality (represented by the testimony obtained from physical presence of presiding officers at a polling station) and evidence of and trust in writing (in genres like the pink sheet) as a remnant of Ghana's colonial encounter with Europe. Afari-Djan's argument explains the tension that can exist between oral testimony and written evidence, a tension productively understood with recourse to history and cultural imaginaries surrounding such matters in the postcolony.

In the election dispute deliberations, that history is best explained by specific reference to what the historian Sean Hawkins, writing about the legacies of colonialism in Ghana, has referred to as the "world of experience" and the "world on paper."[23] In *Writing and Colonialism in Northern Ghana*, Hawkins discusses the ways in which colonialism in Africa was facilitated and sustained through the medium of writing and the worlds associated with it.[24] Hawkins's reference to writing is concerned with the colonial use of literacy and activities associated with the written word. With the example of the thoroughly oral society of the Dagaaba of northern Ghana of the time, Hawkins argues that colonialism in this community was an encounter between a world of experience and the world on paper.[25] Although Hawkins focuses on British colonial rule in northern Ghana by the end of the nineteenth century, his argument, in the main, applies just as much to southern Ghana, where the processes of colonialism took a firmer hold much earlier in the century.

It can be argued that the difference between colonialism in the north and the south is not so much a difference of kind as of degree. For Hawkins, the world of experience of the Dagaaba entails the society's "knowledge, practice, and speech," while the world on paper involves "a world that existed beyond the immediate and local experiences of the [Dagaaba]," one that by the early twentieth century "had become the *official arbiter of legitimacy, a regulator of authenticity, and a source of power*."[26] On each side of this bifurcation, knowledge systems exist that are either valued and privileged or degraded and subordinated. Hawkins maintains that writing intersected with colonialism in this society by reconstituting the social practices of colonial subjects into those envisioned by British colonizers: culture, religion, and politics were all transformed in this reconstitution.

For Hawkins, only by attentiveness to the dynamics of "authority, orality, and literacy" as processes of the colonial relationship can the legacies of colonialism in this African society be fully appreciated.[27] For the encounter between the world of experience and the world on paper did not imply a total displacement of the lives of the Dagaaba, nor of Ghanaian society more generally. Where both worlds intersected, "the [Dagaaba] were forced to adapt, appeal, or defer to the assumptions and expectations of the world on paper."[28] Indeed, while formal colonial rule ended, the dynamics of the two worlds wrought by the encounter transform and adapt to changing circumstances. Colonial legacies remain manifest and steadfast in institutional practices and citizens' social and political lives in the postcolony. One of such means is through deference to the written word. In relation to African rhetorical traditions, rhetorical scholars have argued against the teleological advance and untenable binarism posited between orality and literacy in ways that discount the complexity of African rhetorical knowledges.[29] What I suggest is that beyond what rhetorical scholars have come to know as an untenable teleology, this distinction between a supposedly superior written culture and a so-called inferior oral culture be reconsidered here as a combination, with uses for appropriate situations. That combination would entail creolized forms of rhetorical phenomena such as has been argued by Erik Johnson.[30]

Concerning the dispute deliberations, Afari-Djan argues that it is impossible to provide a faithful account of events of Election Day because both he and his interlocutors in court were absent from polling stations. By suggesting that physical absence from the polling station makes evidence from the pink sheet insufficient, Afari-Djan reveals the necessity of both the physical, embodied presence of the presiding officers and the evidence on the pink sheet in the search for evidence. In that search for evidence during deliberations, there are limitations on the primacy of the written word in a postcolonial context influenced profoundly by a culture of orality.

As rhetorical scholars have argued, considerations of rhetorical production in its many manifestations—embodied, written, spoken, gestural—make for a fuller account of rhetorical phenomena.[31] A long tradition of scholarship on African societies has too often dismissed knowledge from the continent as unimportant precisely because of the oral medium through which it has been articulated. Rather than defer to the authority of the (written) genres as the official arbiter of legitimacy, Afari-Djan points to the careful negotiation that necessarily must attend the quest for authority, legitimacy, and authenticity of the genres in the postcolony. Instead of either "world" supplanting the other, the world of experience and the world on paper exist simultaneously in the postcolony. They mutually enrich understanding of social life and pose challenges to the perceived superiority of the written word as *the* world and perhaps the only valuable means of establishing truth, authenticity, and knowledge. Deferring to a combination of both worlds also pays homage to African knowledge systems rooted in its oral cultures.

Like most postcolonies, the modern postcolonial Ghanaian state is perennially confronted with "competing norms." It faces an almost impossible choice between "the wholesale adoption of modern institutions and media with all their associated norms, and operating foreign institutions within a cultural frame of reference."[32] The chair of the EC operates within this postcolonial cultural frame of reference by negotiating a careful balance between, on the one hand, the affordances of oral testimony or truth ascertained by means of physical presence and, on the other hand, documentary evidence. His arguments function as an indirect case for the necessity of including African knowledge systems in global intellectual contexts, a point persuasively argued by such decolonial theorists as Bagele Chilisa.[33]

A recourse to this cultural frame of reference further shapes arguments about the pink sheet concerning the limits of the BVDs. In response to a question by Philip Addison, a counsel for the respondents in court, Afari-Djan explains the human element that shapes the facticity of the evidence recorded in the form of the written, pink sheet genre. Notice, in this rhetorical exchange from June 5, 2013, his discussion of the needed balance between technology and human intervention:

ADDISON: Would you say that the introduction of this biometric verification had in fact eradicated these practices [impersonation, etc.] from the last election?

AFARI-DJAN: I would be right to say so.

ADDISON: You are right to say so?

AFARI-DJAN: Yes, you see, if I say possibly, it has eliminated the human dimension from the election, the machine itself. But there is a human element in the administration of the election.

ADDISON: When you say human element in the administration of the election, what are you talking about?

AFARI-DJAN: Well, let me give you an example of what I'm saying. We know that to become a candidate you must have your name in the Voters' Register. On Election Day, I'm the presiding officer, you come to the station, the machine takes your picture but is not able to take your fingerprint. If I were the presiding officer, I will let you go and vote. I will let you go and vote because the essence of verification is to establish the true identity of the prospective voter. That is the human element.

ADDISON: I don't really understand what you have just said in relation to . . . You're trying to justify voting without verification?

AFARI-DJAN: My Lords, I don't know what he's asking of . . . He's asked of the human element, I've given it.

ADDISON: So, you're telling this court that your presiding officers, they have a discretion in allowing people to vote without verification?

AFARI-DJAN: I have not said that, My Lords. I've said, for example, let me give you. For example, the paramount chief of the town comes to the polling station. We know him to be the paramount chief, we know his name, he's in the Voters' Register, and that machine won't take his fingerprint, then we say Nana [title for a chief in the Akan language], you can't vote?[34]

On the one hand, Afari-Djan's response may be construed as a contravention of the principle of equality before the law. By his own stipulation, without verification, citizens cannot cast a ballot. On the other hand, Afari-Djan recognizes the human dimension that is inescapably involved in the use of even the best technological systems. This human dimension implies that in addition to technologies, it is individuals' work that determines how the elections are conducted. Technological utopianism holds no sway in the facticity of the results of the elections. If, therefore, poll workers' roles are just as crucial as those of technologies or the facticity accorded genres like the pink sheet, how should the promise of technological accuracy be balanced with the probability of system failure? Afari-Djan's argument contradicts Philip Addison's seeming befuddlement that voters could be and actually were allowed to vote without biometric verification.

Although the electoral regulations allow for verification other than by the use of technology, there still remained an underlying expectation by some election stakeholders that technology would *completely* eradicate the challenges that gave rise to the adoption of the BVDs. That expectation manifests in the arguments stemming from recourse to the role of the pink sheet: expectations about its facticity and authenticity as an arbiter of truth. That expectation also simultaneously exposes the necessity of allowing African knowledge systems, action, and being that tend to favor relationality and contingency and delinks from dominant Euro-American modes of thought.[35]

Furthermore, there is a point to be made about Afari-Djan's claim that "the essence of verification is to establish the true identity of the prospective voter." In the interaction, the example of a paramount chief is instructive for its lessons about the malleability required to balance evidence in terms of embodied presence on the one hand and deference to the written word, on the other hand. Influential and well-regarded nationally, paramount chiefs are traditional authorities of the local communities over which they preside. Within the framework of a hybrid parliamentary and presidential executive system practiced since 1992, the Ghanaian Constitution guarantees the position of the paramount chief, alongside their traditional councils established by customary law. In Ghana's postcolonial democracy, the institution of chieftaincy operates as a (micro)state within the larger nation-state, albeit subordinate in law and governance to the nation-state. This postcolonial condition of a state and the dispositions it engenders within the nation-state is significant for understanding arguments about genres like the pink sheet and their place in studies of deliberation. In suggesting that the chief can be verified other than by the use of the BVD, Afari-Djan exposes the unavoidable condition into which a presiding officer may be thrust in determining a balance between equality and expediency, between technological efficiency and human action, and between the "world of experience" and "the world on paper."

But Afari-Djan's argument about conducting verification through means other than the BVDs is not to be considered as limited to the example of the paramount chief alone. Prior to Election Day, a key part of the voter registration process involved the public display of the Voters' Register at polling stations. The objective here was twofold: to offer voters an opportunity to correct errors in their own biodata details and to challenge or object to names of unqualified voters—any objection may then be settled by a magistrate. What is assumed here is that community members would know voters and can tell when minors and other unqualified persons attempt to register to vote. In a country with national biometric ID card implementation challenges, such additional local solutions become necessary for identity verification.[36] The community determines its own ways of verification when the affordances of literacy become limiting. Their doing so speaks to a recognition of local knowledge that destabilizes the primacy—and fetishism—of the written word by which colonial knowledge continues to be entrenched.

At first glance, Afari-Djan's claim concerning the paramount chief may suggest preferential treatment given to powerful personalities. However, a closer look would reveal that the EC's corresponding decision to display the Voters' Register (a legal requirement in the Ghanaian electoral system) demonstrates the commission's own recognition of the limits of technologies like the BVDs. That display of the register also addresses, through practices of oral evidence rooted within Ghanaian culture, additional means of verification. I contend that in Ghana's postcolonial democracy, the hybrid of the world of experience and the world on paper is manifested in how the BVD, the Voters' Register, the Captured Voter Information Form, and the collation forms, among other genres, were deployed to shape arguments about the pink sheet. The world on paper works in tandem with, rather than in opposition to, the world of experience, and deliberations about both "worlds" are legible by attentiveness to the pink sheet genre and the arguments it enables. In the deliberations, the pink sheet genre is exposed not as the singularly authoritative guarantee for establishing the petitioners' claims but as a document limited in its capacity to inform the quest for authenticity.

In another interaction on June 6, 2013, between Philip Addison and Afari-Djan is a reference to evidence "on the face of the pink sheet" and the argument that it was imprudent to restrict the quest for evidence to the pink sheets:

ADDISON: Now, Dr. Afari-Djan, do you realize that the pink sheet as you have it there is what was used in the declaration?

AFARI-DJAN: Yes.

ADDISON: So, can we limit ourselves to what is on the face of the pink sheet?

AFARI-DJAN: My Lords, I have a bit of difficulty limiting myself to what is on the pink sheet for purposes of determining deeper questions.

ADDISON: Now, Dr. Afari-Djan, if a polling station in addition to its register also has an Absent Voters' List and a Transfer Voter's List, it can affect the number of registered voters eligible to vote at that polling station, am I right?

AFARI-DJAN: My Lords, definitely.

ADDISON: Are you in a position to tell if in fact there was an Absent Voters' List at this polling station?

AFARI-DJAN: From the list I can't tell.

ADDISON: If there was, it will be indicated on the number of voters eligible to vote there, is that not true?

AFARI-DJAN: You're right.

ADDISON: In which case that number can differ from the number on the register.

AFARI-DJAN: Yes, the point, My Lords, that we've been trying to explain all the time that it was, when we talk about the register it is not just simply this document. It says other things that may be there. If there is an Absent Voters' Register, that number is supposed to be taken from out of the number noted there. If there's Absent Voters' Register, it is additional and so yes. So, when we talk about the register, it does not refer, that is why we prefer to say the number of persons eligible to vote at that polling station.

ADDISON: Good, so that in this instance we always have to go by what is on the pink sheet because the register by itself would not tell us.

AFARI-DJAN: No, no, we don't always have to go by. I disagree.[37]

The notion of what is "on the face of the pink sheet" first came into prominence during the deliberations when the lead witness of the petitioners, Dr. Mahamadu Bawumia, routinely remarked that "the evidence is in the pink sheet, and that is why we are in court."[38] Bawumia's commentary suggests that the genre of the pink sheet is the incontrovertible proof for the claims of overvoting, voting without verification, and counting unsigned pink sheets made by the petitioners in court. In seeking to limit evidence to the pink sheet, Addison takes a position reflective of Hawkins's argument, discussed earlier, that colonialism wrought a condition of dependency on the practices associated with the world on paper. In that world, the written record is the official arbiter of legitimacy, a regulator of authenticity, and a source of power. Addison's suggestion presumes that documentary evidence on the pink sheet offers accurate, undeniable proof for his claims. For Afari-Djan, however, limiting evidence merely to what is available on the pink sheet takes away from the task of "determining deeper questions."

These deeper questions, I suggest, are those that can be answered by recourse to the other genres like the Voters' Register and the Transfer List, and, indeed, credible polling agents. In recognizing that determining the authenticity of the results cannot be limited to what is "on the face of the pink sheet," Afari-Djan shifts attention from a singular focus on the pink sheet. Then, in response to another one of Addison's questions about the discrepancy between numbers recorded on the pink sheet and those on the polling station register, Afari-Djan reiterates the limits of the pink sheet. Notice his discussion of the genre:

> My Lords, I have no way of knowing, you know, you keep saying what is gleaned from the face of the pink sheet. We have seen here where what is written on the face of the pink sheet, that is what is the number of voters on the pink sheet is written twelve, but if we refer to the register itself, it's quite a different number so there's always going to be a difference between what is gleaned from the face of the register and what the reality is. . . . I'm saying that on the pink sheet, there could be a great difference between what you add up on the basis of what is on the face of the pink sheet and what the actual situation is according to the register.[39]

The difference apparent here is one between reality and appearance, between the affordances of the world of experience and the world on paper, between local norms and expectations and colonial legacies of legitimacy and authenticity. Afari-Djan's claim also suggests that meaning-making is a site of constant tension and contestation. What constitutes legitimacy and authenticity in this context has deep roots in British colonial practices. Here, the postcolonial critic Peter Leman's discussion of the idea of testimony and documentary evidence in colonial Kenya is instructive for understanding colonialism's relationship with writing and speech. Leman's work also informs how we might think about marked African knowledges and unmarked European ones that unfold in deliberations afforded by genres.

In 1952, British colonial authorities put the Kenyan anticolonial, nationalist leader Jomo Kenyatta on trial for his involvement in the Mau Mau liberation movement. Leman recounts the colonial authorities' dilemma in court in what was a challenge to the legitimacy of British rule in East Africa: in this predominantly oral culture, should an audio recording of one of Kenyatta's speeches to the mostly unlettered followers of the Mau Mau liberation movement be admissible as documentary evidence in a case of incitement to violence leveled against him? Leman argues that authorities' reluctance to recognize the audio recording as documentary evidence is indicative of the anxieties of colonial modernity as it grappled with African modes of knowledge. This anxiety, for Leman, is in accord with "[colonial] law's traditional stance toward oral culture," one that insists literacy, rather than or in addition to orality, is the singular mode for legitimating truth and knowledge.[40]

Leman reminds us that, like in most African societies, in the Kenyan context, oral traditions and culture provided an alternative route to law and knowledge, and colonial authorities' recognition of this threat to their rule led them to restrict and diminish the validity of orality.[41] By diminishing the validity of oral traditions and culture, the "[English] Crown confronts Kenyatta with the authority of the written word, pitting text against speech as has been done in the colony for decades" in maintaining that "if it is not written down, then it must not be true."[42] The audio recording was discounted, and Kenyatta was consequently sentenced to a seven-year jail term. Leman concludes that at least in terms of law, echoes of the debate concerning the tradition-modernity divide still linger on in postcolonial Africa. The debate underscores "the legacy of the late colonial period and the crises and contradictions that destabilized colonial binaries—orality/literacy, uncivilized/civilized, illegal/legal, and ultimately, tradition/modernity—and their postcolonial variants."[43] The crises and contradictions, then, demand critical attention to a decolonizing approach to deliberation that accounts for the tensions and fissures inherent in arguments about evidence, such as those based on genres like the pink sheet.

Leman's analysis offers significant insights into our understandings of the role of genres like the pink sheet in studies of deliberation. Specifically, Afari-Djan's argument recognizes the inescapably intricate nexus between the genre as a written record of the elections and its limit in a postcolonial society where the value of testimony and the status of speech remain valuable and unavoidable. Thus considered, Afari-Djan's argument exposes testimony and documentary evidence as practices on a continuum, rather than in opposition, even as a struggle emerges in the quest to establish truth and the legitimacy of the votes. By insisting on the limits of the pink sheet genre, Afari-Djan demonstrates that the colonial binaries are woefully inadequate in explicating social life in a postcolonial context like Ghana's. A recognition of this limit, then, ought to guide our studies of deliberation. Of course, the tension between testimony and documentary evidence is not a uniquely postcolonial concern. However, this tension is heightened particularly in the postcolony precisely because of the interplay of colonially derived practices and traditional African modes of knowledge production rooted in the oral. The genre of the pink sheet operates as the site of this contention and arguments surrounding it evince the ideologies at the heart of deliberations in this postcolony—authenticity and legitimacy of the written word as the arbiter of truth over oral traditions.

The Status of Documentary Evidence in the Postcolony

Closing arguments in court typically provide a summation of key arguments by petitioners and respondents. In the deliberations, the petitioners and respondents' claims exposed their contradictory positions on the role of the pink sheet as evidence. While the petitioners argued that the genre represents a predictable, incontrovertible record of election records, the respondents saw in it a document with only limited capacity to fully authenticate the truth of the votes. For the petitioners, the pink sheet constituted a primary record of the elections, but its features authenticate it as a genre as well. Among these features is the required signature of the presiding officers, which the petitioners argued lent credibility to the genre. Because of this authenticating feature, the petitioners believed the absence of the signatures nullify the votes recorded on the pink sheets. This argument would come to hold important implications for the judges' declaration of the election results for at least two reasons.

First, the controversy about the signature can easily be considered as a legal quibble of a plaintiff advancing all possible arguments to win a case. In fact, in law, as in administrative procedure, a signature identifies the author of a document, authenticates the contents of that document, and thereby lends it credibility. The "Declaration" section on the pink sheet states, "We, the undersigned, do hereby declare that the results shown above are a true and accurate account of the ballots in this polling station." Here, while the petitioners' arguments follow standard expectations of appropriateness in law, electoral procedures, and commonsense reasoning, what is significant in terms of deliberation is their insistence on the ideological character of the genre—that it is *an accurate representation of truth and effectiveness*. One key claim by a member of the petitioners' team was that duplicate serial numbers on pink sheets invalidate those pink sheets, and this claim was considered by the court as a sort of printer's error with no actual impact on the results of the election.

The second reason the pink sheet held immense implications for the arguments in court hinges on two major refrains of the petitioners during the deliberations: "You and I were not there" and "the evidence on the face of the pink sheet." Both expressions featured constantly in arguments about the pink sheet and suggested that not just documentary evidence—the ethos of which derives from the practices of "the world on paper"—but the features of the genre (including the signature that authenticates it) make the genre what the petitioners believe it is: the exclusive and incontrovertible arbiter of truth. By emphasizing what is "on the face of the pink sheet" to the exclusion of all other forms of evidence, the petitioners maintain documentary evidence and it alone, without witnesses such as polling agents, reveals truth and knowledge. Truth subsists only in what is written, and the physical, embodied presence of witnesses does not detract from belief in that truth. This argument reflects what John Comaroff and Jean Comaroff refer to as "textualizing relations," a mode of politics during colonial times which, to Africans, "appeared to make humans into fragile 'paper persons'" in a manner that disembodies social relations altogether.[44]

A contradictory argument to the genre-as-arbiter-of-truth perspective is proffered by respondents during the deliberations. Of the petitioners' arguments, Tsatsu Tsikata, the lead counsel for the respondents, observed that the exclusivity of the pink sheet's documentary evidence was undercut by the petitioners' own admission that the pink sheet can offer only an incomplete picture of the elections. Referring to Dr. Bawumia's testimony, Tsikata argued, "He [Dr. Bawumia] acknowledged that on some pink sheets, there was not enough information. He claimed in some cases that where there is a blank, it means zero. Now, your lordships certainly will be hard put in my respectful submission to accepting such a claim that a blank in a form means zero."[45] Tsikata unpacks the limits, even in the petitioners' own arguments, of reposing absolute faith in the documentary evidence contained in the pink sheet. For Tsikata, if information on the pink sheet is to be taken at face value, interpretation becomes a matter only of what is seen "on the face of the pink sheet," a practice that disavows all rhetorical insights into interpretation. The petitioners' truth would be limited insofar as the genre may contain errors, omissions, and misrepresentations that impact the veracity of the valid votes cast. Tsikata's argument implies that the petitioners' neglect of polling agents as witnesses and sources of knowledge and evidence is directly tied to those petitioners' exclusive reliance on the force of documentary evidence in establishing the truth of the votes. Such a reliance appears at odds with understandings of rhetorical phenomena as multimodal and embodied.

The position of polling agents is guaranteed in the electoral laws of Ghana, and agents act as observers for their political parties during elections. In contrast to the petitioners' argument, another member of the team of respondents, Tony Lithur, buttressed Tsikata's arguments on the limits of the pink sheet genre as an absolute record authenticating the truth of events on Election Day. Delivered on August 7, 2013, the following excerpts from Lithur's closing arguments sums up the crux of this position. Notice here the reference to the role of polling agents in relation to the limits of the documentary evidence:

> By Dr. Bawumia's own admission, no polling agent was questioned about what they claimed they had found on the face of those pink sheets. In proving their case in this court, the petitioners wave pink sheets at everybody. According to them the evidence is on the face of the pink sheets and coupled with Dr. Bawumia's mantra, "You and I were not there," the petitioners sought to limit discussion about this serious exercise to the face of the pink sheet. But he admitted himself during cross-examination that he didn't ask polling station agents about the figures, about what he claimed, the discrepancies on the face of the pink sheet. But my Lords, you begin to ask very, very simple questions indeed: "Were these polling agents not appointed as agents of the first petitioner in this election?" Dr. Bawumia and the first petitioners must have spent resources training these polling agents to protect their interest at the polling station level. They were actually trained by the Electoral Commission as well. In fact, polling agents themselves cannot honestly say that they were not aware of the roles to perform on behalf of the petitioners, so surely if there were any irregularities at those polling stations, of course one would expect that from their training, they would know how to report those irregularities.[46]

Given the witness role they can play in the evidence matrix, polling agents' exclusion from the quest for evidence reveals the persistence—and limits—of colonially inspired ideologies that place undue emphasis on the infallibility of the written word. As the respondents were quick to point out, such ideologies hold immense implications for citizens' constitutional right to vote. As Lithur goes on to assert,

> If the petitioners' view of the evidence is "on the face of the pink sheet" and "You and I were not there," if this were to be the position, there'd be no need for any party to appoint polling agents. We might as well sit back at our homes trusting that the Electoral Commission would perform their duty and when they finish, we will collect pink sheets without reference to any incident at all at the polling station. We'll lock ourselves in a room, point out figures on that pink sheet and come to your lordships and say annul the votes, the constitutionally exercised rights of individuals, because the evidence is on the face of the pink sheet and my lords, "You and I were not there."[47]

In terms of democratic deliberation, it is important to consider here not so much the legality or reasonableness of the constitutional provisions, but the petitioners and respondents' arguments that highlight two competing impulses about evidence and knowledge-making. On the one hand, a defining feature of the petitioners' argument is the hope they repose in the incontrovertibility of the pink sheet as the final arbiter of truth. Their claims construct the pink sheet as an objective artifact that settles the argument about the election dispute, and neither potential errors nor omissions appear to invalidate the pink sheet genre. On the other hand, the respondents' argument alerts us to the limits of the pink sheet genre and the dangers of reposing absolute faith in its evidentiary role. The pink sheet genre operates in the respondents' arguments as a necessary but limited genre within a postcolonial context where the balance between speech and the written word, and between the written word and embodied presence, is a most unavoidable phenomenon and indeed necessary condition of existence and knowledge-making. Regardless of the potential unreliability of polling agents' accounts, the respondents' closing argument seems to suggest that the oral evidence polling agents may furnish can provide a fuller accounting of the events on Election Day.

Held together, arguments by both petitioners and respondents expose the competing ideologies at the heart of democratic deliberation about the election dispute case. Absolute faith in the incontrovertibility of documentary evidence furnishes only a partial view of events on Election Day, as would an exclusive emphasis on polling agents' accounts. Both of these perspectives further show the necessity of these competing ideological standpoints working in tandem if, in studies of democratic deliberation, we are to more fully understand the practices of deliberation afforded by "the world on paper" and "the world of experience" concerning evidence and knowledge-making more generally.

The Supreme Court and the Rhetorical Construction of Evidence

Thus far, we have seen that, at least in the case of the Dagaaba, British colonial courts framed, constituted, and legitimated the sociopolitical life of Ghanaians through written judicial rulings. The court was a central constitutive institution of the colonial state that (re)ordered the world of the colonized. As Hawkins demonstrates, court records indicate that it was through written law and legal institutions of the colonial state that the British refashioned, among other things, the Dagaaba society's notions of laws governing marriage, (Western) conceptions of God, and the relationship between men and women. It was also through such rulings that "the particular ideologies implicit in colonial writing . . . affected issues of identity, sovereignty, legitimacy, legality, and patriarchy."[48] I contend that this constitutive role of the colonial court echoes in Ghana's postcolonial Supreme Court, as well, through the ways the role of the pink sheet is rhetorically constructed. Like the petitioners and respondents, the judges articulated two key opposing positions on the status of the pink sheet as evidence in a 588-page verdict: that the genre was a sufficient, incontrovertible record of the election and that it held only partial truth in need of complementary evidence from other sources.

The first argument articulated by the judges is that the pink sheet exists merely as the primary record that it is, so its position in the larger scheme of political legitimacy is circumscribed by other records that can lend credence to the elections. The presiding justice of the court, William Atuguba, argued that "no one [in Ghanaian or other judicial contexts] has given it [the pink sheet] a conclusive effect," and so, "I would not infer from the constitution and Electoral laws that its reputation as the primary record of the election means anything more than that it is the ready and basic document to resort to, *for a start*, when one wants to ascertain how the elections fared in a particular polling station."[49] This perspective on the pink sheet makes room for other genres and persons—voter registration documents, Collation Forms, and polling station agents—to shape the nature of evidence that determines the legitimacy of votes. Such judicial position also stands in contrast to the petitioners' argument that the pink sheet, and it alone, remained the legitimate record of authenticity. In making room for the possibility of records and forms of evidence beyond the pink sheet genre, Justice Atuguba highlights not just the ecology of genres that might more fully evince the authenticity of the votes but the limits of an exclusive focus on the pink sheet as an unfailing guarantee of truth. That limit manifests in the idea that polling agents would be present at the polling stations. As active observers and signatories to the events of Election Day, these agents have a constitutional facility to give witness to the truth of the electoral process beyond the evidence provided on paper.

The second, opposing view advanced by the judges held that the pink sheet as a genre constituted a defining document containing complete information on the elections. For instance, Justice Ansah argued that the pink sheet "contains a summary of information on *what exactly took place* during the voting and the number of ballots issued for the day, what use they were put to and the results of voting at the end of the poll."[50] While recognizing that "other documents like the register for a polling station, collation forms, etc., etc. may come in handy," Justice Ansah insists that "there is no other comprehensive record of how the polls were conducted at the polling station."[51] This position ignores the possibility that both genres and human witnesses can overcome the insufficiency inherent in the pink sheet as a genre. But even important, this perspective appears rooted in colonial—and later postcolonial—forms of legal reasoning that place variable emphasis on documentary and oral forms of evidence. Justice Ansah asserts that "in the law of evidence, documentary evidence prevails over oral evidence. . . . The reason is not far to see. Documentary evidence if not challenged, is often the best proof of matters in controversy. In fact, it *should* prevail over oral evidence."[52] Yet documentary evidence may be forged. It may also not be challenged. And it may contain errors, falsifications, and other such disqualifying qualities that undermine its truth-value. Documentary evidence is associated with the regime of "writing on paper," in contrast to the oral evidence that *also* remains a feature of a predominantly oral society's practices of knowledge-making, including those related to the search for truth and authenticity.

The pink sheet is significant as a genre in that alongside practices of evidence associated with a predominantly oral society, it exposes the challenge of deliberation within postcolonial Ghana. It underscores what I argue are remnants of the world on paper in tension with the world of experience. It also reflects the ideology instantiated in the Ghanaian pidgin language expression, presumably influenced by colonial ideologies, that "book no lie"—books contain only truth. Arguments about the rhetorical work of pink sheets in the courtroom deliberations mirror the nature of the postcolonial state itself, wherein the worldviews of both worlds—of experience and on paper—operate in tandem, if also in an uneasy interrelation.

This unavoidable condition in the postcolony also evinces the values and beliefs instantiated in arguments by the petitioners, respondents, and the court based on the pink sheet genre. On the one hand, the arguments demonstrate a firm faith in the authenticity of the written word in terms of documentary evidence. And this reliance on the sufficiency of the written word has roots in a colonial ethos that valorized documentary evidence, and writing more broadly, over other forms of knowledge as the official arbiter of authenticity and the source of legitimacy. On the other hand, the idea that authenticity exists beyond the realm of the written word underlines not only the vestiges of the world of experience that remain in and shape deliberative life within the postcolony but also the anxieties associated with a deference to and fetishism of the written word.

Conclusion

What do the kinds of arguments advanced based on the pink sheet offer our theorizing of deliberation within the postcolony and beyond colonial modernity's investments in the idea that the written is the only legitimate means of knowledge-making? To begin with, the pink sheet operates as a charter-like document, beating a path for what votes came to be counted as valid or invalid and authorizing certain perceptions about the election and disavowing others. Not only did the genre constitute the typified rhetorical action that is based in the recurrent situation (or results, in this case) of practices of Election Day, but it also served to direct arguments that unfolded about the events of that day. While the pink sheets invariably became the dominant form of evidence during the deliberations in court, the networks of genres and persons shape the forms of evidence the genre allows. By recognizing that the pink sheet genre is one node in a network of several others, the influence of these other genres on the evidence provided comes to the fore.

The generic features of the pink sheet, the arguments based on it as the primary form of evidence, and the postcolonial cultural imaginaries that situate the arguments expose the "archive of cultural imprints" regarding ideologies in deliberation in Ghana's postcolonial society.[53] Those ideologies imply that in theorizing deliberation within the postcolony, the cultural terrain wrought by colonialism becomes most salient in extending understanding beyond dominant approaches to studying democratic deliberation. That cultural terrain is never fully a monolithic category. Instead, it consists of interactions between institutional practices that are legacies of the colonial encounter and residual, yet forceful, expressions of local African practices of orality. For studies of democratic deliberation, genres considered within a network remain relevant in understanding the interconnections that shape deliberative activity. Although a single genre, the pink sheet is only fully understood when considered within the system of other genres. Further, rather than oppositional elements, genres may combine usefully with the oral testimony rooted in the oral culture of a people to provide a fuller account of evidence within context. Our reliance on other such modes of knowledge-making can help undermine the colonial logics at play in the exclusive deference to the written word.

Methodologically, in researching democratic deliberation, a reliance on genres can help interrogate the disjunctures, fissures, and seeming contradictions inherent in arguments within context. It is common in studies of democratic deliberation to focus solely on stakeholder arguments to map the deliberative terrain. However, as the analysis here demonstrates, the genres about which deliberations are held can themselves be the point of departure for studying arguments, rather than just the products of those arguments. They can evince the ideological and cultural contexts of the arguments and direct the path that deliberations take. Genres can be crucial sites for examining not just an archive of cultural imprints, particularly those of a postcolonial society, but also the competing, yet complementary, ideologies evinced in deliberations.

CHAPTER 3

Deliberating Participation

Digital Publics and Analogue Political Realities

In postcolonial democracies, it is crucial where we look for citizens' democratic practice. Although citizens may deliberate in publics created to advance institutional imperatives, this opportunity is not available to everyone. As spaces for deliberation, publics are differently conditioned to reflect the relationships citizens have to each other and the state. And those relationships are themselves embedded in the historical and social conditions that structure postcolonial life. In a pivotal essay examining the concept of publics as a critical keyword in rhetorical scholarship, Robert Asen turns attention to the relational dimensions of the term. He emphasizes that the concept is best understood not necessarily in terms of "interpersonal, dyadic interactions" but as "networks of relationships that contextualize particular engagements."[1] Digital publics that emerge on platforms like Twitter reflect a component of this network of relationships. The nature of the engagements and the networks citizens build can be conditioned by histories, structures of power, and forms of political organization. Moreover, these relationships are not merely located in one site of operation; because of their fluidity, a "particular network," Asen writes, "may link up with other networks, sustaining wide-ranging, large-scale discussions."[2] This sense of connection is critical to understanding the formation of publics and the networks of relationships publics enable for democratic practice.

Yet, though crucial to the idea of publics, the nature of relationships, as Asen further observes, remains undertheorized in scholarship on publics. To enrich rhetorical studies' understanding of the nature of relationships, Asen employs the example of neoliberalism's ascendancy in Western democracies. He explains that relationships deriving from this politico-economic system of social organization enable the formation of a certain kind of citizen-subject whose mode of existence with their environment, other citizens, and institutions of state shape their engagement as political subjects. According to Asen, neoliberalism allows citizens to operate only within a limited set of predefined economic and political choices, thereby limiting their ability to transform their communities. Neoliberal publics emphasize logics such as homogeneity, singularity, and universality of the human experience, and they obscure important differences across race, class, gender, and sexuality. As a result, the logic of neoliberalism ultimately "denies relationships their transformative power" by widening inequality, injustice, and racism.[3] As a constitutive force, then, neoliberalism as a vision of political and economic organization operates as a consequential force shaping publics, their purposes, and their actions.

We may extend Asen's neoliberalism example in another idiom. Historically contingent processes such as colonialism and its postcolonial legacies function like neoliberalism. They constitute citizen relationships to the nation-state, deliberation, and democratic practice. Like the constitutive mechanism of neoliberal logics, colonialism and its afterlives function to shape relationships and publics and ultimately prove consequential for citizen participation in democracies. As Achille Mbembe argues of African societies, state institutions during colonialism existed fundamentally to compel and maintain obeisance to the colonial order, and laws operated to serve just this end of violence. In their practice of democracy, postcolonial African regimes inherited and furthered these purposes and ends to varying degrees.[4] To understand democratic practice within African contexts, then, we must pay close attention to legacies of colonialism that reveal citizens' relationships to the state.

The conditioning mechanism constituting the publics that citizens form to participate in non-Western, African democracies exhibits peculiar characteristics arising from the enduring legacies of colonialism. Citizens' position(alities) in relation to state infrastructures and democratic institutions arise from the peculiarities of state formation in the postcolony. And these citizen positions(alities) are by no means uniform across African societies. They differ situationally based on localized contexts and cultures. As several African scholars have long maintained, the logics of public formation for political participation in Africa have historically followed a more distinct trajectory than did those of nations of the North Atlantic.[5] Omedi Ochieng, for example, has argued that publics in such contexts should be understood as embedded in "ecological, historical, and social structures."[6] This embeddedness would reflect "the vicissitudes of power, chance, and luck" and reveal the constitution of "embodied persons who stand in a variety of complex, layered, imaginary, and entangled relationships with one another."[7] In this vein, citizen participation and contribution to politics in African societies proceed differently given the state formation processes that have shaped engagement with democratic institutions. Digital publics like Twitter afford a view into deliberations in "multiple forums not exclusive to those of the official political realm," wherein participants are constituted in "multiple, local, interactive webs of meaning and commitment that arise through discourse."[8]

This chapter examines the nature of relationships in terms of colonialism and its legacies that shaped citizens' participation and deliberation during the 2013 election dispute case in Ghana. Shifting attention away from the institutional contexts of analysis in the previous chapters, I direct the inquiry here toward a digital public that emerged and coalesced around four key, interrelated hashtags during the dispute, namely #GhanaDecides, #ElectionPetition, #TheVerdict, and #SupremeCourt. I argue that these hashtags, the use of which unfolded primarily on Twitter—and accompanying blog posts, opinion articles, and YouTube videos—constituted a digital public. That public reveals a paradigm of new possibilities for citizens' democratic practice beyond the institutional boundaries delimited by the postcolonial state. These possibilities then enable citizens to transpose, (re)frame, and reconstitute analogue political realities in digital contexts through popular cultural resources and literacies. I suggest that the publics are best understood primarily within the framework of state/institutional and nonstate/noninstitutional domains of democratic practice wrought by the postcolonial condition.

As I will argue shortly, within the postcolonial setting, the nation-state operates as an ancillary ingredient of publicness, not the primary one. The cases analyzed here buttress the theoretical claim I make that we understand postcolonial publics and their unfolding not relative to national consciousness, but in the everyday practices that inform them. By so doing, we can establish both a necessary, inextricable link between citizens' offline political realities and rhetorical practices in digital contexts. We can also then gain a view into the cultural imaginaries that underscore democratic deliberation and territorialize democratic practice to reveal the ways it is experienced on a society's own terms.[9]

(Digital) Publics, Democratic Participation, and Citizenship

Historical conditions connect analogue political realities to the emergence of digital publics. When publics emerge on Twitter, for example, they are best understood relative to the offline political realities that produce citizens' relationships with one another. Scholarship in rhetorical studies has typically tended to consider publics in terms of their connection to democratic participation and citizenship. In doing so, publics have been viewed in terms of their situatedness relative to the Westphalian nation-state. Following Jürgen Habermas's study of the bourgeois public sphere of the seventeenth and eighteenth centuries,[10] research on publics has intimately been bound up with citizens' participation within democratic societies. In contrast to the exclusivity of the Habermasian public sphere, a large body of research continues to point to a multiplicity of publics operating within and competing with dominant visions of the common good in varying cultural communities.[11]

This pursuit of multiplicity is irreducible to solely human relationality, however. The character of participants' webs of meaning and their interactions have been shown to extend beyond human interactions and interdependencies and toward the historical, social, institutional, and political processes that shape those very publics. Indeed, Asen's argument with which this chapter opens invokes this logic of the networked nature of publics. In pursuit of a similar line of inquiry, rhetorical theorist Byron Hawk, for example, examines how in the era of digital media, musicians circulate music by forming publics, connecting with other publics, and producing "social ecologies around and through music."[12] This emphasis on the ecological dimension to the study of publics allows Hawk to interrogate how publics intersect with webs of networks. Hawk's argument rests on a counterposition to Michael Warner's view, well-discussed in the scholarship on publics, about the formation of publics based on temporality and circulation.

According to Hawk, Warner's notions of temporality and circulation are shaped by the print culture from which his idea of public formation emerges. In contrast to the immediacy of circulation of digital media in the twenty-first century, circulation of printed texts between the seventeenth and twentieth centuries relied on a slow, gradual process of text transmission, in terms both of time and speed. For Hawk, temporality and circulation have come to acquire new meanings in digital spaces. Situating publics within the context of their emergence in digital and new media, Hawk asks, "How do digital writers invoke complex rhetorical ecologies; imagine and negotiate multiple audiences and purposes; enact the circulation and effects of their digital texts—in short, how do these writing practices co-produce publics?"[13]

Hawk's concerns resonate with emphases on the networked nature of the publics that form in digital spaces. However, they also imply a grasp of the nature of digital publics and their formation, and indeed other publics—both physical and digital—with which they intersect.[14] From this linkage between the physical and digital, Hawk advances a networked view of publics, arguing that the connections that emerge from such a conception of digital publics entail "both humans and nonhumans, digital networks and physical environments." What is important for Hawk concerning digital publics is the inextricable link discernible between the digital and the physical. On what he calls sphere publics—to emphasize the sense of interactivity between the digital and physical—Hawk writes,

> As we know from Facebook and elsewhere, the lines between digital (nonplace) and physical (place) overlap and interlink considerably. Sometimes texts from searches are recirculated to others in digital networks. These connections generated by digital protocols can be specifically designed to create public events (concerts) and connect real people, music fans, promoters, managers, artists in digital spheres. Publics, then, emerge from these spheres of densely packed connectivity—a kind of materiality that encompasses the digital and the physical to form sphere publics.[15]

If Hawk's claims about the connectivity between the physical and digital hold relevance for digital writers, even more crucial are his arguments when extended specifically to the domain of politics and citizens' participation in the context of digital media. For research on democratic practice historically located within Greek and Roman practices of antiquity, a sense of the physical and digital allows us to shift the ground to, as Ralph Cintron explains, territorialize democratic practice wherever it is experienced.[16] That territorialization is important because even as networked forms of public spheres become common, the cultural dimensions that inform their emergence have not been given much attention in our theorizing. Damien Smith Pfister has observed that theories of the networked public sphere have paid little attention to "much of the world that remains un-networked by information technology."[17] Digital access, of course, remains a feature of the inequalities of the networked public sphere, but other concerns such as the interrelatedness of digitally mediated practices and their offline historical and physical conditions are significant if we are to understand digital publics as culturally contingent formations.[18]

As publics form in digital domains like Twitter, for example, their connection to physical spaces, institutional logics, and the political histories of their emergence reveal the nature of politics and citizen participation. The linkages between physical and digital contexts, to institutional logics, and territorial spaces therefore necessitate a rethinking of how we conceptualize digital publics vis-à-vis citizen participation. By attending to the physical-digital dynamic, we avoid the analytical risks rhetorical scholar Dan Ehrenfeld cautions about the study especially of digital publics: universalizing narratives of place, time, history, and politics.[19] Ultimately, we foreground the cultural imaginaries of deliberation and their potential for reimagining how publics are constituted, operate, and contribute to democratic practice.

Inscribing cultural imaginaries into the work of digital publics demands attentiveness beyond familiar and extant notions of the nature of publics as they relate to the nation-state and to citizenship. Rhetorical scholarship demonstrates that publics and nation-states' affinity to citizen narratives remain a dominant leitmotif in conceptions of citizen participation and the nation-state.[20] Ideas about this affinity derive mainly from Western democratic traditions, and thus represent only a limited view of citizens' relationship to the nation-state in general, especially when societies outside the North Atlantic are considered. State formation processes and citizens' relationship with the nation-state have proceeded differently elsewhere. As Kundai Chirindo observes, colonialism interrupted state formation processes in places like Africa south of the Sahara. In such places, "nationalist ideology is not as entrenched as it is among societies of the North Atlantic."[21] Consequently, manifestations of citizenship in postcolonial Africa cannot be expected to proceed according to traditions pertaining in the Westphalian state system.

Colonialism disrupted previously constituted socialities and reconstituted them in ways that set citizens' participation within postcolonial African democracies on a path distinct from those of Western democracies. That path has expanded the boundaries of what could count as political. The political, as Chirindo further discusses, entails "a wide range of experiences that ordinary people mundanely negotiate beyond the stereotypically discontinuous rituals of democracy like voting, activism, or lobbying legislators."[22] Ordinary citizens in the postcolony participate in ways extending beyond official domains of politics using cultural resources available to them. As we pursue interest in the multiplicity of and variance in publics, attention to counterpublicity can be complemented by an emphasis on cultural and geographical specificities.[23] Such an emphasis remains relevant to expand the purview of research on publics in undertheorized cultural contexts and rhetorical traditions. More importantly, emphasizing such contexts is significant for disrupting universalizing narratives of citizen engagement vis-à-vis the nation-state.

Research in African Studies on state formation and state-citizen relations highlight the exclusivity of notions of the public and extend the conversation to include cultural specificities.[24] In "Rethinking Publics in Africa in a Digital Age," Sharath Srinivasan, Stephanie Diepeveen, and George Karekwaivanane highlight one such specificity. They explore the ways that Kenyans are constituting themselves around the hashtag "Kenyans on Twitter" as a collective voice in the country's political life. As they say, their concerns relate to "the nature and possibilities of publics from within African historical experience," particularly in terms of the emergence of digital publics amid "wider contemporary social and political realities and not somehow separate from them."[25] They argue that African digital publics constituted on Twitter entail forms of citizen engagement such as popular culture and notions of spectacle and appearances that highlight quotidian expressions of democratic practice on the continent.[26] Such modes of democratic practice operate on at least two levels. First, they function alongside traditional notions of deliberation, those that unfold within formal contexts of politics like parliaments, board meetings, and the like. Second, they address the exclusivities produced by historical understandings of the public sphere, making legible previously undertheorized forms by which citizens engage with the state and perform citizenship.

But that these forms of engagement are digital does not mean they lose their connection to the physical and material conditions that produce them. In linking digitality to materiality, Srinivasan, Diepeveen, and Karekwaivanane write further that publics are "tangible in the media, texts, images and words through which people make themselves known."[27] Local, sociocultural values drive digital publics and their work, in ways that expose the linkages between cultural imaginaries and digitally mediated formation of publics. As local idioms, values, and norms are transposed from physical spaces to the digital, historical continuities that hinge on local modes of communication come into clearer focus at the same time that such communicative modes intersect with the media on which publicity unfolds.[28]

Two compelling cases of this digital-physical nexus serve to exemplify the point about such continuities. First, take the East African country of Tanzania. Here, African Studies scholar Irene Brunotti examines digital publics in the aftermath of an election impasse in Zanzibar, a semiautonomous region of the country. Brunotti invokes the concept of *cyberbaraza*, her idea of a digital manifestation of a *baraza*, or "a stone bench at the front of the houses of Zanzibar Town . . . a place, which is known for the stories associated with it, for its specific history, as well as for the people meeting there."[29] For Brunotti, such meeting places, with their cultural imaginaries, social practices, and modes of communication find their way into digital spaces where citizens are constituted into publics for deliberative activity. Brunotti sees in the concept of *cyberbaraza* a manifestation of the "discursive tradition of Swahili orature, among the variety of communicative genres available to debate, inform on and reframe conflicting deliberations."[30] Zanzibari citizens' ability to mobilize their cultural discursive resources to deliberate represents, for Brunotti, a sort of "mastery of their social imaginary" in a way that exposes the meeting place of culture and digital media.[31] A concept like *cyberbaraza* illustrates "how the challenge of defining a digital public can be addressed by grounding it within specific sociopolitical and cultural contexts."[32]

A second case of such continuity relates to Kenyan politics. In her aptly titled *Digital Democracy, Analogue Politics*, the Kenyan political scientist Nanjala Nyabola studies the ways that the internet shapes democratic practice in Kenya.

Nyabola examines citizens' use of digital media in the context of previously colonized Kenya by observing the tensions that arise as Kenyans contest with institutional structures of the state for participation in politics. In practicing democracy in digital spaces, Kenyan citizens draw upon the affordances of their exclusion from larger discursive arenas of politics. The political conditions of their country—dominance of state media, little access to opportunities to frame political debates, and so on—have spurred them on to digital spaces. In digital publics their "digital democracy" of advocacy and democratic participation becomes informed by their "analog politics" of exclusion from the formal sites of participation delimited by the state. By 2007, given official government policies that muzzled the Kenyan press and restricted citizens' political participation, new digital spaces like Twitter and blogs provided avenues for popular politics, including by Kenyans in the diaspora. For Nyabola, these developments in Kenyan politics reveal the necessity of accounting for historical and cultural specificities that shape conditions under which democratic practice in Kenya, and indeed anywhere else, unfolds.

Because government policy served to exclude several Kenyans from political life, these new digital spaces served to forge new visions and narratives of statehood and identity espoused by Kenyans both within the country and in its diaspora.[33] According to Nyabola, platforms and online communities like #Kenyans on Twitter created discursive arenas for Kenyans to give voice to a collective sentiment about new visions of statehood that extended beyond, and against, single, dominant narratives upholding governmental agendas. These visions were more diffused and more pluralistic, and they entailed the Kenyan peoples' collective hopes—a new nation of multiple stories, aspirations, and freedoms. Nyabola's analysis reveals that "our digital public lives are predicated on our lives offline."[34] The network of participation in a society like Kenya has come to include its diasporic communities, extending, therefore, the boundaries of identification to the state, from bounded communities to more diffused spaces.

The preceding examples lead us to at least two major conclusions. First, the peculiar relationship of citizens to the state in Africa and the legacies of colonialism that shape politics on the continent necessitate including such historical conditions in our analysis. Second, to fully account for the inextricable link between digital and physical spaces, we ought to interrogate historical processes and politics in the analogue. We must do so at the same time that we examine digital publics. The idea of cultural imaginaries can help territorialize and highlight digital publics' emergence. Deliberations on Twitter during the 2013 election dispute case in Ghana exemplify this digital-physical dynamic, and it is to the analysis of these that I now turn.

Peace Narratives and/as Democratic Aspiration

A major part of the online deliberations about the 2013 election dispute case in Ghana concerned peace. Citizens engaged in advocacy for peace and called on others to promote measures within their communities to foster peace and prevent conflict. This emphasis on peace represents the highest frequency in citizens' deliberations online, which is unsurprising given the rhetorical exigence of the deliberations. Elections remain a contentious affair, with competing interests that occasionally lend themselves to incredibly volatile situations. While electoral violence had not erupted on a large scale in Ghana, that absence of an all-out strife was no bulwark against a future eruption of violence. On Twitter, citizens' persistent advocacy for peace as a nonviolent strategy during the election dispute can be understood, therefore, in terms of the need to protect law and order.

The peace narratives stem from both regional and national concerns. On the one hand, they feature in the national political consciousness because media reports of electoral violence experienced by regional neighbors alerted many Ghanaians to the possibility that similar violence could erupt in the country. On the other hand, a national concern for peace grew because of years of military intervention in politics that heightened anxieties about the potential outbreak of violence. The peace narratives therefore signal not an inherent capacity on the part of citizens for violence but the dictates of political expediencies. Insofar as peace is a bedrock for governance, citizens' calls can be viewed both as a yearning for a strife-free political environment and a celebration of a cultural ethos of nonviolence. The following examples on Twitter demonstrate these claims:

> @KobbyGregg: #Ghana, one of the world's most peaceful country's [*sic*] is going to get more peaceful after the #supremecourt verdict tomorrow. @GhanaDecides

> @Ghanathink: "No matter what happens, peace must win."

The emphasis on peace is rhetorically significant because although the election dispute case was not related to concerns about peace per se, citizen deliberations on the events unfolding in court suggest some saw peace as the most important outcome of the deliberations. Several tweets celebrated a cultural ethos of peace and touted a national peaceful political atmosphere. Such an ethos has become widely accepted across the country as a necessary precondition for democratic practice. It is the same reference to peace that is manifested in tweets such as "In Kumasi [Ghana's second largest city] & everywhere else in this country, Ghana shall be the winner today. #electionpetition."[35] In suggesting that peace must win at all costs, citizens proffer peace as an antidote to the likelihood of conflict. They do so in hopes that efforts expended in the service of this value would protect and sustain democracy. The notion of peace features, then, prominently in the Ghanaian democratic imagination. Reading both analogue and digital contexts in tandem, we can understand the peace narratives here not as some sort of exceptionalism, but as a value that aligns with a national ethos cultured to celebrate it.

Peace operates as a god term insofar as it is a desired democratic value.[36] However, not all citizens deliberating in these digital publics express similar positive sentiments of this nationally cherished value. In circulating peace narratives, numerous commenters suggest the focus on peace might serve to occlude other equally important aspects of the deliberations. A commenter, @Kwabena, observed, for instance, "I don't feel like going to church tomorrow cos I feel the sermon will be heavy on peace. I've heard enough. #ElectionPetition #Ghana." Another person, @Bossinit, laconically declared, "JUSTICE JUSTICE!! JUSTICE=PEACE! #verdict #ghana #SupremeCourt." And a third commenter, @EEHayford, expanded on a similar sentiment: "While we pray for peace to reign in Ghana, lets [*sic*] also pray for justice to prevail. #TheVerdict."

What appears evident from these examples is a sense of "peace fatigue" informing citizens' critique of the limits of "peace talk" as a desirable democratic value. By "peace fatigue," I refer here to a rush to achieve the objectives of peace without a systemic and corresponding commitment to the work of justice. Citizens construe peace without justice to be meaningless peace. As a positive attribute, the notion of peace operates for citizens as a god term, but peace does have its limits even for a people for whom it is a cherished value. In the tweet from @Bossinit, the emphasis on justice as coterminous with peace reveals yet another complexity in a commonplace idea for democracy among

Ghanaians. Although only the word *justice* is repeated and correlated with peace, it is reasonable to infer a certain semantic opposition, one in which justice would entail the discomforts associated with deliberation. By asserting that justice equals peace, the commenter suggests a focus on due process, the rule of law, and attention to the contentious issues that sparked the dispute case in the first place. Where @Bossinit's tweet is subtle in its reference, @EEHayford's is explicit: justice must exist alongside peace, and peace can operate only as a prerequisite for justice. The commenter here refers not to the idea of negative peace, "the mere absence of violent conflict engagement," but to the notion of positive peace, "a comprehensive understanding related to the institutionalization of justice and freedom."[37]

The notion of peace as a Ghanaian democratic aspiration is also ultimately bound up with the belief that Ghana's success as a democracy is linked with the larger project of Africa's democratic experiment. This belief is revealed in the dataset by multiple commenters, one of whom, @HertzbergHege, notes that "Africa's black star stood the test. Woke up to a peaceful Accra today. Ghanaians can be proud of themselves! #electionpetition #Ghana." Another commenter, @KwesiTheAuthor, similarly pointed to Africa, writing about the verdict on the dispute thus: "Big day for #Democracy in #Ghana today. I have no doubt though that #Ghana will be an example to the rest of Africa once again. #TheVerdict." In both tweets, and similar ones, commenters highlight the notion that Ghana's experience successfully adjudicating the election dispute case signifies a victory for Africa's democracy more broadly. Ghana stands as the proverbial city on a hill to which the continent can look, aspire, and sustain its democracy.

This leading role assumed by Ghana—as the Black Star of Africa—is redolent of a pivotal moment in African nationalist politics. On March 5, 1957, on the cusp of Ghana's independence from British colonial rule, the country's first prime minister and leading pioneer of Pan-Africanism, Kwame Nkrumah, declared that the independence of Ghana was meaningless unless it was linked with the continent's total liberation from political domination. In fact, in the years that followed, Nkrumah would bolster this declaration with monetary and strategic support to colonies across the continent to achieve independence. Echoes of this sentiment of Pan-Africanism reverberate in Ghanaian politics even in these tweets that suggest the success of the dispute case is a victory for African democracy. To understand these sentiments, one needs to consider politico-historical contexts outside the immediate tweets, those rooted in the cultural imaginaries that celebrate peace as an ethos of democracy in Ghana.

But what are the sources of these peace narratives as a democratic value to which citizens aspire? I argue they are to be located in Ghana's quest to entrench a cultural ethos of peace. This aspiration led the country to enact legislation in 2011 to institutionalize and promote peace among its citizenry. By many accounts, Ghana is perceived to be a relatively peaceful country, particularly in a continental subregion occasionally plagued by pockets of strife, including those of electoral violence. For example, a 2021 Global Peace Index Report indicates Ghana ranks second most peaceful country in Africa's fifty-four countries.[38] Côte d'Ivoire (in 2010), Togo (in 2005), and Burkina Faso (in 2011), all Ghana's neighboring countries to the west, east, and north, respectively, have experienced some form of widespread political violence in the recent past.

Against this backdrop and a growing sense that intermittent internal ethnic and political strife would undermine the country's democratic growth and shining example, the Ghanaian government took steps to enact legislation to promote peace as a bedrock value for democracy and development. The government laid before the country's parliament a bill to establish a National Peace Council. The Council's mandate was expressly "to promote peace in the country" and "help institutionalise a culture of peace as well as make the institutions responsible for the maintenance of law and order more proactive in the discharge of their duties and obligations."[39] This institutionalization of a culture of peace was to take many forms. Chief among them was a decentralized approach geared toward the establishment of peace councils at all levels of governance, including at regional (state and provincial) and district (local) levels. In a strong bipartisan support, legislators on both aisles of Ghana's parliament endorsed the bill with hardly any dissent. Debates on the draft law during parliamentary sessions preceding the enactment of the National Peace Council Act provides critical insights into the nature and objectives of the law.

In discussing the background to the legislation, the chair of the Committee on Defense and Interior, Alhaji Sumani Abukari, argued for the bill's nation-building potential. He suggested the bill would promote "understanding about values of reconciliation, tolerance, confidence building, mediation and dialogue as responses to conflict among others," all values widely accepted as ideals in many democracies the world over.[40] The premise here is that peace would be a necessary precondition that both enables and nurtures these values for Ghanaian democracy. But beyond this objective of the bill, the debates highlighted a socialization dimension. A ranking member of the committee, William O. Boafo, proposed a sort of national socialization drive, in which "the Peace Council would establish in the various schools and colleges, in the churches and in the communities, peace clubs—as we have debating societies in various schools and colleges—to inculcate into the students and our youth the need for peace and stability in the country."[41]

There is a similarity posited here between debating societies as sites for cultivating rhetorical skills for citizen engagement and peace clubs as associations that instill democratic values at all strata of national life. The associative thinking is that peace, like debating societies, enables the formation of democratic dispositions and habits. By establishing peace clubs and educating citizens about peace and its associated values, democracy would consequently be promoted and would thrive. Peace would yield, in political philosopher Chantal Mouffe's phrasing, a "democratic habitus," highlighting "the historical and contingent character of the discourses that construe our identities."[42] Rhetorical scholar Dana Harrington argues that eighteenth-century debating societies facilitated the development of democratic dispositions.[43] Like these societies, peace clubs envisioned by Ghanaian legislators would instill in citizens democratic dispositions. The attorney general and minister for justice, Martin Amidu, summed up the sentiment surrounding the bill's prospects, concluding that the debates on the floor pointed to one thing—that "in all our differences, we are all moving towards one thing: a peaceful nation in which we will have democracy and rule of law."[44] The bill was passed into law with continuing support from both the Ghanaian government and international peace organizations. Peace narratives remain a defining feature of Ghanaian democracy.

In a sense, my argument that peace operates in the tweets as democratic aspiration recalls Erik Doxtader's observation about the idea of reconciliation, a concept almost analogous to peace. For Doxtader, the concept of reconciliation served multiple functions as South Africa pursued a postapartheid democracy: it created the occasion that made the idea of transition possible at all; it operated as a form of communication enabling citizens' ability to forgo the injustice of oppression in favor of the promise of liberation; and it made the idea of political representation possible.[45] In operating on these three levels, reconciliation "preceded, conditioned, and followed the transition from apartheid to democracy," and by doing so, it became "an example of how speech invents the potential for politics."[46] The analysis here of how peace operates within the Ghanaian context can be seen in a similar vein: peace makes the practice of politics possible at the same time that it gives meaning to Ghana's democratic aspirations. But more importantly, a focus on the peace narratives reveals the interconnection between the digital and the physical as digital publics emerge on Twitter.

Ghana's historical and political realities led the country into a period of aspiration for peace as a democratic value. That value—and politics offline in the form of the parliamentary debates and advocacy for a cultural ethos of peace—informs the deliberations on Twitter. The notion of peace also was the mechanism that shaped the kind of digital public that simultaneously advocated for and pointed out the limits of peace as a democratic value. Recalling both Hawk's call for an interplay between the digital and the physical in understanding digital publics and Nyabola's attention to the Kenyan political realities that shaped the democratic visions of multiple voices on #Kenyans on Twitter, I suggest that understanding the (concerns of the) digital public on Twitter requires not just attention to the digital democratic practices that unfold, but also the analogue politics that inform the value of peace in the first place.

Like the concept of the *cyberbaraza* that exposes the meeting place of culture and digital media, we see revealed here the cultural underpinnings of the peace narratives in the tweets. The theme of peace as democratic aspiration is rooted in citizens' relationships to the state, a relationship that manifests in a commitment to avoid political violence. That commitment also reflects in offline environments, parliamentary debates, and historical time, space, and agency, informing the desire for peace. It is carried over into digital contexts, ultimately structuring and shaping the relational dimensions of the publics citizens create, form, and participate in.

Humor Use as a Popular Culture Form of Democratic Practice

The rhetorical uses of humor in the election dispute case are a testament to a form of democratic practice by ordinary Ghanaian citizens. Rhetorical theorists have argued that humor can function as a form of citizen engagement within a democracy.[47] It can serve as persuasive discourse, enable citizens to speak truth to power, and "enhance public argument."[48] As a counterpoint to the institutional discourse of democratic rhetorics, vernacular rhetorics highlight the quotidian modes by which citizens form publics and engage democratically. In *Vernacular Voices: The Rhetorics of Publics and Public Spheres*, Gerald Hauser notes that such modes of engagement entail discursive practices involving those symbols and meaning-making rhetorical strategies peculiar to cultures that provide a basis for deliberation.[49] Political scientists Jensen Sass and John Dryzek also write that the interplay between culture and deliberation is evidenced in "publicly accessible meanings, symbols, and norms" that inform democratic practice.[50] Part of these publicly accessible practices would include humor, storytelling, and silence, a focus on which can reveal the nexus between culture and politics.[51]

In particular reference to postcolonial African societies, this connection manifests under the rubric of popular culture. These are modes of citizen engagement that cultural studies scholars Stephanie Newell and Onookome Okome call "the episteme of the everyday." In *Popular Culture in Africa*, Newell and Okome put forward the idea that especially for African contexts, popular art forms provide avenues for cultural production and dissemination that foreground the lives of people "outside the limits and hierarchies of officialdom."[52] Indeed, the discussion on peace narratives partly reflects this very upending of hierarchies of officialdom as it spotlights ordinary citizens' lives on Twitter.

Moreover, as Newell and Okome posit, citizens' visions embedded in popular cultural art forms consist of "desires for future alternatives, for emergent possibilities," and the use of popular cultural forms has the potential for "destabilizing the relationships set in place by the postcolonial state in Africa."[53] Given that many citizens in postcolonial African democracies are frequently excluded from participation in the official realms of politics, popular cultural forms of participation provide a viable means by which they engage the political order. For example, beyond the reprieve it offers from the drudgery of dealing with officialdom in the postcolony, humor also operates as a potent symbol of discursive power, of survival, and of the possibility to resist societal systems. It can be used by society's subalterns to "caricature those in power, subvert authority, and in some instances, empower themselves."[54]

Citizens' tweets bear out the rhetorical uses of humor as a form of democratic practice. As can be seen in table 1 in the appendix, the use of humor was a crucial popular cultural art form of rhetorical activity, constituting some 16.93 percent of all tweets. For example, a commenter, @kofiemeritus, stated that "the next title for a Ghanaian movie by Agya Koo will be 'The Verdict' #ElectionPetition #TheVerdict." With a cultural subtext, this commenter sees a hilarious dimension to the entire election dispute case by likening it to popular Ghanaian comedian and actor Agya Koo, widely known to Ghanaian audiences for his tendency to create humor out of serious sociopolitical issues. The election dispute is a crucial part of the governance process. The verdict was intended not only to confer legitimacy on political leadership, but also to entrench acceptable democratic norms of resolving electoral disputes in Ghana's democracy.

Thus, removed from the officialdom of the entire dispute case, this commenter engages the political process but in a different way. A cultural valence is evident here in the use of humor. Although the case is a serious matter of politics, the commenter takes a lighthearted approach to it, likening the entire dispute to a comedic show of sorts, one in which Agya Koo plays a part. To the Ghanaian audience of this tweet (and this sociocultural context is important), the humor invoked manifests in the figure of the comedian, one who evinces what some citizens consider was a theatrical election dispute case, and who pokes fun at the process as a means by which to engage democratically with that process. The recourse to Agya Koo's comedic ethos resonates with the Ghanaian audience and serves to enhance the persuasive appeal of conceiving the election dispute case in lighthearted terms.[55] Culturally contingent, then, this use of humor allows for broader discursive participation in the election dispute case by the "the people," a majority of whom are excluded from the law courts.

As in the contempt of court cases discussed earlier, the Supreme Court judges considered themselves guardians of democracy, those on whom the Constitution confers a bounden duty to protect and safeguard laws. In contrast to this perception by the judges, citizens find avenues to participate democratically through pathways such as humor. They assert the primacy of "the people of Ghana," those "in whose name and for whose welfare," the Ghanaian Constitution stipulates, "the powers of government are to be exercised."[56] By engaging the political process through familiar and accessible ways, citizens' use of such quotidian practices as humor evinces the possibilities of participation beyond boundaries delimited by the postcolonial state.

Similar registers of humor are reflected in the tweets. Some of these may be only indirectly related to the case, but they retain the local, popular cultural meanings that, within context, suggest their purpose as forms of political participation. Commenter @ofoli_kwei remarked that "it's actually good to see and be in a queue at the kelewele seller's. #Ghana still be Ghana after #TheVerdict." This tweet does not directly engage the election dispute, but it shifts attention to an everyday element of Ghanaian social life, that of queuing to buy *kelewele*, or spicy fried ripe plantain. For many Ghanaians, the *kelewele* seller's (if it exists in an open-air market, as do most Ghanaian markets) operates as one of those spaces that quickly turns into what the economist Virgil Henry Storr has referred to as a "site(s) of extraeconomic sociality in addition to extensive economic activity."[57] Such physical markets create space for convivial social relations independent of the economic activity at hand. In relation to the dispute case, and with the Ghanaian social media users who would be the primary audience in mind, this commenter creates a humorous effect with the tweet focusing on the mundane activity of food purchase. The commenter suggests that social life after the court verdict will continue as before; whatever verdict is handed down may not change life after all. Like this commenter, another person, @ GhRainmaker, noted, "Ahead of the verdict I am drinking coke with my bestie @jessicacitifm! #electionpetition." Revealing a lighthearted aspect to the entire dispute case, this commenter sought to create humor out of the process. The tweet conjures familiar popular cultural imaginaries of one who smugly prepares themselves to derive amusement from an otherwise serious issue. But like the gadflies of the peace narratives discussed earlier, some commenters occasionally considered these attempts at humor potentially destructive. As one person, @Abocco, observed, "We're taking these #electionpetition jokes too far. Peace loving people sharing funny pictures with weaponry all over? #Ghanadecides." The idea of the peace-loving Ghanaian is highlighted here yet again and contrasted with the caution to create only constructive humor.

Perhaps the most compelling use of humor as an aspect of popular culture was a YouTube music video repurposed from a dance form and circulated as tweets. An urban Ghanaian dance, *azonto* gained popularity among Ghanaians home and abroad by 2011. According to cultural anthropologist Jesse Weaver Shipley, the dance signified a paean of sorts to the figure of the "azonto girl, . . . a disreputable outcast or a sexually promiscuous woman."[58] As it became digitally mediated and moved through transnational circuits of circulation across Africa, Europe, and the United States, the dance's semantic references broadened, often with ameliorative valences that expanded its meanings from the pejorative to the praiseworthy. Shipley writes that the dance transformed "the image of the outcast into that of the irreverent urbanite and technologically savvy street hustler," ultimately serving to embody "a new social persona for young Ghanaians around the world to emulate."[59]

This new persona is one of cultural iconoclasm. It represented for the youth "a tacit yet subtle form of defiance towards expected norms in Ghanaian society."[60] The expansion of *azonto*'s referents allowed young people, otherwise excluded from the official domains of politics, to engage the election dispute case on their own terms. One repurposed *azonto* dance, dubbed "Election Zonto," circulated as tweets (and on YouTube) and embedded references to the courtroom deliberation.[61] Crucially encoding a summation of pivotal moments in court, the lyrics accompanying the dance are reproduced here. They signify a compendium of the official deliberations in court from the perspective of the ordinary Ghanaian:

> You and I were not there
> On the face of the pink sheet
> I put it to you
> You and I were not there
> On the face of the pink sheet
> People have grown horns
> Will you shut up?
> Humbled by baptism of fire
> Possessed by Gbeshie Spirit
> Court Rise

Because the election dispute case was televised nationally, snippets of legal arguments entered popular parlance, becoming commonplaces of shared reference for social interactions. In court, during cross-examination, one petitioner's constant response to a query about evidence and polling station staff was "You and I were not there." The statement suggested that regardless of the availability of the Statement of Poll and Declaration of Results Form (the pink sheets analyzed earlier), neither respondents nor petitioners can make definitive claims about events at all polling stations on Election Day. The statement disputes the credibility of evidence apart from human witnesses. Pivotal as it was to the quest for evidence in court, the remark quickly entered popular parlance, becoming a referent for the insufficiency of documentary evidence in establishing truth and falsehood.

Furthermore, the legalese "I put it to you" recalls the Supreme Court judges' claim that the contemnors (discussed earlier) "have grown horns" (become recalcitrant and disobedient to the law) and conduct themselves as though hypnotized (possessed by an evil spirit called *Gbeshie*). The idea that the contemnors have had a "baptism of fire" by the Supreme Court represents the court's excessively punitive approach to citizens' deliberation about the case. Concluding with "Court Rise," the dance dramatizes the election dispute itself and injects its major discourses into the popular imagination. It also renders the complex, often exclusionary courtroom deliberations among judges, lawyers, and the formally schooled into a popular culture art form with which citizens can relate and by which they can politically engage with the entire process. In doing so, the humor it creates and circulates enables an engagement with the process regardless of physical proximity to the courtroom. The "everyday" popular *azonto* dance is elevated to the level of the political, and the concerns of the dispute case are superimposed on the mundanity of the dance itself. Citizens' use of the dance in this fashion therefore powerfully signals claims to (discursive) power. It signifies their reclamation of a space for deliberation in a way consonant with Uchenna Okeja's contention that deliberation in African societies ought to be understood as an exercise of agency.[62] The dance moves from the mundane to the consequential, from levity to seriousness, from entertainment to politics.

As communication scholar Admire Mare found in his analysis of genres of popular communication in African societies, such uses of humor rhetorically "poke fun at the ruling elite."[63] They also serve, in the context of African social media platforms, as an evocative example of cultural netizenship, or the "use of play and performance . . . to resist the analogue expressions of state hegemony."[64] Through these popular cultural art forms, citizens created productive spaces of sociality to poke fun at the process while retaining the discursive power that the platforms offer. In terms of digital publics, there is a connection between the physical and digital in the use of humor and popular cultural art forms more generally. In particular, the *azonto* dance draws on the ubiquity of this popular cultural art form offline, transposes the art form onto YouTube, and enables its circulation and connection to other audiences on other digital platforms like

Twitter. In integrating the courtroom drama into the popular culture form that is *azonto*, citizens establish a connection between cultural art forms offline and politics online, as they circulate the dance on multiple platforms. In "A Discourse Theory of Citizenship," Robert Asen reminds rhetoricians that citizenship engagement need not be construed solely in terms of the "somber and solemn action"; playful moments can equally sustain future aspirations.[65] It is such playful moments—in the idiom of humor, and through popular culture—that constitute the means of participation thus far discussed.

In a sense, the relationships cultivated by citizens through communal uses of popular cultural art forms depend not so much on affinities with the nation-state as with fellow citizens. Because the institutional domains of democratic deliberation are generally limited in the postcolony, citizen participation through popular cultural art forms provide one way relationships and socialities between citizens are forged. And as scholars such as Omedi Ochieng have argued concerning publics, these relationships are usefully understood as conditioned historically, socially, and politically. To understand these relationships and the role of the humor here is to account for the cultural imaginaries that condition politics in digital publics.

Democratic Interventions and Civil Society Organizations: Blogging Ghana's Ghana Decides Initiative

Advocacy for peace and rhetorical uses of humor toward democratic ends were central to citizens' strategies for deliberating about the dispute. However, educative initiatives organized by citizen groups equally served in encouraging participation by ordinary citizens. These initiatives reveal the role and intervention of civil society groups in furthering democracy in Ghana. As can be seen in table 1 in the appendix, approximately a third of the tweets referenced the activities of Blogging Ghana (BloGh). BloGh is a civil society organization that describes itself on its social media pages as a community of bloggers and social media users documenting the Ghanaian experience online. One of the organization's key projects is Ghana Decides, a nonpartisan initiative committed to promoting youth and marginalized voices in Ghanaian society. The Ghana Decides initiative was significant in the lead-up to Election 2012 through its educative projects that encouraged citizen participation in the electoral process. During the dispute case deliberations, BloGh embarked on similar initiatives to promote debate around the case from the perspective of citizens.

Many tweets referred to the Ghana Decides program organized in relation to the election dispute case, revealing the crucial role of this civil society organization in mobilizing citizen participation. One tweet, for example, referenced activities outlined by BloGh ahead of the verdict: "#GhanaDecides Activities ahead of SCROG [Supreme Court of Ghana] Verdict on #Election-Petition."[66] Another provided links to online videos on behind-the-scenes activities documenting the organization's collaboration with other civil society organizations to ensure a fair, free, and peaceful conduct of the elections. These videos showcased BloGh's initiatives in organizing a presidential debate before the elections; developing community training camps for youth groups, other civil society organizations, and public institutions; and facilitating other election-related campaigns and consciousness-raising activities, including circulating resources on the Ghanaian Constitution to citizens.

One of BloGh's primary initiatives was the promotion of social media use for democratic engagement. The organization led efforts to accomplish this goal, supplying evidence in the aftermath of Election 2012 to demonstrate citizens' responses to the success of the BloGh's initiatives. These initiatives were especially crucial at a time in the early 2010s when social media use was only beginning to gain popularity among a majority of urban, educated Ghanaians. For example, the organization supplied results of a brief poll they conducted, indicating, "Of 100 respondents, majority used BOTH social media & traditional media during Ghana's 2012 elections. #GhanaDecides." BloGh further noted citizens' recognition of the social media use for Ghana's democracy more specifically: "Most respondents think social media shd [*sic*] be considered as viable tool for enhancing democracy in Ghana. #GhanaDecides."[67] And in an apparent reference to one of the organization's training camps, another commenter saw in BloGh's promotion of social media use the promise for increased and more effective citizen participation: "#GhanaDecides showed us in a practical way what a powerful tool social media could be. #eyeopener #BlogCamp13."[68] These tweets reveal BloGh's efforts at encouraging the deployment of social media toward citizen mobilization around common democratic causes, an objective the organization accomplished by actively engaging citizens online and offline.

BloGh constituted a public around which online communities could rally. They did so by mobilizing citizens around common hashtags in advance of the momentous verdict by the Supreme Court. A tweet by @peagama informed online audiences of hashtags: "The #Hashtags on twitter and Facebook for tomorrow is #TheVerdict and #ElectionPetition. Don't forget. Join the Discussion as #Ghanadecides." As with many social media technologies, these hashtags certainly enabled topical markers that constituted a public to collectively advance nonofficial perspectives on the dispute case.[69] The hashtags also functioned as technologies that enable users "to embody/perform a talking back . . . aimed at disrupting hegemonic orders of intellect, epistemologies, and cultures."[70] In the unregulated, noninstitutional political context of the dispute deliberations on Twitter, the hashtags unmoored the deliberations from officialdom, disrupted official perspectives, and invested in this "marginalized literacy" values,[71] experiences, and perspectives of the Ghanaian citizenry. On Twitter, BloGh's project received resounding commendation, as when one commenter, @Miss_Quainoo, noted, "I think #GhanaDecides deserves a big applause @BloggingGhana #BlogCamp13 #ContentIsKing." Indeed, BloGh's activities thus exemplify Gerard Hauser and Chantal Benoit-Barne's claim that "the grassroots resources of civil society are the major cultural resource for deliberative democracy to thrive."[72]

In addition to their online promotion of social media use, another key initiative undertaken by BloGh was an hour-long Google Hangout event broadcast on Twitter and YouTube. BloGh assembled a panel of six members drawn from a section of the Ghanaian online community to deliberate about the Supreme Court's verdict. For the panelists, it was "people who are plugged into Ghanaian issues"[73]—ostensibly those outside official government circles—that were the best to talk about the issue. The idea itself reveals the exclusionary politics that tends to be at the heart of civil society organizations' practice (for it is predominantly educated, well-connected citizens for whom such opportunities for deliberation are available). Additionally, it also highlights the spaces available for postcolonial African political practice: official, governmental arenas of democratic practice and nonofficial, more diffused arenas, those often directly affected by decisions of state institutions.[74]

In deliberating about the dispute case, the panelists shared ordinary citizens' perspectives. Kajsah Adu, a political scientist and blogger, for example, observed the dispute case represented a watershed moment for Ghanaian democracy, as the court's unprecedented decision to televise the proceedings created a national atmosphere of transparency and a sense of fairness and due process. But that transparent atmosphere did not completely solve the problem of exclusion embedded in the dispute deliberations operating predominantly in court. For an academic such as Adu, the process was a "sign of democracy" but was "too technical as time went on," in certain cases becoming incomprehensible even for educated persons. Transparency, then, was not enough to qualify these deliberations as entirely democratic because the deliberations were just as exclusionary. The deliberations included exclusively educated persons whom some panelists opined were "plugged into Ghanaian issues," presumably citizens actively involved in the process largely because of the benefits of their education. Then, as another participant, Nana Yaw discussed, many citizens reported feeling economically impacted by the dispute deliberations in court. Even as these persons became invested in the proceedings, Nana Yaw recalled they occasionally found the deliberations an impediment to their and others' productivity.[75] Citizens spent just as much time invested in the proceedings as other activities and expressed anxieties about the consequences of the outcome for their daily lives.

Beyond economic impact, the dispute case also indirectly facilitated political socialization across the country. The panelists agreed it offered an avenue for knowledge acquisition on electoral systems and processes as well as the role of electoral officials at polling stations. Panelists saw in such knowledge the promise of a more politically educated citizenry equipped for effective democratic practice. Using knowledge of electoral processes, and through deploying social media in service of storying the dispute case, citizens ensured marginalized perspectives were circulated across platforms. From the tweets that circulated and the Google Hangout postverdict deliberations, citizens—and BloGh in general—disseminated news about the case. They also critiqued the deliberations, brainstormed ideas about the postverdict direction of governance, and created a space for envisioning possibilities beyond those familiar within the confines of institutional structures in Ghana's democracy. What the work of BloGh demonstrates is the democratizing role of civil society organizations, especially in postcolonial contexts like Ghana's where many citizens find themselves excluded from official domains of politics.[76]

Of course, the Google Hangout event and other initiatives by BloGh cannot be limited to the digital platforms on which they unfolded. A more complete accounting of the organization's role demands attentiveness to the politics offline that makes the online initiatives possible in the first place. The digital publics are informed by the political realities offline, where civil society organizations, especially urban-based ones, have been shown to mobilize citizens around "a space of sociability outside the reach of a traditionally overbearing state."[77] Such a role, in the case of BloGh, is carried over onto digital platforms. There, it culminates in a networked public in which the offline activities of the organization—advocacy, campaigns, behind-the-scenes election work—emerge online, and where multiple audiences, offline and online, are organized around mutual commitments to an improved democratic practice in Ghana. Importantly, the offline and online activities of BloGh are not to be considered in separate, bifurcated terms. The nature of the publics that emerge must be understood in terms of their connection to the cultural imaginaries that expose the materiality of the publics themselves.[78] And as with the deployment of humor and circulation of peace narratives, the relational dimensions of the publics revolving around the democratic interventions of BloGh manifest chiefly in the shared commitment of the panelists and commenters to a better democracy.

The Paradoxes of Freedom of Speech

Earlier I discussed the contempt of court cases involving Stephen Atubiga and Ken Kuranchie's critique of the court's perceived selective dispensing of justice. Citizens certainly debated the ongoing dispute in a variety of forums. However, Twitter was one important site where they staked their claims to freedom of speech through critique and praise of the case in a public they themselves created. The significance of such a public for critique and praise depended especially on the fundamentally exclusionary characteristic of the postcolonial nation-state's realms of political participation. As a counterpoint to these exclusionary realms, citizens demonstrated the utility of digital media for the unencumbered expression of freedom of speech, be that a critique of the judges, praise of the process, or other commentary on the case more generally. In this, the public they formed evinced the spirit of palabre, wherein their online interactions were intended to keep them together even as they disagree and discuss the outcomes of the case.

Yet in exercising this freedom, commenters evinced a certain paradox toward the nonnegotiability of freedom of speech, on the one hand, and citizens' expectation that the court protect the nation's democracy, on the other hand.[79] Recall that when the judges insisted during the contempt cases that they were the guardians of democracy, and thereby sought to protect it from citizens' "violent speech," they were treading a similar tightrope. In reference to the contempt case, a commenter, @julietbawuah, noted, "As much as i don't support this #Supremecourt ruling but [*sic*] 'Freedom of speech comes with responsibility.' #Ghana." What the commenter acknowledges is a paradox of sorts. Freedom of speech is a necessary foundation for democratic practice, but citizens are norm-bound to communicate in nonviolent ways. There is an expectation that they comment on the case in ways that weigh those freedoms against an ethos of peace thought to be foundational to the practice of democracy in Ghana. Other tweets share this paradox. One commenter, @javvn, wrote, "Comments made can put off public interest in Supreme Court rulings #supremecourt #Ghana." Expressing anxieties about the judges curtailing these freedoms, another person, @UmaruSanda, tweeted, "I smell the Fear of the Gavel emanating from media houses all around town. I hope Freedom of Speech is not struck. #SupremeCourt #Ghana." This latter comment reveals the shadow of the "culture of silence" that still underpins dispositions toward the place of speech in democratic practice in Ghana. These anxieties are not unfounded, however. Five days to the verdict, a tweet linked to an online news portal warned of "police on the lookout for rumour mongers on social media ahead of #ElectionPetition verdict."[80]

Like the journalist Kuranchie's suggestion that the judges' decision to track down every offending commenter was impractical, the announced national clampdown by the police on the abuse of speech did seem similarly unrealizable. But given a media landscape that had only until barely a decade earlier experienced repression under Ghana's Criminal Libel and Seditious Laws,[81] this warning—and the consequent paradox concerning the limits of freedom of speech—speaks to anxieties about specters from the past. It recalled a period of political retaliation and a culture of forced silence that hampered democratic deliberation.[82]

Citizens' paradoxical relationship with freedom of speech reflects also in their ability to critique the court or the judges and to render praise where they felt it was due. For example, commenter @Le_Kwaku tweeted, "I'll be going to the bank and I won't sign. #SupremeCourt is telling me no signature is 3nny3 hweeeeee [is inconsequential] #Ghana #ElectionPetition #Injustice." More derisively, another commenter, @glovben, observed, "The nine wise wo(men) at #Ghana's #SupremeCourt have succeeded in holding us all hostage. #ElectionPetition #TheVerdict." The first comment points to one of the primary issues around which the case revolved: whether or not statements of poll without a signature were valid. Part of the petitioners' request was for the court to annul invalid statements of poll (those without signatures). Regarding this request, the commenter's critique concerned one of the judges' opinions that the absence of a signature does not invalidate the results of the polls. By drawing an analogy between an unsigned bank check and the judges' decision, this commenter critiques the seeming incongruence, for citizens, between commonplace understandings of action and result (sign a bank check, withdraw cash) and the judicial opinion which held that unsigned statements of poll may still be considered valid. The second comment implies another critique. It suggests that the nine-member panel of judges, acting as the supposedly wise biblical Magi, not only delayed but also delivered an uncharacteristically brief verdict that left citizens confused about who won the case.

While these critiques were common in the dataset, there were corresponding examples of praise. Concerning the courts' decision on the contempt case, one person, @joseikofi, commended the president of the panel of justices thus: "Justice Atugubah is speaking!! Noone [*sic*] is above the law, no one, no one!! #SupremeCourt #Ghana." @EfoChris remarked, "Honestly Justice Dotse stole my heart with his example on what politicians should discuss today in court #ElectionPetition."A third person, @OforiAkuffo, added, "But JSC Atuguba is my hero. He handled this matter with finesse, humour, kid gloves or iron fist when it was demanded #ElectionPetition." Together, these instances of praise stand in contrast to the criticisms of the process, and concerning the expression of opinions, they reveal the paradoxical stances citizens held toward freedom of speech as a democratic value. Regarding digital publics, a grasp of the paradox displayed online requires attention to the historical dynamics and political realities offline. These realities are understood in terms of a layered history of a "culture of silence" provoked by political intimidation and repression and freedom of speech guaranteed in the era of constitutional rule. It is in this history that we can situate citizens' fraught relationship to the notion of freedom of speech.

Resisting the Postcolonial Election Library

Reference to Ghanaians' confidence in their democracy as an exemplar for other African countries was common in the tweets. But another way commenters registered their commitment to democratic practice was through resistance to what we might call the *postcolonial election library*. Historicizing the depictions of Africa in the global imagination, the Congolese French historian and philosopher V. Y. Mudimbe observes in *The Idea of Africa* that from the fifteenth century onwards, European depictions of Africa(ns) cohered in a corpus of discourses, ideas, and epistemologies, what he calls the "colonial library." The colonial library would later provide dubious justifications for colonialism. The library operates as an archive from which Africa's relationship to the world came to be—and is mostly still—parsed. Mudimbe maintains that the colonial library "constructs stereotypes, allocates remarkable adjectives to Africans and other "primitives," and establishes [Europe's] civilizing mission."[83]

That civilizing mission did not end when colonialism formally ended. Rather, it is a process that is constantly transformed, negotiated, and reconfigured to suit a variety of purposes across time and space. The civilizing mission unfolds in the image constructions of the West as Africa is pathologized as a counterfoil to a perceived superior West. As Achille Mbembe explains, "Africa still constitutes one of the metaphors through which the West represents the origin of its own norms, develops a self-image, and integrates this image into the set of signifiers asserting what it supposes to be its identity."[84] A negation of Africa, then, is imbricated in the very image and imagination of the West. It is partly against this backdrop of perceived primitiveness and pejorative narratives of ineptitude that Africans would come to resist the colonial enterprise. In his speech declaring independence from British colonial rule, Ghana's Kwame Nkrumah, for example, defiantly spoke about the newly independent countries emerging on the continent: "That new Africa is ready to fight [its] own battles," he proclaimed, "and show that after all the black [person] is capable of managing [their] own affairs."[85] The colonial library persists in the face of this hopeful defiance, regardless. Specifically, in electoral matters, there is what I call a *postcolonial election library*: discourses, ideas, images, and epistemologies in Western media and institutions that essentialize, circulate, and exaggerate Africa's challenges with electoral processes as an inherent incapacity by Africans to govern themselves.

It seems hardly necessary to substantiate claims of biased reportage in Western media institutions about electoral processes in Africa.[86] Western institutions and media have frequently been perceived in African countries as biased regarding striking a fair balance between offering solidarity to citizens where needed and turning on a gaze that feeds the curiosities of Western audiences. This reality of biased reportage explains the critique of foreign media manifested in Ghanaian citizens' deliberations on Twitter. One commenter, @MrAyitey, noted, "Ok, now all the international pressmen who were waiting to "flee" Ghana can leave. We proved you wrong again. #TheVerdict #ElectionPetition." Another person, @Keg2han, challenged the perceived appetite of major British and American news organizations for negative news about the outcome of the case: "Hey @BBCWorld and @CNN, there can't be war in Ghana. Go back to Syria for the news you are craving for. #theverdict." Commonly perceived as tending toward a bias for negative reportage of the continent, the BBC and CNN are told to turn their attention toward Syria, a country embroiled in civil conflict at the time. The statement "We proved you wrong again," then, negates the perception that the election dispute case would degenerate into chaos, and that Ghanaian democracy would not live up to "foreign" expectation, whatever those may be. Indeed, other tweets in the dataset link to foreign journalists' and major news organizations' reportage on the case. Reuters, Voice of America, and Aljazeera all had commentary on the case, as did blog posts in such famous outlets as the now-defunct Toronto Review of International Affairs.

Beyond media outlets, foreign embassies were not spared the critique, either: "Dear @USEmbassyGhana," @oralofori wrote, "am a little :-([sad] u sprung into panic prior to #TheVerdict on #ElectionPetition but I hope u know #Ghana is matured now!" The critique reflects a resistance against the postcolonial election library that depicts Africa—and Ghana, in this case—as a place from which international organizations ought to flee because of perceived postelection violence. In anticipating and rejecting Western media coverage of African sociopolitical issues, these commenters were acknowledging, as research continues to show, the problematic coverage of Africa in Western media.[87] Indeed, in the lead-up to the court's verdict, the US embassy cautioned American citizens in Ghana against the possibility of an outbreak of violence. Presumably the tense national atmosphere and the novelty of the case led the embassy to caution American citizens in Ghana against the possibility of violence.

It is possible to see in the embassy's circular a proactive administrative measure aimed at protecting foreign citizens. However, given the unbalanced geopolitical power dynamic and the historical relationship of domination between Western, often more resourced countries, and emerging African economies, the source of the criticism by the commenters becomes apparent; they denounce the embassy's caution precisely because they believe it is rooted in dubious perceptions of inherent violence by Africans. In criticizing Western media institutions and the United States for what they perceive to be their meddling in Ghana's democracy, these commenters also highlight the sovereignty of Ghana's democracy. They exercise their agency to revise the colonial record of negative African representation. In all, we can fully understand the resistance and the public that coalesces around it online only vis-à-vis the offline historical relationship from which it emerges, one of Africa's continual resistances to the colonial library, or, more appropriately, the postcolonial election library in this case.

Conclusion

There are cultural, historical mechanisms that underpinned the digital publics that formed and deliberated about the election dispute case. I have expanded on the notion of the centrality of relationships to scholarship on deliberations in digital publics by exemplifying how cultural and historical legacies of colonialism in Ghana inform the kind of publics in offline political contexts that then transpose in online spaces. As rhetorical scholarship extends the study of publics beyond the logics of its dominant formations (Habermasian, exclusionary, fundamentally Western), we can arrive at more capacious notions of publics, including digital publics that attend to and are informed by other historical processes, say, of colonialism, in previously colonized contexts.

More specifically, by grounding the analysis in a matrix of digital and physical conditions, what emerges here is a host of considerations about deliberations about the election dispute case: a Ghanaian cultural ethos of peace inflecting democratic practice; the uses of humor as a popular culture mode of political participation; the role of civil society organizations operating in offline and online contexts; a paradoxical stance on freedom of speech informed by the anxieties of speech in the postcolony; and resistance toward dominant Western notions of African ineptitude with electoral processes. From the physical spaces of the Ghanaian nation-state, these ideas are transposed into the digital contexts. Much like Brunotti's notion of *cyberbaraza* or Nyabola's digital democracy–analogue politics dynamic, what is realized here is the analytical utility that is to be derived from grounding, defining, and studying digital publics by reference to the specific sociopolitical and cultural contexts of their emergence—their cultural imaginaries. It is in this contextual grounding—one that attends to the relationship of citizens to the nation-state, the cultural elements of peace as a democratic aspiration, citizens' paradoxical relationship to the constitutional guarantee of freedom of speech, and so on—that the cultural imaginaries of the deliberations emerge. Ghanaians' analogue political realities are revealed here to be best understood in concert with the digital publics that deliberated about the election dispute case.

Publics exist as a function of relationships between individuals. These relationships have manifested here through their connection to historical underpinnings rooted in the legacies of colonialism and its afterlives. A cultural imaginaries orientation to understanding the deliberations in digital spaces accounts for the role of colonialism and historical trajectories in creating spaces for democratic practice *on the Ghanaian society's own terms*. Along this orientation, the goal of the analysis departs from a mere inclusion of Ghanaian rhetorical practices, for their own sake, in the canons of rhetorical studies of deliberation and democratic practice. Indeed, a mere inclusion will be limiting. On a meta-analytical level, what the analysis offers is not "some hidden code for non-Western rhetorical practices," but an orientation that "recognizes and honors the cultural specificity of *all* rhetorical practices/productions."[88] The paradigmatic example of postcolonial Ghana's deliberations about the dispute case enriches the meta-analysis. Where a networked view of digital publics demands attention to "digital networks and physical environments,"[89] our sense of the interconnectivity between postcolonial democratic practice and digital public leads to opportunities to decolonize our conceptions of (deliberations about) democratic practice. If we approach the analysis here as "stories from the perspective of colonized cultures . . . working to delink from the mechanisms of colonialism," we can rethink universalizing narratives about what and how deliberations about democratic practice can mean beyond any one specific iteration of the idea.[90]

CHAPTER 4

Deliberating Memory

Contested Remembering, National Identity, and the Re/production of Postcolonial Histories

In January of 2002, a year after taking office, the government of John Agyekum Kufuor in Ghana established the National Reconciliation Commission (NRC). According to the legislation that established it, the NRC's mandate was "to seek and promote national reconciliation among the people of this country" toward securing "redress for persons who have suffered any injury, hurt, damage, [or] grievance or who have in any other manner been adversely affected by abuses and violations of their human rights arising from activities or inactivities of public institutions and persons holding public office during periods of unconstitutional government."[1] The work of the NRC was inspired by end-of-the-millennium global discourses about transitional justice and accountability for human rights abuses. In these discourses, citizens, governments, and global agencies were increasingly reckoning with the demands of historical injustices and devising legal, social, and cultural solutions to them. South Africa's Truth and Reconciliation Commission became an iconic symbol of this global phenomenon.

In Ghana, for the first time, a reckoning with decades of citizen abuse under several military regimes provided the immediate local exigence for a national dialogue to confront memories of a painful, regrettable past. The government's objective was to fashion a national future built on trust, peace, and reconciliation. Citizens responded to that call. They filed petitions, appeared at televised public hearings, and debated the past. The government itself circulated photographs of military brutality that it then used to justify calls for the NRC hearings. Two years of public hearings saw more than four thousand petitions brought to the commission. By July of 2004, when the commission concluded its work, memories of a violent collective past had been forced and etched into the national imagination. The commission's recommendations for redress, including payment of reparations to victims, offered hope to aggrieved persons. But as Abena Ampofoa Asare persuasively demonstrates in *Truth Without Reconciliation*, although the commission "did not produce unimpeachable truths" nor "did it fix the country's politics," its work represents something perhaps even more important: it led to "an unprecedented public accounting of Ghana's past, by Ghanaian people, at the turn of the twenty-first century."[2]

The commission's public accounting project highlights the important role of *history* in national political culture, but it also affirms the *memory* of historical events in that culture. By history, I refer here to "the reconstruction, always problematic and incomplete, of something that is no longer."[3] On the other hand, I understand memory here in its public manifestation, as recollections about "fundamental issues about the entire existence of a society: its organization, structure of power, and the very meaning of its past and present."[4] Whether articulated in the singular or plural, histories and memories are multiple, never fully stable, and always in a flux. Rhetorical scholars Marouf Hasian and Robert E. Frank argue that history and memory are complementary and their rhetorical dimensions "help us understand how particular ideologies are accepted, modified, and sometimes rejected."[5]

Both memory and history work in recognition of a shared national past based on which presents and futures can be forged. In this sense, they are interconnected in relation to democratic practice, specifically how citizens engage with issues of common concern. The present chapter takes as its point of departure the organizing principle based on which the NRC's work was established: the idea that memories of an event tend to fashion citizens' self-understandings of their presents and futures. This chapter attends to memories of the 2013 election dispute case in Ghana as they manifest in an important documentary, *The Election Petition*. Artifacts of memory such as the documentary lend themselves to political uses and the rhetorical constructions of a past that can anchor democracy.

The documentary arranges memory—and its counterpart, forgetting—into a rhetorical and cultural lens with which to see not just how electoral disputes have and can be resolved, but also visions of what democratic practice can look like. I suggest that as it memorializes the election dispute, *The Election Petition* serves as a form of historical production that attunes audiences to a public pedagogy of citizenship. It positions audiences to locate and understand what their role as citizens is within the broader story of Ghana's democratic practice, what orientation to adopt toward electoral politics, and what kinds of electoral outcomes are worthy of emulation and aspiration. Understanding the political and rhetorical uses of memories such as those of the dispute remains salient for establishing a link among memories and democratic practice. For without memory, we understand democratic practice only in the abstract, devoid of the texture that citizens' concretized and territorialized experiences can offer. More than this, in relation to the dispute case, memory affords valuable vistas into how electoral politics and democracy are "created, institutionalized, disseminated, and understood."[6] In postconflict, postcolonial democracies with fractured national histories in particular, memories linger on in a variety of places, showing up as they do to shape citizens' sense of national identity and action. What is remembered, forgotten, and ignored all at once feeds democratic practice, not in a teleological or deterministic sense, but in an *influential* manner, in the capacity of rhetoric to shape civic, democratic life.

In establishing this connection between memory and democratic practice, I conceptualize the narrative of *The Election Petition* documentary itself as a story. I do so in much the same way that cultural rhetorics scholars consider stories as fundamental to an appreciation of a culture. As artifacts of memory, documentaries tell stories, and in those stories are embedded the meanings that cultures offer for their values, beliefs, and practices. This chapter further builds on Nathan Atkinson's notion of *celluloid circulation* to argue that *The Election Petition* documentary positions its Ghanaian viewers as audiences for whom the dispute case comes to be entangled in historical production. With *celluloid circulation*, Atkinson contends that nonfiction films (like documentaries) operate simultaneously as "record and performance of an event" in ways that broaden their utility as public address. For Atkinson, the characteristic of nonfiction films as record and performance alike is what calls the audience into being as a form of public. Considered this way, such films can blur and combine both the sense of record (actual historical event) and performance (treatment of that record).[7]

This chapter contends that *The Election Petition* documentary straddles this binary. It combines the status of record and performance by calling into being a public and memorializing the election dispute case into ongoing contentious postcolonial historical production in Ghana. In addition to responding to the exigence created by what its producers call the need to "tell the Ghanaian story from the perspective of the Ghanaian," the documentary extends perspectives on Ghanaian postcolonial history. It inserts electoral histories into a broader story of Ghanaian democratic practice while simultaneously unfolding as a public pedagogy of citizenship.

As it is implicated in extant discourses about nationalist histories and the production of postcolonial Ghanaian history, *The Election Petition* operates, then, for its Ghanaian audiences as a canvas upon which contested memories about democracy in Ghana come to be scripted. Given the significant political capital held by its producers and the media platform on which it is broadcast, *The Election Petition* reached a broad audience.[8] Writing about the rhetorical function of documentaries, Thomas Benson and Brian Snee suggest that documentaries can serve a political agenda by framing courses of action for audiences.[9] They can be deployed to frame contentious public and political issues and unfold as the "creative treatment of actuality."[10] They can further shape public opinion, serve ideological purposes, and be deployed toward entertaining ends. Even for those documentaries that depart from the expectations of the genre, only appropriating the form, that form is sufficient to lend the subject matter credibility. Although audiences may be skeptical of documentaries' objectivity, the rhetorical force behind the genre lends it some degree of truthiness.[11]

The sources upon which documentaries rely may be products of individual interpretation by the documentarian, but those products tend to be believable. On political documentaries concerning national elections, there is, Benson and Snee go on to note, a "lingering rhetorical aura," giving documentaries "a special claim on truth telling, however tenuous."[12] What is valuable about a documentary—at least rhetorically—is the uses to which it is put, its persuasive treatment of an event, its pedagogical capacity. In our case, that use, persuasion, and pedagogy manifest in the ways that nationalist political histories can function as scaffolds for democratic practice.[13]

To this end, then, this chapter examines political implications of knowledge production and the dissemination of memories as a resource for democratic practice. Although the documentary is advertised as a historical record, it also unfolds as a paean to the political career and service of the first petitioner of the election dispute, Nana Addo Danquah Akufo-Addo, who went on to become Ghana's president. To be sure, memories do not serve democratic practice in a deterministic way, but they do shape how that practice is understood, lived, and practiced. In terms of the election dispute case, for example, memories of the elections inform practices, procedures, laws, and general citizen dispositions toward future elections. A decade since Election 2012 in Ghana, *The Election Petition* documentary remains perhaps the only record of its kind with extensive reach that has systematically attended to the historic event. In so doing, it bears a pedagogical value: it treats for citizens the pasts, presents, and futures of Ghanaian democratic practice in terms of electoral politics.[14]

There is a note of caution, however, as we attend to the documentary's pedagogical value in terms of historical production aimed at democratic practice. Because texts make meaning only in context and in relation to other texts, attending specifically to *The Election Petition* documentary is not to suggest that the documentary is single-handedly responsible for Ghanaians' recollection of the dispute case. Instead, doing so is to follow Marouf Hasian and Robert E. Frank's position that single texts do not create collective memories, they are aided by other contextual factors.[15] I articulate some of those factors here as political histories and the anxieties of historical production in postcolonial Ghana.[16] Of course, postcolonial histories of Ghana's political trajectories cannot be told and remembered in a single teleological fashion. However, by bringing the events of the election dispute to the fore of political and politicized memory, the producers supply an interpretive prism through which citizens would come to parse memories of the election dispute and its significance for democratic practice. For rhetorical studies of democratic practice, then, this chapter articulates a culturally contingent manifestation of memory in the postcolony, with power at its core, toward democratic ends.

The rest of the chapter is organized as follows. I begin by briefly examining key themes in *An African Election*, a documentary that offers background context on the immediate African, and specifically Ghanaian, electoral realities against which *The Election Petition* can be read and understood. Next, I explore historical production in Ghana as a practice of the exercise of memory and forgetting in the service of democratic practice. This exploration paves the way for an analysis of *The Election Petition* documentary as an instantiation of this practice. I conclude by examining how we might reconsider historical production, memory, and forgetting in relation to democracies, and specifically postcolonial democracies.

Documenting Africa's Electoral Realities in *An African Election*

Jarreth J. Merz's 2011 documentary, *An African Election*, offers a historical snapshot of African electoral realities in the recent past. The film's focus is Ghana, with attention to the twenty-eight days leading up to the national elections on December 7, 2008. For the first time since a return to multiparty rule in 1992, both the New Patriotic Party (NPP) and the National Democratic Congress (NDC) had alternately held the reins of government for two four-year terms each and entered campaign mode for a third tenure. The Ghanaian electorate were in the throes of a keen national electoral contest dominated by both political parties. Both the discovery of oil in commercial quantities the year before and projected revenues that could help fund the national economy had raised the stakes of the contest. *An African Election* powerfully captures the momentousness of this historic election.

For its producers, the award-winning documentary was intended to provide a view into the behind-the-scenes actions of key stakeholders in the election. The producers described the documentary as a look into the "political machinery of a third world democracy struggling to legitimize itself to its first world contemporaries."[17] This characterization suggests that African elections are oriented to the gaze of Western audiences. There were specific moments in the documentary itself when key Ghanaian political stakeholders saw the election as a test of the perceived leading role Ghana has played in Africa's democracies. With this recognition, such stakeholders called on citizens to be alert to the historic nature of the elections. As the NPP's Akufo-Addo filed presidential nomination documents at the Electoral Commission headquarters, he made two observations: "The eyes of the world are on us here in Ghana for this election," and "We know what is happening on the rest of the continent," namely electoral incidents. Akufo-Addo goes on to bemoan these incidents and expressed the hope that none of those "will mar the process that we have initiated this morning." This expression of hope would be shared across the political spectrum in the days leading up to the elections. A former president, the NDC's Jerry John Rawlings remarked similarly to a visiting African Union Observer delegation that "Ghana's case now is going to be a test for all of us." The idea that Ghana is an exemplary democracy among and to its peers is here brought into focus.

The documentary articulates an expectation of hope that Ghanaian democracy would be an exercise in continental image restoration: "The people of the Republic of Ghana are getting ready to choose their next president," it begins, and "the international community hopes that the Ghanaian elections will repair the image of democracy in Africa—damaged by allegations of electoral fraud, followed by violence in Kenya and Zimbabwe and military coups in Mauritania and Guinea." This list of continental electoral challenges fed into negative perceptions in the global imagination, and the producers of the documentary hoped Ghana's Election 2008 would help counter such perceptions. Thus, insofar as *An African Election* portrays Africa's electoral realities through the lens of Ghanaian elections, it offers key thematic ideas as scaffolds for understanding *The Election Petition* documentary. The election dispute case of 2013 has historical roots in the momentous Election 2008, and the producers of *The Election Petition* claimed their inspiration for the documentary came from seeing Ghana's story told in *An African Election*.[18]

Two key themes would be sufficient to inform an appreciation of the *Election Petition* documentary. First, *An African Election* is concerned with the idea that Ghanaian democracy is and ought to be considered exceptional in Africa's democratic journey. As Akufo-Addo articulated this sentiment, he also signaled the major pitfall to be avoided: political violence. In the documentary, delegations from across continental bodies and notable personalities alike echo similar sentiments. For instance, two days to the elections, as delegations from the regional political and economic body, the Economic Community of West African States (ECOWAS) paid a crucial last-minute visit to Jerry John Rawlings, he uses the occasion to sound a note of caution. In remarks to the president of ECOWAS, Professor Amos Sawyerr, Rawlings emphasizes the need for a successful election. Like Akufo-Addo, Sawyerr recognizes Ghana as "the trailblazer in West Africa on democratization," going on to observe that "what happens in Ghana affects all of us [continental neighbors], positively as well as negatively." Rawlings called for vigilance among the observer mission groups in order to safeguard the lives of twenty-million-odd Ghanaians who would otherwise be affected by political violence. Electoral politics in Ghana is understood here, then, not as a local issue so much as a regional, continental, even global concern.[19]

Second, the documentary highlights the intricacies of knowledge production about Africa for global audiences. These intricacies are evident in the producers' motivations for creating the documentary, namely, to showcase to the world a so-called third-world democracy's struggles at legitimizing itself to its first-world counterparts. *An African Election*'s framing in this way posits a hierarchical relationship between African democracies and those of Western societies. It also simultaneously creates interpretive space for Africans themselves to narrate their stories on the interplay between African politics and democracy, on the one hand, and global politics, on the other. In the documentary, Hannah Tetteh, at one time Ghana's foreign minister, articulates the nature of this relationship through the hope she expresses for a change in the power dynamics of what Ghanaian democracy could be for both Ghanaian and Western audiences:

> I want people to look at my children and my children not to feel that being African is something to be ashamed of because Africa is always looked at as a basket case. And more importantly, I want the Western world to come and learn from what we have in Africa because I think that we have a lot of wonderful things here that are overlooked because we are considered to be poor and backward and unstable, and to show that as a community we respect, we learn, we grow together.[20]

Tetteh's hope was for a revision of what I have referred to in this book as the postcolonial election library, those sets of discourses, ideas, images, and epistemologies in the Western imagination that essentialize, exaggerate, and circulate Africa's challenges with electoral processes. Told in Africans' own words, democratic practice would no longer be about Africans being the putative learners with Euro-America, paternalistically, as teacher.[21] Tetteh's orientation to politics is a recognition of African agency and knowledge production, one that even inverts the relationship of Africa as student and "the world" as teacher. As shall become apparent, this idea gains significance later in *The Election Petition*.

In the years since the release of *An African Election*, the documentary has been significant for understanding African electoral politics. To one reviewer, it poses a challenge to long-standing depictions of Africa, at least by outsiders. It depicts African politicians as "people who do desire democracy and political stability just like their counterparts anywhere else, and not as individuals prone to turn into bloodthirsty dictators once they seize power."[22] It has also been widely screened in several African countries and around the world especially in advance of national elections. In so doing, the objective has been to keep in the public imagination both the lessons citizens can draw from Election 2008 about resilience in the face of daunting challenges and the critical role of formal and informal institutions in sustaining democracy.

As producer Merz observes in an interview, one key objective of the documentary was to showcase a good example of a successful African political practice, "to create a prototype of something to be proud of."[23] *An African Election* was a major impetus for *The Election Petition*; the thematic considerations explored in the former—Ghana's democratic example to continental peers and the intricacies of knowledge production about Africa—offer a foundation based on which the story told, and arguments advanced in the latter, can be much better understood. To do so, however, requires an understanding of the ways that historical production in Ghana functions rhetorically as memory that in turn tries to shape democratic practice. It is to this intersection between historical production and memory that we now turn.

Historical Production and Memory in Ghana

History and memory intersect in Ghanaian politics in symbiotic, mutually reinforcing ways.[24] In *States of Memory*, memory scholar Jeffrey Olick argues that "memory has long been the handmaiden of nationalist zeal, history its high counsel."[25] This triptych of history, memory, and the nation rests on both the formal and informal education of citizens who in turn re/produce ideas about politics for generations. In Ghana, political parties are a conduit through which this education furthers history more informally. In discussing a tradition of change in continuity in Ghanaian history education, Samuel Adu-Gyamfi and

Eugenia Anderson contend that debates about historical production in Ghana have revolved around the traditions of politics envisioned by mid-century independence nationalists Joseph Boakye Danquah and Kwame Nkrumah (and both leaders' political progenies).[26]

In their vision for the new nation, Danquah and Nkrumah differed on at least three grounds. First, whereas Danquah's United Gold Coast Convention (UGCC) party favored "independence in the shortest possible time" from British colonial rule, Nkrumah's Convention People's Party (CPP) launched a campaign for "independence now."[27] Second, Danquah advocated for the preservation of the powers historically vested in chiefs, so they could continue to manage (revenue from) stool lands. Nkrumah, on the other hand, envisioned a new nation with limited powers for the chiefs, wherein local governments would be democratized and administer revenues from stool lands.[28] Finally, while Danquah called for a federal system of government, Nkrumah thought a unitary state was more conducive to Ghana's economic and historical conditions.[29] The two major political parties in Ghana today, the NPP and NDC, each trace their political traditions to what have come to be called the Danquah-Busia and Nkrumahist parties, respectively.[30] For Adu-Gyamfi and Anderson, the continuity and change in Ghanaian history have their roots in the actions of political actors like Danquah and Nkrumah, who in turn influenced the production of history.

During colonialism, Europeans circulated ideas for centuries to deny Africans' humanity and agency, producing these ideas as de facto histories. Across Ghana, a major part of self-determination efforts in the immediate postindependence era was to repopulate the national imagination with histories about Africans told by Africans themselves as a counterpoint to earlier dehumanizing narratives. Adu-Gyamfi and Anderson argue that in this effort, civilians and military governments over time took steps to shape historical production in ways that further political ends. As they put it, "the two main competing political ideologies [Nkrumahist and Danquah-Busia] have sought to use political power to influence how history is written and studied."[31]

These uses of history toward political ends came with their own perils. Historian Joseph Adjaye observes that in rewriting Africa into histories of the world, Ghanaian historians did not fashion a sense of nationalist history in terms of fostering an ideal around which the diverse multiethnic cleavages at independence could be bridged.[32] Instead, in the quest for self-definition, several forms of local, rather than nationalist, historiographies emerged.[33]

Local historiographies strategically focused on specific ethnic groups. For Ghanaian history, this has historically been the larger and more researched Akan group.[34] Over time, these privileged local histories achieved the status of national histories, dislodging histories of relatively smaller ethnic groups and cementing the place of select historical personalities and events in the national imagination. Whether ethnic or positivist as Adjaye contends, nationalist histories have political implications. They can be used toward defined rhetorical and political ends. In Ghana, such implications of history, history writing, and political legitimacy have been all too clear, most recently in what came to be known as the "Battle of the Apostrophe." This controversy concerned the drama of the midcentury independence movement, its key protagonists, their roles, and their significance for nation-building.

In this respect, political parties are implicated in historical production in Ghana through commemorative acts. In historicizing the controversy of the "Battle of the Apostrophe," the historian Edem Adotey reports that the two dominant political parties in Ghana, the NDC and the NPP, have used commemorative acts like holidays in producing (politicized) history. With a leaning toward the political ideologies of the first president of Ghana, the NDC government in 2009 introduced Kwame Nkrumah's birthday, September 21, as "Founder's Day." The important point here is the positioning of the apostrophe. Controversy followed this declaration, particularly from the NPP. It was unsurprising, then, that less than a decade later, upon coming into office in 2017, the NPP government reversed this holiday in some sort of "argument-by-apostrophe." The party redesignated the day instead as "Founders' Day," set at August 4, and ostensibly intended to embrace a multiplicity of historical actors as founders of Ghana. Rather than a flippant placement of an apostrophe, this controversy reflects the very idea of "legitimacy, and who has the pedigree to rule contemporary Ghana."[35]

As we shall see momentarily, such notions of political legitimacy offer insight into how we might read *The Election Petition* documentary. The trope of "founding father" relies on the constitutive capacity of rhetoric, and both founding myths of a national past and hagiographies of national heroes can serve to legitimize political agendas, shape subjectivities, and pinpoint future trajectories.[36] Such political fictions, or a culture's stories of "political heroes, villains, and the births and deaths of governments,"[37] are sustained by the repetition and circulation of contested national histories in *The Election Petition*.

Such fictions also serve to strategically legitimize specific narratives of Ghanaian histories of democracy. Thus legitimized, they unfold in artifacts of memory such as *The Election Petition* as tools of public pedagogy, teaching citizens who they are and how they may practice democracy.

In public, the circulation of historical accounts like those just discussed depends upon public memory, defined here as memories concerning "fundamental issues about the entire existence of a society: its organization, structure of power, and the very meaning of its past and present."[38] Debates about these issues illustrate the nomadic character of memory itself, in the sense that we remember historical accounts differently depending on multiple conditioning mechanisms, whether those be of time, place, or purpose.[39] The contingent, variable character of public memory means that memories may be imbricated in other purposes beyond those of the original, even as they circulate across time and place. Their domain is not one of "stability but [an] ongoing redistribution or, better still, re-membering."[40] This sense of instability is intimately bound up with another character of and counterpoint to memory: forgetting.

Both memory and forgetting constitute two prongs of the same fork of remembrance; what societies choose to remember is as important as what they decide to forget. Expanding this idea elsewhere, Bradford Vivian posits in *Public Forgetting* that "forgetting is not merely the opposite of memory; it parasitically haunts the act of recollection, thriving by virtue of a stealthy but lethal attachment to its host." Although forgetting is often posited as a counterfoil to the more valorized memory, Vivian calls for attention to forgetting because of the "positive, formative role it can play in the works of public memory." Part of that formative role in public memory practices reflects in the capacity of forgetting to "maintain, replenish, or inaugurate vital cultures of memory writ large." In its symbiotic relationship with memory, forgetting can be necessary in contexts of memory when recollections such as those of, say, injustice and violence would threaten communal unity.[41]

Vivian further writes that "uncommonly pivotal moments in the evolution of communal time, history, and memory" define the practice of public forgetting. Such moments would be characterized by an articulation of both a rationale for the imperative to forget and "a novel public idiom" through which the past, present, and future of the community ought to be parsed. This momentous, explicit practice of forgetting is set against "ordinary and often unnoticed patterns of selective interpretation or partial recollection."[42] What this formulation emphasizes is an explicitness at the heart of calls for forgetting unlike those of practices of memory that may not necessarily require that explicitness. But Vivian also rightly observes that practices of forgetting, like those of memory, are "irreducibly contingent in nature" and may become popular "within public speech, language, or symbolism as a *situational response* to contingent needs and interests."[43]

One may argue that forgetting may be *enacted* and not specifically *inaugurated* by interpretive practices that only remember certain events, places, and people, but not others. This manner of approaching public forgetting might imply that in addition to the explicitness that Vivian advances for public forgetting (like those evident in public history projects and state-sanctioned memorials), interpretive practices of remembering may invariably *enact* forgetting. Through silence and silencing, deflection and selection, interpretations may, intentionally or not, work in the service of public forgetting. They may begin the work of public forgetting by tapping into already existing practices and discourses. Interpretations may also engender forgetting especially through selective disregard of key features of an event being commemorated. Consider the fact that there are several plausible interpretations and ways to memorialize the election dispute case. However, as a record and performance of the events, *The Election Petition*'s interpretation of key events of the dispute, its silences on some incidents and emphases on others, all work to foster and enact specific public memories, while de-emphasizing and engendering public forgetting of others.[44] How history, forgetting, and memory intersect in the service of democratic practice is the subject of the analysis of *The Election Petition* that now follows.

Recording and Memorializing Ghanaian Electoral Histories in *The Election Petition*

SOAS and Spurs, the producers of *The Election Petition*, indicate they have been inspired by Jareth J. Merz's *An African Election* to tell their own story—"the story of the massive legal challenge that was mounted to an election to elect the President of the country (Ghana)."[45] The definitive title, *The Election Petition*, signals the producers' authoritative perspective on the subject. However accurate Merz's depiction or noble his intentions, the story told by the documentary suggests that the accounts of electoral realities in *An African Election* are, to some degree, an outsider's perspective of an internally African affair. Although the documentary features mostly Ghanaians telling their own stories about Election 2008, and Jarreth Merz makes the savvy editorial decision to avoid voice-over narration, the camera in the hands of anyone at all is itself of great import. It offers both the ability to see, to select, to deflect, and to avoid seeing altogether. Besides, while Merz had spent formative years in Ghana, he is a white man of Swiss origin. To this extent, he could be considered by some, like the SOAS and Spurs producers, a Ghanaian "outsider." Positionality in knowledge production about Africa was therefore at the heart of the making of *The Election Petition.*

Although a private media organization, SOAS and Spurs held enormous public sway on remembrances of the election dispute case. This is significant in a country where the state largely dominates memorializing initiatives regarding national historical narratives. The documentary premiered in Accra on January 24, 2018, five years after the case had been adjudicated. At its premiere, there were in attendance several dignitaries, including Ghana's president Nana Akufo-Addo, who was the Special Guest of Honor. Under the auspices of SOAS and Spurs, the noted Ghanaian political journalist Paul Adom-Otchere directed and narrated the documentary. SOAS and Spurs has produced other political documentaries, including *Voices of Political Campaign in Ghana* and *From Gold Coast to Ghana*, a Ghanaian independence story. Across these, the organization's emphasis has been to stage an interplay between politics and democracy in Ghana. Adom-Otchere's stature in this enterprise is noteworthy. He cut his journalistic teeth hosting and discussing sociopolitical issues across media organizations in Ghana. For nearly two decades, he has been the host of the popular current affairs political show, *Good Evening Ghana*, on the Accra-based Metropolitan Television (Metro TV). Here, he has superintended over one of the longest-running political talk shows on Ghanaian television. Both *Good Evening Ghana* and Adom-Otchere owe their credibility as news and media sources in part to this longevity. Thus, when Adom-Otchere premiered a documentary on the election dispute, first at the Accra International Conference Center to an audience of citizens and distinguished politicians and later on *Good Evening Ghana*, it was sure to garner much political interest. The enormous institutional media support behind Adom-Otchere's documentary demonstrates that even localized acts of remembering, those initiated by private individuals, can work in the service of state-sanctioned ways of remembering.

The sixty-minute documentary is not clearly delineated in any specific sense. However, it proceeds in four discernible progressions that narrativize Ghanaian political history pre- and postindependence. The first progression spans the electoral history of Ghana from the immediate post–World War II period to the postindependence period. These eras are marked, respectively, by agitations for national liberation across European colonies and the interruption of several civilian governments by military dictatorships. A second progression moves to the sociopolitical background of the key petitioners of the election dispute. Both the dispute case proper and testimonials from key protagonists follow, and the implications of the case for future elections concludes the documentary. This narrative arc rhetorically situates the election dispute case in a larger context of Ghanaian political history and memory while tying the event to ideas about democratic practice more specifically.

The documentary opens with a reference to Cicero: "Justitia est constans et perpetua voluntas jus suum cuique," to wit, "Justice is the constant and perpetual wish to render everyone his right." The Ciceronian quote immediately locates the exigence for the election dispute in the domain of justice, presumably a quest for justice for the petitioners (the NPP) who filed a suit challenging the Electoral Commission's declaration of the NDC's John Mahama as president. That quest for justice was to render a fair trial in the controversial election dispute case. The narrator indicates that the documentary is based on "a true political story from the leading democracy in Africa—Ghana in West Africa." Other audiences aside Ghanaians may be inferred here. It is for Ghanaians and these imagined audiences (who may presumably be unaware of Ghana's geographical location) alike that *The Election Petition* is produced.

The narration of electoral history in this first part works not merely as a chronicle of electoral procedures over time. Especially for other-than-Ghanaian audiences, it can be explained overall in Fanonian terms as a narration of African time. This opening gambit and harkening back into electoral time, as it were, signals a deft move to locate Africa in time, much against popular discourses that locate African electoral democracy outside of time. That writing of Africa into time accomplishes an important decolonial objective. Channeling Frantz Fanon, Achille Mbembe explains in *Out of the Dark Night* that Fanon's sense of decolonization was about writing Africa into history, reinscribing it into time, against prevailing colonial discourses that "natives were not simply people without a past and without history," but that they were also people "radically located *outside of time*."[46] Part of the effectiveness of colonial discourses depended and still depends on logics of repetition, and only through these logics are the discourses circulated and cemented in the global imagination. Mbembe understands this writing into history as a practice of decolonization and a subversion of the law of repetition. If the perceived inability of Africans to self-govern is to be upended, the notion that Africans were located outside time would be undone effectively through a reinscription of Africa's electoral histories in larger political histories. This would be done however checkered, difficult, or (in)glorious those electoral histories may be judged to be.

In the attempt to write Africa into electoral history, the producers relied on somewhat unrelated histories. Specifically, they deployed one of the major catalysts for the keen contest of Election 2012—the sudden death in office of President John Atta Mills five months before the polls. Mills's death is cast as an unforeseen event that prematurely ushered Vice President John Mahama into office. Given his late-game entry into the presidential race, Mahama's electoral victory five months later was therefore anomalous. Almost as a nod to the idea we have already seen in *An African Election*, *The Election Petition*'s narrator recounts the now-acclaimed position of the country in Africa's democratic enterprise. By doing so, the narrator centers the perception that Ghana is "widely seen as a modern beacon of African democracy," being also "the first to win political independence from colonial rule in 1957."[47] This rhetorical move reinscribes the nationalist and continental role the country played in the midcentury African independence movements into a history of democracy writ large. And by doing so, it serves a public pedagogical purpose of teaching citizens to be proud of their national political heritage.

Several key events in Ghana's electoral history that came to profoundly define both political and electoral history in the country are brought to the limelight. The narrator traces some of these through timelines: Ghana's electoral history stretches back to the colonial Gold Coast when, in 1951, parliamentary elections were won by "the party [Convention People's Party] of Ghana's famous first president, Dr. Kwame Nkrumah." This victory by Nkrumah was to be followed by two more, in the elections of 1954 and 1956, the latter a momentous one at the cusp of independence. Nkrumah won these elections against his main political opponent, Dr. Joseph Boakye Danquah, his United Gold Coast Convention (UGCC) from which Nkrumah had splintered, and its successor party. The narrator proceeds to acknowledge the first military coup d'état that overthrew Dr. Nkrumah's government in the 1960s, to be followed by alternating civilian and military governments through the 1970s. We see here a historical periodization from political independence onwards. In the wake of military interventions, the return to civilian rule ushered in other constitutions, the latest being in 1992.

What is evident from this account is that the NPP and the NDC trace their political ideologies and traditions to the two main parties at independence—Nkrumah's CPP and Danquah's UGCC. While the NPP's direct genealogical links to the party of Danquah is evident from history, the NDC's associations with the Nkumahist political tradition is more strategic and pragmatic. Given its roots in military rule and perhaps to legitimate a historical political tradition, the NDC seems to have appropriated Nkrumah's legacy, in turn pitting itself in opposition to the NPP's long-standing, if also historically nonlinear, Danquah-Busia tradition.[48] *The Election Petition*'s chronicle and memorializing of this electoral history in this way stages a juxtaposition between the traditions, recalling not only the roles they played or failed to play in Ghana's electoral democracy but also the continuing influence of these political parties on democratic practice.

This juxtaposition, however, is not just historical. It also resonates with Adotey's claim that the "Battle of the Apostrophe" concerning Nkrumah's holiday was a matter of political legitimacy.[49] Political histories extol Nkrumah's founding-father role in Ghanaian politics, and his position as the first prime minister and subsequent president of Ghana is a matter of historical record.[50] However, the documentary offers a slightly divergent perspective of this fact. It notes that the first ever presidential elections were held in 1979, seven years after Nkrumah's death. Previous elections, it goes on to point out, were to elect prime ministers, and Nkrumah only automatically became president in 1960 because Ghana attained republican status from British rule. What followed Nkrumah's overthrow were military governments and elections of prime ministers and, in some cases, ceremonial, unelected presidents. The elections through which Ghana's president Hilla Limann came into office in 1979 were therefore the first ever presidential elections. This semantic precision is not without rhetorical and political merit. Although the act of memorializing and the concern for historical accuracy is of public pedagogical value, the underlying logic also questions the position of Nkrumah as president per se. The logic here is that elections confer legitimacy to rule; therefore, if Nkrumah was not *elected* by the people as president, but only became one by virtue of Ghana's republican status, his position was not a result of the people's will.

Another way the documentary highlighted political legitimacy was in connection with electoral losses between the NPP and the NDC over the decades. Having lost the general elections to the NDC in 1992, the NPP leveled allegations of electoral malpractice and boycotted the subsequent parliamentary elections. These allegations are memorialized in the party's report on the elections, *The Stolen Verdict*, written by the eminent Ghanaian historian and politician Albert Adu Boahen. Adu Boahen's 1993 report was defining in its call for electoral reforms in subsequent elections. After a two-term tenure in office, the next electoral cycle saw a peaceful transition from the NPP to the NDC in 2009. As was observed in *An African Election*, Election 2008 was momentous precisely because "it was the first time in Africa that power was changing hands in a peaceful and democratic way." If Ghana's assumed lead role in Africa's democracy is instructive, Election 2008 was a defining election.

With this memorializing, then, overall, *The Election Petition* writes Ghanaian electoral history into time. It details the glorious and sore spots and memorializes promising beginnings and challenging times along the way. It also simultaneously selects, addresses, and memorializes historical controversies of political legitimacy, foregrounding as it does events and personalities that have substantially defined Ghanaian politics. In memorializing the election dispute case, the narrator suggests that Ghana's political history made Election 2012 "a major test case of Ghana's electoral systems, judicial maturity, and political stability." The documentary weaves the election dispute case into Ghana's political and electoral history and traces a genealogy of electoral politics in Ghana. It connects history to politics by memorializing what counts as legitimate political history. In this way, it lays the foundation for audience perceptions of the ways that Ghanaian political history shaped electoral democracy over time. If its audiences are to develop knowledge of credibility and legitimacy of the political parties' positions during the election dispute, the documentary would play a crucial role in that endeavor. *The Election Petition* serves a pedagogical function evident in this first part, in the (dis)positions it invites viewers to take vis-à-vis electoral politics in Ghana.

On Portraits of Heroism and Political Legitimacy

The memory practices observed in the documentary are themselves in accord with observations about memory in postcolonial African societies. In *Memory and the Postcolony*, Richard Werbner identifies a link between political subjectivity and the significance of the ultimate sacrifice for the nation. This observation is in evidence in Zimbabwe, where a "modern memorial complex . . . [unfolds in] a distinctively postcolonial form, glorifying above all the individuality of great heroes of the nation."[51] Like the Zimbabwean example, and more than a fascination with communal dimensions of democratic practice, Akufo-Addo is presented in *The Election Petition* as yet another rightful occupant in a pantheon of political actors whose sacrifices and dedication to country have helped built Ghanaian democracy. He is portrayed as an epitome of what in the postcolony has been "the historic sacrifice of life in the cause of the nation-state."[52] This portrait serves to foreground his political legitimacy.

The second progression of *The Election Petition* concerned the sociopolitical background of key petitioners in the case. These political players determined the outcome of the case through the arguments they presented in court, as did the respondents who equally argued and the judges who adjudicated the case. Thus, when the documentary spotlights the background of the key players, such focus can be understood as memorializing historical actors who shaped Ghanaian electoral democracy. Like all genres, documentaries select and define their objects of representation in ways that simultaneously deselect and detract from other equally plausible representations. This process of representation is the way memory and forgetting are enacted through silence, selection, and interpretation. In positioning itself as a historical record, *The Election Petition* presents a picture of the petitioners that is at once historical and hagiographic. In this twin representation, electoral histories become mobilized toward specific political ends. If the duration allotted to key ideas is indicative, then the documentary's significant spotlight (a little more than ten minutes of the entire sixty minutes) of the first petitioner, Akufo-Addo, demonstrates a hagiographic account with the potential to be wielded toward power and more-than-historical ends.

The spotlight on Akufo-Addo accomplishes one such end of power and legitimacy. *The Election Petition* harkens back to Akufo-Addo's days as attorney general and foreign minister in the NPP government of President John Kufuor in the early 2000s. This period preceded his candidature for president for the first time in 2008. Akufo-Addo is portrayed as a progeny of a family who have dedicated their political careers to nation-building. His "antecedent father, Edward Akufo-Addo and two maternal uncles, J. B. Danquah [of the UGCC] and William Ofori-Attah," the narrator recalls, "were all founding members of Ghana's first political party, the United Gold Coast Convention formed in 1947." Especially from the 2000s onward, Ghanaian political historiography has tended to drift toward an almost exclusive focus on the so-called Big Six, a group of six men whose contributions to the country's anticolonial rule has increasingly been accorded pride of place in the national independence story.

If the dominant focus on Ghanaian men as historical actors is at all indicative, we must pay attention to how that focus itself excludes others who just as significantly contributed to what became the new nation of Ghana. In addition to the ethnic-based histories identified by Joseph Adjaye as limiting the development of nationalist histories, Ghanaian history has also mostly valorized the place of men in politics. This valorization has been accomplished through the circulation, in various media, of the heroic role such men played in the independence struggle. Nancy Henaku has argued that despite their significant contributions, Ghanaian women politicians such as Nana Konadu Agyeman-Rawlings have been elided from the country's political and rhetorical history.[53] For Henaku, this is especially the case in the founding-father debates, revealing "the lack of recognition for female political agency in the Ghanaian postcolony."[54]

In *The Election Petition*, the exclusionist and masculinist perspective on politics is suffused into the independence narrative yet again through the spotlight not only of the Big Six, but also of their descendants like Akufo-Addo, even if the roles they played were noteworthy. Indeed, like Henaku's reclamation of Agyeman-Rawlings's contributions, historian Jean Allman has explained that this feature of exclusion is pervasive in accounts of the roadmap to independence in Ghana. Allman found that when Ghana celebrated its golden jubilee in 2007, for example, the elaborate ceremonies that characterized the jubilee celebrations, namely street naming initiatives, unveiling of statues, and historical reenactments, conspicuously neglected the valuable contribution of women during the period. For Allman, this exclusion was a case of "sanctioned forgetting," a phenomenon she blames on "nationalist metanarratives, and state and diaspora histories . . . [which have] all conspired, sometimes unwittingly, in the . . . disappearance of African women as named historical subjects."[55]

As a memorializing not only of the dispute case but also of Ghanaian national and political history more broadly, *The Election Petition* likewise pursues this path of exclusion and avails to its audiences a version of history that participates in this sanctioned forgetting. The documentary genre necessarily includes and excludes, and the editorial control exerted by the producers has implications for the kind of history that is memorialized. For democratic practice in the postcolony, this combination of memory and forgetting works together as a public pedagogy of citizenship, highlighting in part for citizens how they may locate and understand their roles, place, and subjectivities within the broader story of Ghana's democratic practice.

Important also are the rhetorical uses to which Akufo-Addo's political career is deployed in the documentary. If his familial lineage would mean the audience could not be persuaded by the suggestion of ascription, the narrator was sure to remind viewers of Akufo-Addo's own accomplishments. Here, he is portrayed as one who "had dedicated most of his youthful years to political mobilization toward democracy and legal battles toward human rights." A paradigmatic example is offered. Harsh economic conditions during the NDC's tenure in the 1990s fueled widespread dissatisfaction with the government. On May 9, 1995, citizens organized a major political protest, dubbed *Kume Preko* (Twi language for "You might as well kill me"), to protest the government's implementation of a Value Added Tax.[56] In what has been considered one of the biggest national protests to date, Akufo-Addo is featured in the documentary as a key organizer whose concern for human rights is noteworthy. In addition to his accomplishments in politics, the audience is also reminded of his famous contribution to media freedom in the repeal of criminal libel laws from the statute books. In a parliamentary debate spotlighted on the issue, he is shown in a fervent argument on the floor against the status quo: "The bill before this house is very much in accordance with the sentiments of the Ghanaian people, and those who still yearn and hanker after a return or maintenance of the status quo which allowed governments to prosecute journalists are completely out of step with public opinion in our country today."[57]

Occurring in the context of histories of military interruption in Ghanaian politics, the repeal of the criminal libel law led to expansions in legal provisions surrounding freedom of speech and expression, themselves central tenets of many democracies. While the hagiographic accounts of Akufo-Addo's political life were indirectly related to the election dispute case, memorializing the account served to tie his political history and Ghana's democracy together. A deputy attorney general in the government of the NPP, Godfred Dame, praised Akufo-Addo's incredible contributions to constitutional law in Ghana, concluding, "If ever there'll be a legal hall of fame or Book of Ghana Law, Nana Akufo-Addo's name will undoubtedly receive favorable mention." Dame points out that when it comes, for example, to fair and balanced coverage of political parties by the state broadcaster, the Ghana Broadcasting Corporation, it was Akufo-Addo's legal cases that helped develop Ghana's constitutional law in that regard.[58] In *The Election Petition*, the history of Akufo-Addo's political career intertwines with national history as two sides of the same coin.

But this sort of history production is not alien to Ghanaian politics. Kwame Nkrumah's publication of his autobiography, *Ghana: An Autobiography of Kwame Nkrumah*, coincided with political independence in 1957. Some have argued that the book's title and its publication date were not accidental but instead a strategic political move to symbolically meld the new nation with the personality and national vision of Nkrumah. This melding—whether directly as in Nkrumah's case, or more subtly in the documentary's portrayal of Akufo-Addo—reflects a postindependence, postcolonial African historiography that has been positivist, one that turns the spotlight on and celebrates so-called great rulers, who are mostly men.[59]

Memories of political persecution by military governments also suffuse the documentary and are kept alive to shape citizens' understanding of democracy in Ghana. The public pedagogical purpose appears to be that the current democratic dispensation is worth safeguarding since nobody wishes to return to a brutal past. As the opening paragraphs to this chapter show, the NPP government had taken a major step to initiate a national conversation to redress historical wrongs. The National Reconciliation Commission (NRC) was a key result of this effort and helped foster a national dialogue on truth and reconciliation. As the key government official to have launched the initiative, Akufo-Addo's role as attorney general and minister of justice looms large in the documentary's recall of the period. Almost as a Manichaean juxtaposition between right and wrong, Akufo-Addo's lead role in the NRC initiative is immediately followed in the documentary by the appearance at the commission hearings of none other than former president Jerry John Rawlings. It was

Rawlings's military government of the Provincial National Defense Council of the 1980s that morphed into the NDC. Indeed, this strategic juxtaposition is a matter of memory and forgetting.

The election dispute case was in no way directly related to the reconciliation initiative; however, the inclusion of the latter in the documentary helps posit good against evil, and democracy against military rule. Rawlings appears in *The Election Petition* to deny charges of extrajudicial killings that occurred during his tenure as a military ruler. In the 2000s, the reconciliation initiative had been denounced by the NDC as, in reality, a "'Nail Rawlings Commission,' designed to besmirch and delegitimize the legacy of the party's founder."[60] The documentary juxtaposes the role of Akufo-Addo of the NPP and Rawlings of the NDC in this epochal memory-making: where one seeks peace, the other does not. If Rawlings contributed to a painful past that called for reconciliation, Akufo-Addo worked to redress that wrong in the present; where Rawlings divided the country, Akufo-Addo unified it.

Recalling and centering this piece of history which has little direct link to the election dispute case demonstrates the ways that culturally contingent historical production and memory can work in the service of democratic practice in the postcolony. Memory in the postcolony is itself plagued by the dislocations of time wrought by the colonial encounter, and a linear sense of memory in the postcolony, like anywhere else, is itself anomalous. As memory scholar Michael Rothberg suggests, in the postcolony in particular, memory unfolds not in the continuities often emphasized for nations and civilizations but in fractures that mirror "the structural dislocations produced by an imperial world system."[61]

Such dislocations remain and are evinced if we consider memory through cultural imaginaries—the values, politics, and histories that drive democratic practice. As we have seen, the history of the NRC is crucial to an appreciation of Ghanaian history and politics because it sparked a national conversation around a culture of repression in the hands of state and nonstate actors. Writing about colonialism and the posthumous "diseases" of memory, Mbembe notes that the national divisions resulting from the politics of memory can be explained in part by "the capacity of memory to reawaken the wounds of a difficult past" in shaping national founding narratives.[62] In the postcolony, those founding narratives are in turn capable of being used in the service of political legitimacy. Thus, although Ghana is generally considered a peaceful nation, that label is best understood in the context of a history of military repression and political intimidation that followed alternating periods of military and civilian rule. The NRC was designed to offer citizens a platform to publicly narrate their own stories of abuse in the hands of the state and its actors. More than two decades since the conclusion of the work of the NRC, "the stories [of victims] remain as glimpses of Ghanaians' political and historical consciousness."[63]

The Election Petition's references to the commission's work operates in this context, then, as a recall of a past that continues to shape understandings of citizens' relationships with the state and with each other. But the references work as a prism through which histories, specifically those of democracy, are produced, negotiated, understood, and articulated. Perhaps to complete the portrait of the nationalist, *The Election Petition* presents Akufo-Addo as more than a politician concerned with justice. Phillis Maria Christian, a lawyer and consultant, says of Akufo-Addo, that he has "a very fascinating side and [is] somebody who is very fun loving." More than this, he also "would sit at the feet of his elders and learn from them" and "loved good music," too. This way, he embodied "two sides of a good coin." The overall portrait is that of an all-round stateman, one dedicated to the state and its peoples. Besides this portrait of Akufo-Addo, a historical account of the sociopolitical life of the second and third petitioners in the dispute case took a mere minute each respectively, in contrast to the more than ten-minute focus on Akufo-Addo.

Thus, *The Election Petition*'s representation and interpretation of key events (re)produces—through repetition, selection, and forgetting—historical accounts that its producers deem are worthy of remembrance and forgetting. The documentary positions protagonists and antagonists in the decades-long story of national politics. Relative to political others in the documentary, Akufo-Addo is portrayed heroically in *The Election Petition* presumably because of what appears to be the narrator's political sympathies toward his party.[64] Aspects of Akufo-Addo's sociopolitical background may appear indirectly related to the election dispute case. However, the documentary's rhetorical choices reflect a concern with historical re/production that valorizes ideas, historical actors and events, and particular perspectives even if these might also be tangential in context.[65] For rhetorical studies of democratic practice, the postcolonial context offers important avenues for rethinking connections between history, memory, and forgetting, especially where national heroes, continuities, and discontinuities are concerned. To understand democratic practice in this context is to attend to the role that sanctioned ways of remembrance and forgetting plays in shaping citizens' understanding of politics.

Afterlives of Legal Arguments in Public

In its third and fourth progressions, the documentary stages the political controversy between the NPP and NDC over the broadcast of the election dispute case. It also reveals the afterlives of the arguments in public. Although the NPP had argued to the Supreme Court that public broadcast of the case would demonstrate institutional transparency, the petitioners indicate that the NDC had "vehemently opposed live coverage" of the proceedings. In an unprecedented administrative decision, the chief justice permitted the live broadcast of the case. Some citizens' reflections on this decision highlight the important role that such transparency played in public trust of the judiciary in a postcolonial context with limited citizen trust in public institutions. For example, for a professor of communication, Audrey Gadzekpo, the live coverage helped ease tensions across the country and ensured transparency. Gadzekpo noted that in issues of high salience that generate much enormous public interest (like the election dispute case), the live coverage helped "lessen the burden on those who make the decisions." For Moses Foh Amoaning, a law lecturer, there was even a legal rationale to broadcast the case: Ghana's Constitution allows that "except for matters of public order, public safety, or the security of the state, all proceedings of the court are supposed to be in the open." For Amoaning, a practical interpretation of "public" in this case would demand that the proceedings be broadcast, since the case concerned "the exercise of the sovereign will of the people" and live broadcast would broaden access for all.[66]

The political parties in court played a key role not only in seeking justice but also in articulating what citizens came to understand about their democracy. In this, the documentary indicates that for most people who saw the live broadcast, the case was defined by two sets of actors: Philip Addison versus the Electoral Commission, and Tsikata versus Bawumia. In a key episode in the interaction between the NPP's lead counsel, Addison, and the chair of the EC, Afari-Djan, the latter is depicted as a witness who skirts around evidence, simply repeating "I will not be able to tell." Addison asserts that Afari-Djan "was quite an irritant witness" because he was "very reluctant to say the truth even in very obvious cases." This suggestion pits the NPP against the EC, subtly making the claim the EC's evidence and posture was designed to aid the NDC. When it came to the interaction between the NDC's lead counsel, Tsatsu Tsikata, and the NPP's key witness, Mahamadu Bawumia, what the audience sees is a struggle to allow Bawumia to show the court key evidence substantiating the NPP's claims of overvoting. Tsikata is depicted as a cross-examiner who would rather not have key information shared with the court.

But perhaps the final day of the case, August 29, 2013, was the most consequential of all key representations of the case; "Tensions were high, shops were closed, and people remained at home," the narrator tells the audience. One may see this state of affairs as a consequence of the peace narratives circulated throughout and especially in the days leading up to the verdict. In response to the allegation that they unnecessarily delayed the verdict for more than two hours on August 29, the chair of the nine-member panel clarified that any haste in declaring winner versus loser could risk jeopardizing national peace and order. "The length of the wait," the panel's chair clarified, "was commensurate with the length and gravity of the matter we had to decide." The case was clearly "a most delicate and important national matter," he goes on to say, and the day of verdict was "volatile" and demanded tact in all forms.[67]

In the aftermath of the case, then, the documentary portrays the decision of the judges as the most practical in the moment. But apart from the judges' perspectives, the documentary's differential framing of President John Mahama (the declared winner) and Akufo-Addo is worthy of note. While Mahama welcomes and jubilates over the judicial decision validating that he had been legitimately elected president, Akufo-Addo is positioned as the statesman with knowledge of the terrain of politics. He understands what it means to win and lose, and having lost the case, he deploys this understanding to great, patriotic effect. In a concession speech touting his patriotic credentials, he says: "Everything in my bones and in my upbringing and in what I have done with my life thus far makes it imperative that I accept the decision made by the highest court of the land, however much I dislike or disagree with it."[68]

As suggested earlier, the dispute case had several political implications for understanding democratic practice in postcolonial Ghana. It solidified appeals to using democratic tools for the resolution of electoral disputes and opened the intricacies of the electoral process to the eyes of citizens. But perhaps it is in the 2016 electoral cycle that the resonances of the case came to be most felt. The 2016 cycle provided a political laboratory to test reforms advocated by the political parties in the wake of the 2013 verdict. The foundation for these reforms manifests first in the political goodwill with which Akufo-Addo went into Election 2016. In *The Election Petition*, the NDC's legal counsel, Tsatsu Tsikata, opines that Akufo-Addo "actually gained more in stature by that concession," and that this gracious concession "certainly helped him subsequently in the minds of the Ghanaian population." Indeed, while a multifactor explanation would explain his victory in Election 2016, Akufo-Addo's depiction as a peace-loving and unifying statesman, one who privileges national peace and interest over self-interested contest for power, put him in a positive political light.

All this is not to assume that the 2013 verdict enjoyed broad bipartisan support, however. In discussing what he saw as the disconnect between the arguments presented in court and the judges' verdict, a former president of the Ghana Bar Association, Sam Okudzeto, posits that based on the judges' own arguments, one would see they were, in fact, in favor of Akufo-Addo. This criticism of the judges reflects ordinary citizens' fraught relationship with the justice system during the dispute case and brings into sharp focus specters from earlier Ghanaian elections such as of 1992, in the aftermath of which the NPP published its *Stolen Verdict*. The trope of the "stolen verdict" pervades Ghanaian electoral history at critical junctures and has been used toward strategic political ends to assign praise and blame where its users deem it fit.

Audience Challenges to Dominant Memories

Social media offered a viable platform for audiences to engage with the memory of the election dispute. These audiences' engagement with the documentary complicated the narratives about the dispute case contained in *The Election Petition*. As Ekaterina Haskins has argued, institutions of memory (in this case, the narrative of the dispute case supported by the Ghanaian state) tend to promulgate official ideologies of ruling elites, while purporting to speak on behalf of ordinary people.[69] On Facebook, Sammy Bee commends the narrator Adom-Otchere "for letting the so-called youths knows [*sic*] where we were before." Phylix Sackey similarly offers high praise, commenting, "Congratulations.

For documenting our history. We need more of this." These commendations reveal the public pedagogical value of the documentary for posterity and expands its purview beyond a narrow attention to the dispute case.

But even as congratulatory messages poured in, criticisms of the documentary's memorializing followed, too. In the same breath that he praises the producers, Sackey continues by asking, "But was the documentary on Nana Addo's victory or on the petition?" Gpi Gunners follows up, observing, sarcastically, "Such a nice way of reporting a one-sided history. You show the reaction of the NPP in all our elections but refuse to show that of other political parties." In addition to a criticism of the overemphasis on the NPP, other commenters, following Sackey, called into question the documentary's prominent focus on Akufo-Addo's personality. Phelix Appiah Ankuma commented, "I think people have said it all. The election petition which was the main subject took less than 15mins in the narration, but the rest is on the petitioner. Nothing or no pictures of the victors of the petition. The Nana narration was just too much from the start to the end."

For these audiences, then, the documentary serves a political function, accomplished rhetorically: even as it manifests as a historical record on a historical event, it also advances a one-sided, political slant on the NPP's perspective on electoral history in Ghana. This way, for these audiences, *The Election Petition* re/produces a heroes-focus dimension to the making of Ghanaian history. The documentary's specific slant on the case—partial, contingent, multiple, fragmented—has political implications for how audiences remember the case. Even more important, that memory-making shapes a sense of national identity, for this is who the documentary tells audiences that Ghanaians are, who it says they have been. Through repeated recall and imbrication of specific versions and angles of Ghanaian political history in the national imagination, *The Election Petition* enables its publics to, as Vivian argues, "derive their sense of identity by attempting to remember with continuity" at the same time that it "discursively fashion[s] a meaningful relation between the past and the present."[70]

The commenters' apprehensions about the political and ideological uses of the dispute case are themselves not uncommon especially in postconflict situations. In "Memory, Crisis, and Democracy in Africa," Sakiru Adebayo writes of the Angolan ruling government's strategic reading of the country's history through an erasure of its complicity, thereby silencing critics. Adebayo concludes that in terms of postcolonial nation-building, "partisan politics plays a pivotal role in the way memory is instrumentalized for the inclusion or exclusion of certain factions."[71] Whether intentionally or not, the partisan political perspectives that heavily shape the narration invariably includes and excludes while posturing themselves as national projects. As Werbner contends, "Politicized memory is at the heart of postcolonial studies." Like old ones, Werbner asserts that young nations resort to "a myth of political origins for imagining the ongoing formation of the nation." The founding, originary moment of nation-formation may be one, but the myth is "effectively plural," often "the subject of contradictory appropriations in and of which 'the imagined singularity of national formations is constructed daily.'"[72]

It is instructive to consider the work of memory in the context of postconflict situations dealing with democratic practice. In relation to Africa, Latin America's somewhat analogous democratic conditions—histories of coups d'état, political repression, military dictatorship, postconflict political realities—make for a useful entry point. In *Reflections on Memory and Democracy*, political scientists Merilee S. Grindle and Erin E. Goodman establish a close connection between memories of political repression and democratic practice. Memory and democracy are linked in that an understanding of the past shapes practices of the present and future within democracies. Memory is important for democratic legitimacy because it helps beat a path for what kinds of democratic practices should be valued, who should be entrusted with communal power, and how democracy informed by memory should be practiced.

But memories may also undermine democracy. They can stand in the way of the present and future when they inhibit new possibilities. Thus, for Grindle and Goodman, a set of considerations would constitute an important link in the memory-democracy dialectic: "dilemmas of what is remembered, what lessons are drawn from it, how those lessons are used to construct new democratic institutions, and whether a link reaches beyond institutions to citizenship."[73] Even for what appears to be the relatively similar historical contexts of the Latin American societies they studied, Grindle and Goodman caution that these questions ought to be addressed "in the context of individual societies."[74] They have to be cultural. This recognition of cultural specificity resonates with what Vivian has called the "cultural varieties of remembrance."[75] This would mean, in the case of this book, recognizing the embeddedness of the election dispute case in Ghanaian histories and memories of democratic practice more generally.

Of all the ways the dispute case remains integral to democracy in Ghana, its significance lies chiefly in the afterlives of its arguments for the role of law in shaping public life. In court, arguments surrounding the pink sheet (the Statement of Poll and Declaration of Results Form) and the biometric verification devices (BVDs) used in the elections occupied a central role in the judges' verdict. The lessons from the verdict shaped the political parties' engagement with the EC. The NPP sought electoral reforms to avert a repeat of cases of overvoting that the party claimed unduly augmented the NDC's vote margins in Election 2012. The NPP drifted from a total reliance on the EC and put in strategic plans to collate votes at every step of the electoral process, from polling stations all the way to the EC's Collation Center. Among other factors, the party's resounding, unprecedented first-round victory at the 2016 polls could be attributed to this strategic planning. The memory of the dispute case lived on into electoral reform. When in 2020 the NDC filed a suit at the Supreme Court similarly alleging electoral malpractices that denied the party victory at the polls, there was improvement in the judicial procedures of the case thanks to reforms in the aftermath of the dispute case of 2013.[76]

Further, as a public pedagogical tool, *The Election Petition* became useful when, in 2020, it was rebroadcast by media houses in the wake of controversy surrounding the compilation of the Election 2020 electoral register. But it is in the memory of the elections, in what publics come to accept as historical perspective on the dispute, that politics are framed, national histories are fashioned, and positions and identities are cemented for the future. The political uses of supposedly national histories lead us to questions of how historical events are memorialized and circulated in genres to allocate differential positions to various historical actors.

Conclusion

In the immediate aftermath of the 2013 dispute, Ghana received plaudits both home and abroad for amicably resolving the dispute in court. Individuals and institutions saw in the process viable opportunities for the consolidation of democratic practice in Ghana. Through debate on the case, Ghanaians resolved thorny questions about electoral representation and democracy, amid tensions associated with this unprecedented historical event. But the memory of the election dispute case, its meanings across time, and its significance for knowledge on democratic practice in Ghana unfolds later in *The Election Petition* documentary. As one of many possible avenues for historical knowledge production and dissemination, the documentary operates as record (actual historical event) and performance (treatment of that record). As a story in a long arc of a national story, it is suffused with historical knowledge, some unrelated directly to the dispute, but nevertheless of critical import for narrativizing the idea of democracy in Ghana. The documentary reflects the anxieties of fragmented histories of the postcolony as they circulate and are shown to public audiences. By narrativizing Ghanaians' own stories of the case, *The Election Petition* indexes a terrain where historical knowledge about democratic practice can be mapped. In that mapping, historical details are recalled, reframed, and in some cases forgotten. For its audiences, the memory of the case is inextricably bound up with Ghanaian history and politics more broadly.

For studies of memory about democratic practice in the postcolony, how might we rhetorically consider the role of historical artifacts like *The Election Petition*? First, through the interpretive license of its producers, the documentary employs rhetorical strategies that emphasized key historical details (even those not directly related to the case) and ignored other, apparently contextually relevant details. Because histories may be expected to show up anywhere, it is imperative to reimagine how they shape and are shaped by memory and democracy, as well as routes of remembrance and forgetting. The production of historical knowledge about Ghanaian democracy upholds a focus on the heroic role of key political actors to the exclusion of many other facets of history in Ghana. This memorializing orients audiences toward an understanding of the dispute case and its significance for Ghanaian democracy. In this way also, the documentary becomes a sort of by-product of the deliberation, in and of itself constituting a resource for how deliberation and democracy can be understood within context.

Second, the political uses of the documentary represent some far-reaching effects for historical production, memory, and democratic practice. When the documentary was broadcast to audiences prior to Election 2020, it was not because there was another dispute case in clear sight. The goal appears to be an attunement of audiences to a public pedagogy of citizenship: how to locate and understand their role as voting citizens within the larger story of Ghana's democratic practice, what orientation to adopt toward electoral politics, and what kinds of outcomes they might aspire toward or not. Indeed, there are contingencies, especially, with narrating and memorializing postcolonial histories. The multiple ethno-nations that came together to form what is today Ghana did so not voluntarily per se, but by accidents of the organizing mechanisms of colonial border-making and later postcolonial nation-building. Paying attention to such accidents of history is essential to understanding who is memorialized and written into histories, how sanctioned forgetting unfolds, and what histories are invoked as deserving of national aspiration. In this respect, *The Election Petition* represents the anxieties of postcolonial history production in the service of democratic practice and national belonging.

Conclusion

Thus far, I have been arguing for the nexus among rhetoric, cultural imaginaries, and democratic deliberation within the specific context of the 2013 Ghanaian presidential election dispute case. The analyses have demonstrated that deliberation within this postcolonial context remains shaped by cultural imaginaries concerning the nature of rhetorical practices in terms of who can speak, about what, how, and where. The historical context of the deliberations has been analytically important: the Supreme Court of Ghana operates as a crucial postcolonial institution that retains the legacies of the colonial condition even as it grapples with local African norms and expectations of rhetorical practices. This way, deliberation in court is embedded in a balance between upholding indicators of borrowed Western liberal democracy (like freedom of speech) and peculiar African emphases on polite speech (like *obuo kasa*) rooted in traditional understandings of the potential of speech to be volatile.

The analyses have shown that rather than deference to either impulse, there is a constant negotiation and competition of visions between them. In the institutional context of the law court, colonial legacies clash with traditional local norms and expectations, and this in turn delimits the *what* and *how* of citizens' practices of democratic deliberation. What is also evident beyond the traditionally delimited avenues of participation are the new possibilities that exist in digital forums. Here, citizens constitute and form publics with the aim of rhetorically participating in the democratic process. These new spaces create avenues for critique through popular cultural art forms, including those of humor.

In the specific context of Ghana, examining democratic deliberation around the dispute case means attending to who is allowed to speak, about what, where, and how. Beyond the Ghanaian case, and for rhetorical studies more broadly, such knowledge reveals the nature of democracy as it can be studied and understood outside of traditionally Western boundaries and in other, non-Western contexts. In this respect, this book contributes to the study of democratic deliberation as rhetorical scholars seek to understand its character in light of not only its global manifestations but also how those manifestations enable how we might theorize citizens' deliberative practices in democracies.

The two examples of the contemnors analyzed showed how varying interactions with the postcolonial institution of the court delivers differing outcomes for citizens. On the one hand, Stephen Atubiga's docile, civil, and decorous response to the judges of the Supreme Court was a crucial factor in the lenient three-day prison sentence he received. The judges held up his deferential posture as a prime example of responsible citizenship that avoids confronting the established order. On the other hand, the ten-day prison sentence handed to Ken Kuranchie reveals the limits of what Karen Tracy has called "reasonable hostility," or face-attack involving "emotionally marked criticism of the past or future actions of public persons."[1]

In democratic deliberation, strategies such as reasonable hostility have been demonstrated to be purposefully employed to counteract the potential of civility to squelch dissent. However, the cases analyzed in this book have revealed that deliberative norms, including reasonable hostility, are themselves culturally contingent and ought to be so considered. What the court's differing response to both Atubiga and Kuranchie indicates is that democratic deliberation in institutional spaces like the Ghanaian Supreme Court remain shaped by interlocking, competing notions of traditional, cherished communication values (like deference to authority) and the logics of adopted, mostly Western practices (such as ideals of freedom of speech). This tension turns on power and access to resources and fundamentally shapes whose speech is valued, when, and how. In studies of democratic deliberation, this culturally contingent factor and the workings of power ought to engage how we imagine and theorize citizens' deliberative practices, account for them during deliberations, and seek improvements in deliberative outcomes more generally. In doing so, we must emphasize the agency of participants engaged in deliberation.

The notion of freedom of speech is exposed in this book to be one that not only is contingent but follows a cultural logic and is invested with meaning-making practices within Ghanaian society. Also evident is the fact that relative to deliberations, there are limitations on the practice of freedom of speech within Ghanaian society. For rhetorical criticism of democratic deliberation, we see evidence of how that purportedly universal tenet of democratic practice—freedom of speech—operates within the ecology of a society's history and sociocultural condition. By interrogating the historical and sociocultural contexts from which the constitutional guarantee of freedom of speech unfolds, the book highlights for understandings of democratic deliberation the necessity of a culturally informed study of democratic principles that also attends to questions of power.

The analysis of the genre of the pink sheet has exposed the ideological impulses that shape deliberative activity. Like the rhetorical tension between local communication values and colonially inflected practices and ideals of the law court, there exists a rhetorical tension in practices of evidence. Here again, the tension between "the world on paper" and "the world of experience" unfolds in the ways in which both shape each other. Evidence derived from practices of the world on paper did not merely supplant that of the world of experience. Instead, there is a constant negotiation that allows for the continuing relevance of the residual, yet forceful, expressions of local, noninstitutional African practices of oral testimony. Scholars studying democratic deliberation stand to benefit from attention to genres and the rhetorical work they perform in deliberation. Genres can serve as analytical portals for studies on deliberation, exposing the tensions, fissures, and seeming contradictions inherent in arguments within context. Perspectives from the postcolony on genre and deliberation enable us to broaden our sites of deliberative study.

Furthermore, in shifting attention from the genre itself to arguments surrounding it, I have shown how colonial legacies tend to shape what counts as knowledge in democratic practice. Indeed, the coexistence of the notion of "the world of experience" and "the world on paper" in the search for knowledge about evidence here troubles distinctions between the two terms as polar opposites. The rhetoricity of such statements as "You and I were not there" evoke the limits of documentary evidence within a cultural context where testimony interrupts notions of truth anchored exclusively in written texts. This unavoidable condition of the postcolony raises important questions about what sources of knowledge we may consult and foreground in studies of deliberation to disrupt single-factor explanations to complex rhetorical phenomena. As is evidenced from the courtroom deliberations, cultural practices predating colonial rule coexist with institutions wrought by colonialism and practices associated with those institutions. The interruptions citizens make in these colonial legacies therefore signal visions of decolonial futures, a point I elaborate further shortly.

Digital platforms provided a space for the formation of publics and democratic deliberation around the election dispute case and operate in counterposition to the institutional, formal space that is the court. The constraints of deliberation in court—demands for decorous speech, balance between freedom of speech and deference to authority—give way to more expansive possibilities of democratic deliberation. While not forwarding utopian visions of deliberations on such platforms—platform politics and the rise and concentration of tech monopolies are important considerations here—there exists considerable potential for understanding the manifestation of digital publics and their rhetorical work. This is the case especially if we consider digital publics through the frame of cultural imaginaries. The idea of cultural imaginaries allows us to think through the materiality and digitality of such publics as we connect their work to the political logics, historical junctures, and social realities that animate those publics. In explicating the interrelations between the digital and physical environments, the book has shown how we may understand the rhetorical work of publics and public spheres in contexts where the nation-state and its subsequent spheres of publicity have developed quite apart from the Westphalian nation-state system.

The practice of democracy as it has manifested in the analyses in this book is not to be equated to a failed attempt within the Ghanaian context of an aspiration toward a democratic ideal outside of this nation-state. Rather, we need to recognize that democratic practice here is a manifestation of an aspect of democracy as the Ghanaian people conceive of and practice it at a specific moment in history. That practice, of course, has had its promises and perils. John Comaroff and Jean Comaroff argue that African modernities (and I might here add, from which democracies emerge) ought to be understood on their own terms as products of historical processes. Their legitimacy derives not from their similarities to conceptions of modernities elsewhere but from the ways they are enacted within contexts of their own. Writing of modernities, Comaroff and Comaroff state, "Afromodernity has lain implicit in signs and practices, dispositions and discourses, aesthetic values and indigenous ways of knowing. Nor is it best labeled an 'alternative modernity.' It is a vernacular—just as Euromodernity is a vernacular—wrought in an ongoing, geopolitically situated engagement with the unfolding history of the present. And, like Euromodernity, it takes many forms."[2]

The authors' argument about the conceptualization of modernity in the vernacular is in accord with recent research in rhetorical studies on democratic deliberation within the context of culture. Around the world, democracies function for us as a fetish, or "a kind of empty container that gets filled with everyone's private miseries."[3] The concept of democracy is "simultaneously meaning-filled and contentless."[4] When democracy is viewed this way, it becomes understood on its own terms in different places, while its possibilities and limitations as a system of governance that produces specific outcomes for citizens gain salience within context. This notion of the "empty container" also shifts the grounds of conceptualizing democracy and deliberation away from its Western anchors and firmly onto any territory where it is practiced. My argument has been that democracy as practiced within the Ghanaian context, evidenced through deliberations in court about the pink sheet, enacted in digital public spheres, and memorialized in the documentary, has the particular cultural specificity that is a result of a political history of colonialism.

The book also contributes to methodological approaches in rhetoric, digital media, and democratic deliberation. By examining the ways that digital publics are conditioned by cultural, social, and political contingencies, the book further contributes to methodologies of deliberations in networked public spheres by showing how close attention to the physical—social, cultural, and political histories—can illuminate analyses of deliberations in digital spaces.

Throughout this book, I have used the term postcolonial in the sense of the condition of the period after formal colonialism had ended, a period conditioned by the legacies of colonialism. My use of the term in this fashion lays the foundation for what could constitute decolonial possibilities for rhetorical studies. For where the term "postcolonial" has been used to offer an alternative account of rhetoric and democracy in Ghana, decolonial visions would emphasize a reimagining of our rhetorical concepts of democratic deliberation writ large. Democracy as practiced in Ghana remains not just an import from the West broadly construed, but also a local feature within this African space.

In recent years, rhetorical scholarship has contributed to a growing body of work on the need to decolonize understandings of rhetoric. The exigence for this turn has been to "build a foundation, a history, of local knowledges and meaning-making practices that breaks from . . . Western hegemonic models."[5] This mobilization of local knowledge-making and dissemination is itself rooted in an analysis that starts from a cultural vantage point. That vantage point, rather than being anchored in the Eurocentric or European outside, would be centered on the experiences of the people about whom rhetorical practice is studied. Decolonial visions would hinge on knowledge about a cultural context on the society's "local history of language, memories, and political economy and not just from the colonial European center."[6] This book has sought to accomplish such a vision in its examination of the historical context of rhetorical production. It has done so by considering democratic deliberation not necessarily from the Eurocentric understanding of what constitutes the practice, but in this actually existing African context, to adapt Nancy Fraser's apt phrasing.[7]

Another decolonial dimension to the book is in its epistemological stance. By focusing on the rhetorical practices and democratic orientations of a particular non-Western society, the book has drawn attention to the epistemologies of governance rooted within this African context, and in doing so, it has offered a deterritorialized notion of democracy here. The courtroom practices, the rhetorical construction of evidence based on the pink sheet genre, the deliberations in the digital public sphere, and the unfolding of history and memory to serve democratic ends all constitute a corpus of knowledge concerning the practice of democratic deliberation within Ghanaian society. The relevance of the analyses lies both in their resonance with other such postcolonial contexts and in the ways we might reconsider speech, genre, participation, and memory as practices embedded in power for democratic deliberation writ large. For this reason, I urge a thorough application of the insights offered here to other contexts, including those of Western countries.

It is worth recognizing that decoloniality in rhetorical scholarship entails "a primary responsibility to hear/record . . . stories without reducing their irreducible quality, the local histories and human experiences that exist outside

'Western' epistemologies."[8] Concepts such as freedom of speech as an anchor for democratic practice; public deliberations about genres like the pink sheet; the recontextualization of digital publics to embed cultural logics of participation that draw on popular culture; and the interface between memory and history as public pedagogies in the postcolony—these are located within cultural domains and are usefully understood through cultural imaginaries. The explanatory inadequacy of Western normative frameworks of democratic deliberation for the study of non-Western democratic practices implies that we must examine cultural imaginaries that can yield perspectives anchored on a society's self-understandings. In extending scholarship on democratic deliberation into undertheorized African rhetorical traditions and contexts, we might hope for a rethinking of concepts that make rhetoric and democratic deliberation truly global yet localized practices.

Up to this point, if we accept this book's cultural imaginaries orientation to studying rhetoric and democratic deliberation, several implications arise not just for the postcolony but also especially for the Western democracies with which postcolonies share some relationality within the global order. First, the contemporary global rise of antidemocratic populism particularly in Western countries means scholarly attention to democracy has become more and more salient. If there is one lesson to be learned from the U.S. Capitol attack on January 6, 2021, for instance, it is that democracy and its institutions stand in need of constant assessment, recreation, and safeguarding. The events of January 6 coincidentally relate to electoral politics and its associated issues of representation, trust in institutions, and ideas of memory that tend to shape rhetorics of democracy. For any democracy, the risk of coups d'état exist regardless of whether such democracies are a few years old or two centuries established. Consequently, scholars and teachers of rhetoric and democratic deliberation ought to continue dedicating attention to actually existing practices of democracy in Western countries to reexamine if and how rhetorical strategies and practices serve democratic ends.

Second, in African understandings of deliberation, the spirit of palabre as discussion and redemption, rather than discipline and punishment, holds relevance for Western democratic practices as much as for non-Western ones. One of the challenges for any democracy is the ideal of maintaining communal bonds in the midst of difference and disagreement. As this book has extensively argued, this ideal implies a model of critique and public dialogue in which there is a recognition both of persons invested in deliberation and the cultural resources and legacies they bring to the deliberative table. Moreover, because deliberation is structured by logics of power, and power tends to serve interests, unbalancing such logics is germane to accomplishing discussion and redemption rather than discipline and punishment. For Western democracies, this is crucial in redressing historical wrongs of exclusion, of white supremacist ideals, and of oppressive structures that tend to swiftly discipline and punish as ends of justice.

Finally, the imperative to decolonize rhetoric and democratic deliberation must not be limited to previously colonized countries. Colonialism is as much a fact of existence for the West as for the "Rest." Thus, in Western democracies, there exists a just as strongly felt need for the imperative to decolonize. God terms such as freedom of speech ought to be interrogated to address the cultural imaginaries that surround them. So too should the connections among histories, memories, and democracy. All this requires scrutinizing the related concerns of rhetoric and democracy, including questions about who is granted access, who has historically been excluded, what spaces of discussion and redemption might exist, who valorized ideas are designed for, what memories are circulated, and whose interests those tend to serve. It is in examining such concerns that a cultural imaginaries orientation geared toward decolonizing epistemic traditions might find its fullest expression, regardless of our locations.

Appendix

Data Analysis and Methods for Chapter 3

The data for chapter 3 is drawn from deliberations on Twitter between April 16, 2013 (when the substantive election dispute case in court started after procedural hearings), and August 30, 2013 (the day after the verdict was delivered). The tweets came from Twitter's Historical Data PowerPack package. Social media statistics collated by the Irish web traffic analysis firm, StatCounter, show that on average, between April and August 2013, Facebook engagement ranked the highest among eighteen social media types (including Twitter, YouTube, LinkedIn, Reddit, Vimeo, Pinterest), with as much as 79 percent of all engagements. This ranking was followed by Twitter's approximately 12 percent, in addition to 9 percent of engagements distributed across the remaining sixteen categories.[1] In terms of general social media engagement numbers, then, Facebook may seem an obvious choice for this analysis. Since disambiguated numbers for various kinds of social media engagement (politics, entertainment, advertisements, etc.) are unavailable, I rely on other parameters in determining Twitter for the purposes of analyzing political engagement.

For this analysis, I focus on Twitter for two reasons. First, the civil society organization, Blogging Ghana, circulated the hashtags analyzed in chapter 3 on Twitter to coalesce citizens' engagement with the election dispute case. As the analysis shows, these hashtags were used widely to engage politically on Twitter. I do not find evidence of similar active engagement on Facebook. Second, as a platform, Twitter allowed for an easier retrieval and subsequent analysis of messages coalescing around the same hashtag that archived the tweets. For political engagement of the election dispute case, then, Twitter provides a viable platform for analyzing the uses of digital media for democratic purposes in emerging African democracies.

Research indicates that Twitter use in African countries tends to be more political.[2] On this point, Michael L. Best and Amanda Meng point out that Twitter constituted a strong platform for debates surrounding policy and identity during the 2012 presidential and parliamentary elections in Nigeria, Kenya, and Ghana. These authors contend that in the case of Ghana, Twitter provided a platform for citizens to engage politically: Ghanaians discussed educational policy on free secondary education and examined other policies in presidential candidates' political promises. Across six policy term indicators, Best and Meng found more than thirty-eight thousand tweets with conceptual matches, suggesting a relatively highly active Twitter engagement, compared to Nigeria's conceptual matches of 6,565 and Kenya's 6,984, respectively. Based on this study of Twitter use for presidential election debates, the authors conclude that "as democratic deepening occurs, citizens do engage in more discussion of policy on election day, and they are using Twitter to do so."[3]

Informed by the view that Twitter's hashtag constituted a topical marker for constituting publics, I searched four hashtags widely used during the election dispute case: #GhanaDecides, #ElectionPetition, #TheVerdict, and #SupremeCourt. As one of the most notable civil society organizations working for citizens' electoral participation in the country, Blogging Ghana circulated #TheVerdict and #ElectionPetition as hashtags to be used. After an initial survey of both, I included #SupremeCourt and #GhanaDecides to the dataset, as these were also widely used. Of these latter two, #GhanaDecides was earlier used during the general elections in December, before the dispute case commenced in April. Because a similar election dispute case was filed at Kenya's Supreme Court in March of 2013, my dataset entailed only those tweets that referred to Ghana; tweets related to the Kenyan case featured in the dataset were excluded. Also excluded were duplicated tweets, retweets, and tweets on radio station reportage linking to the dispute. Finally, after excluding ads, there were 304 tweets and seven additional links that pointed to blog posts or YouTube videos with some bearing on the case. This latter set provided useful contextual information on the deliberations.

To analyze the data, I adopted Cheryl Geisler and Jason Swarts's two-step approach to analyzing verbal data—segmenting and coding. In *Coding Streams of Language*, Geisler and Swarts explain that segmentation involves separating "the entire data set using some well-defined unit of analysis," followed by the coding of data "segment by segment." The authors claim apart from its benefits of systematicity and replicability, segmenting before coding allows for a focus on the linguistic unit of analysis.[4] In analyzing the tweets, I examine one such unit, the t-unit, defined as "a principle [*sic*] clause and any subordinate clauses or non-clausal structures attached to or embedded in it."[5] Thus, the t-unit operates as a sentence. By examining t-units, I highlight the rhetorical "moves that a speaker or writer makes."[6] In all, after clearing the data of those tweets unrelated to the case, I segmented 313 t-units. For the additional links to YouTube and blog posts, I focused on the texts as a unit with their "well-established boundaries" remaining intact.[7] Doing so revealed both the persuasiveness of the textual data and a certain analytical parsimony that would have been more difficult to achieve were the texts separated into t-units.

Once the tweets were segmented, I followed Geisler and Swarts's second step to develop a coding procedure that focused on the description of and patterns in the t-units. My goal was to "let each segment of the data suggest appropriate categories to describe what is happening with the phenomenon of interest."[8] This categorization involved two steps. In the first, I employed descriptive coding, a first cycle coding method that "summarizes in a word or short phrase—most often as a noun—the basic topic of a passage of qualitative data."[9] My codes included nouns and phrases indicating praise of Supreme Court justices; critique of Supreme Court justices' actions; quiet atmosphere of the election dispute case; peace advocacy; critique of foreign institutions and media; optimism or skepticism about the dispute case; Ghana as a gateway to Africa; social media use; use of humor; advocacy by civil society groups; and emphasis on freedom of speech provisions.

My second cycle of coding—pattern coding—built on the first codes and involved the "development of major themes from the data."[10] In this cycle, I identified patterns across the descriptive codes and included the following themes, pointing out the cultural imaginaries that characterize them: peace narratives and/as democratic aspiration; humor use as a popular culture form of democratic practice; democratic interventions and civil society organizations: Blogging Ghana's Ghana Decides initiative; the paradoxes of freedom of speech; resisting the postcolonial election library. Whereas the patterns identified in the data are categorized primarily by theme, some, like the theme of humor use as popular culture form of democratic engagement, may operate both as a theme or topic and mode of topic. It is not so much that citizens discussed the use of humor as that they used humor in engaging in the process. Similarly, it is not that they discussed paradoxical stances toward freedom of speech, but that they evinced, through their commentary, a paradox that characterizes this constitutional freedom.

Table 1. Themes, Frequency, and Percentage of Total Tweets from Coded T-Units

THEME/FEATURE	FREQUENCY	PERCENTAGE OF TOTAL
Peace narratives and/as democratic aspiration	111	35.46
Humor use as a popular culture form of democratic practice	53	16.93
Democratic interventions and civil society organizations: Blogging Ghana's Ghana Decides Initiative	104	33.23
The paradoxes of freedom of speech	21	6.71
Resisting the postcolonial election library	24	7.67
Total	**313**	**100**

This table shows the themes identified from the dataset of tweets, along with their frequency and percentage totals.

Table 2. Themes, Descriptions, and Examples from Coded T-Units

THEME/FEATURE	DESCRIPTION	EXAMPLE
Peace narratives and/as democratic aspiration	Indicates a reference to the notion of peace, a disposition essentially that advocates an avoidance of (especially) physical violence; celebrates a "Ghana-wins-we-all-win ethos," and/or advocates for citizens to be calm and adopt nonviolent democratic strategies.	#Ghana, one of the world's most peaceful country's [*sic*] is going to get more peaceful after the #supremecourt verdict tomorrow. @GhanaDecides
Humor use as a popular culture form of democratic practice	Deploys culturally situated elements of laughter/humor as forms of participation in or commentary on the election dispute case.	The next title for a Ghanaian movie by Agya Koo will be "The Verdict" #ElectionPetition #TheVerdict.
Democratic interventions and civil society organizations: Blogging Ghana's Ghana Decides initiative	Points out civil society groups' activities, including education, advocacy, and citizen mobilization efforts relating to the election dispute case.	"The #Hashtags on twitter and facebook for tomorrow is #TheVerdict and #ElectionPetition. Don't forget. Join the Discussion as #Ghanadecides."
The paradoxes of freedom of speech	Celebrates and/or expresses skepticism about the limits of constitutional provisions of freedom of speech.	As much as i don't support this #Supremecourt ruling but 'Freedom of speech comes with responsibility.' #Ghana
Resisting the postcolonial election library	Denounces foreign, mainly Western, media for negative press coverage of Ghana's democracy.	Ok, now all the international pressmen who were waiting to "flee" Ghana can leave. We proved you wrong again. #TheVerdict #ElectionPetition

This table shows the themes derived from the dataset of tweets, their description, and paradigmatic examples.

Notes

INTRODUCTION

1. Ghana describes itself as the "Gateway to Africa" because of its leading role in the mid-century independence movements on the African continent. The term "Black Star of Africa" is a symbol of anticolonialism and Pan-Africanism of the same period, both movements championed by Ghana's first prime minister and first president, Dr. Kwame Nkrumah.
2. John Effah and Emmanuel Debrah, "Biometric Technology for Voter Identification: The Experience in Ghana," *Information Society* 34, no. 2 (2018): 107.
3. Isidore Kafui Dorpenyo, *User Localization Strategies in the Face of Technological Breakdown: Biometric in Ghana's Elections* (London: Springer Nature, 2019), 13.
4. According to the Constitution of Ghana, to be declared president, a candidate must have won 50 percent plus one of the valid votes cast.
5. EISA, "Election Observers Interim Report On 2012 Elections," *GhanaWeb*, December 9, 2012, www.GhanaWeb.com."
6. Mabel Aku Baneseh, *Pink Sheets: The Story of Ghana's Presidential Election Petition* (Accra: Graphic Communications Group Limited, 2015), 20.

7. Baneseh, *Pink Sheets*, 35.
8. For an account of the case, see especially Baneseh, *Pink Sheets*, 1–9.
9. In this book, I use the term "election dispute" rather than the term more common in the legal literature—election petition—to emphasize the deliberation at the heart of the case.
10. Jean Comaroff and John L. Comaroff, *Theory from the South: Or, How Euro-America Is Evolving Toward Africa* (London: Paradigm Publishers, 2012), 1.
11. Comaroff and Comaroff, *Theory from the South*, 6.
12. Achille Mbembe, *Out of the Dark Night: Essays on Decolonization* (New York: Columbia University Press, 2021), 25–26.
13. Jeffrey W. Paller, *Democracy in Ghana: Everyday Politics in Urban Africa* (Cambridge: Cambridge University Press, 2019), 12.
14. Christine Keating, *Decolonizing Democracy: Transforming the Social Contract in India* (University Park: Penn State University Press, 2011), 8–13.
15. Although used in a variety of fields, the contemporary emergence of and scholarly attention to the idea of the imaginary is widely attributed to its explication in social theorist and philosopher Cornelius Castoriadis's *The Imaginary Institution of Society* (trans. Kathleen Blamey [Cambridge: Polity Press, 1987]). While valuable, I depart from Castoriadis's orientation given, first, its "staggering Eurocentrism" and "idealization of ancient Greece" and, second, its limitations at the level of abstraction that rarely locates the workings of the imaginary locally and "at specific social-historical conjunctures" (Gaonkar, "Toward New Imaginaries"). For instance, in relation to the first claim, Castoriadis asserts that the idea of human autonomy as a function and driver of democratic practice originated exclusively "only twice in human history, first in the ancient Greek city-states and later in Western Europe" (Gaonkar, "Toward New Imaginaries," 9). Such a perspective suggests a derivative sense of political formulations elsewhere, and it is this very derivative sense that I argue against in this book.
16. Castoriadis, *Imaginary Institution of Society*, 3.
17. Charles Taylor, "Modern Social Imaginaries," *Public Culture* 14, no. 1 (2002): 91.
18. Damien Smith Pfister, *Networked Media, Networked Rhetorics: Attention and Deliberation in the Early Blogosphere* (University Park: Penn State University Press, 2015), 11.
19. See, for example, Majid Yar, *The Cultural Imaginary of the Internet: Virtual Utopias and Dystopias* (London: Springer, 2014); and Christoffer Kølvraa and Bernhard Forchtner, "Cultural Imaginaries of the Extreme Right: An Introduction," *Patterns of Prejudice* 53, no. 3 (2019): 227–235.
20. Benedict Anderson, *Imagined Communities: Reflections on the Origin and Spread of Nationalism*, rev. ed. (New York: Verso, 2016), 6.

21. Taylor, "Modern Social Imaginaries," 107.
22. Ato Quayson, *Tragedy and Postcolonial Literature* (Cambridge: Cambridge University Press, 2021), 4.
23. Kwame Gyekye, *Tradition and Modernity: Philosophical Reflections on the African Experience* (Oxford: Oxford University Press, 1997), 107.
24. See, for example, Kundai Chirindo, "Micronations and Postnational Rhetorics," *Women's Studies in Communication* 41, no. 4 (2018): 383–393; Xiaoye You, *Genre Networks and Empire: Rhetoric in Early Imperial China* (Carbondale: Southern Illinois University Press, 2023).
25. Raka Shome and Radha Hegde, "Culture, Communication, and the Challenge of Globalization," *Critical Studies in Media Communication* 19, no. 2 (2002): 173–174.
26. Phil Bratta and Malea Powell, "Introduction to the Special Issue: Entering the Cultural Rhetorics Conversations," *Enculturation: A Journal of Rhetoric, Writing, and Culture* 21 (2016)
27. Casie Cobos et al. "Interfacing Cultural Rhetorics: A History and a Call," *Rhetoric Review* 37, no. 2 (2018): 141.
28. Bratta and Powell, "Introduction to the Special Issue."
29. Omedi Ochieng, *Groundwork for the Practice of the Good Life: Politics and Ethics at the Intersection of North Atlantic and African Philosophy* (London: Routledge, 2017), 4, 13, 90, 123. The italics in "*transcendental* point of view" are the author's emphasis.
30. Julia Paley, "Toward an Anthropology of Democracy," *Annual Review of Anthropology* 31, no. 1 (2002): 479.
31. Ralph Cintron, *Democracy as Fetish* (University Park: Penn State University Press, 2019), 6, 8.
32. Dilip Parameshwar Gaonkar, "On Cultures of Democracy," in *Cultures of Democracy*, ed. Dilip Parameshwar Gaonkar (Durham: Duke University Press, 2007), 16.
33. Candice Rai, *Democracy's Lot: Rhetoric, Publics, and the Places of Invention* (Tuscaloosa: University of Alabama Press, 2016), 43.
34. Jensen Sass and John S. Dryzek, "Deliberative Cultures," *Political Theory* 42, no. 1 (2014): 3.
35. Sass and Dryzek, "Deliberative Cultures," 4.
36. Sass and Dryzek, "Deliberative Cultures," 7.
37. José M. Cortez, "Of Exterior and Exception: Latin American Rhetoric, Subalternity, and the Politics of Cultural Difference," *Philosophy & Rhetoric*, 51, no. 2 (2018): 146.
38. Cortez, "Of Exterior and Exception," 138.
39. For an example of work arguing against such universalizing narratives, see the examination of hate speech in David Boromisza-Habashi, *Speaking Hatefully: Culture, Communication, and Political Action in Hungary* (University Park: Penn State University

Press, 2012).

40. Lyon explicates a theory of performative deliberation that answers such questions as "How do diverse peoples recognize and respond to each other while respecting differences of being and doing?" Arabella Lyon, *Deliberative Acts: Democracy, Rhetoric, and Rights* (University Park: Penn State University Press, 2013), 8. *Deliberative Acts* advances a *cross-cultural and global* dimension to deliberation, suitable particularly when studying parties for whom a foundational premise or common ground of democracy and deliberation cannot be assumed because of rather extreme cultural difference. Furthermore, Lyon's performative theory of deliberation has as its goal the transformation of the participants and their "interpretive horizons." While theories like Lyon's attend to the constitutive character of deliberation, such approaches depart from the goals of this book. My purposes remain a study of the cultural foundations at the heart of deliberation *within* a particular culture, with the (post)colonial context as an important dimension, rather than a recognition of personhood among diverse peoples and *cross-cultural* deliberative encounters per se.
41. Jean Godefroy Bidima, *Law and the Public Sphere in Africa: La Palabre and Other Writings* (Bloomington: Indiana University Press, 2013), xxvi.
42. Laura Hengehold, "Introduction: Speech, Belief, Power," in *Law and the Public Sphere in Africa: La Palabre and Other Writings*, by Jean Godefroy Bidima (Bloomington: Indiana University Press, 2013), 3.
43. Bidima, *Law and the Public Sphere in Africa*, 21.
44. Bidima, *Law and the Public Sphere in Africa*, 27. See also Michel Foucault, *Discipline and Punish: Birth of the Prison*, trans. Alan Sheridan (New York: Vintage Books, 1977).
45. Bidima, *Law and the Public Sphere in Africa*, 33.
46. Hengehold, "Introduction," 4.
47. Uchenna Okeja, *Deliberative Agency: A Study in Modern African Political Philosophy*. (Bloomington: Indiana University Press, 2022), 4.
48. Okeja, *Deliberative Agency*, 28.
49. Okeja, *Deliberative Agency*, 38.
50. Okeja, *Deliberative Agency*, 27.
51. See, for example, Nancy Henaku and Ruby Pappoe, "African Rhetoric as an Emergent Subfield," in *A Companion to African Rhetoric*, ed. Segun Ige, Gilbert Motsaathebe, and Omedi Ochieng (Pennsylvania: Lexington Books, 2022): 171–194.
52. Segun Ige, Gilbert Motsaathebe, and Omedi Ochieng, eds. *A Companion to African Rhetoric* (Pennsylvania: Lexington Books, 2022).
53. Henaku and Pappoe, "African Rhetoric as an Emergent Subfield," 180–182.

54. Henaku and Pappoe, "African Rhetoric as an Emergent Subfield," 175–176.
55. Yunana Ahmed, "Toward an Understanding of African Rhetoric: A Decolonial Approach," in *A Companion to African Rhetoric*, ed. Segun Ige, Gilbert Motsaathebe, and Omedi Ochieng (Pennsylvania: Lexington Books, 2022), 26.
56. Ahmed, "Toward an Understanding," 29.
57. Erik Johnson, "In the Midnight Hour: Anticolonial Rhetoric and Postcolonial Statecraft in Ghana," *Review of Communication* 22, no. 1 (2022): 62.
58. Omedi Ochieng, "What Is African Rhetoric: The Constitutive Imagination in Olaudah Equiano's *The Interesting Narrative and Other Writings*," in *A Companion to African Rhetoric*, ed. Segun Ige, Gilbert Motsaathebe, and Omedi Ochieng (Pennsylvania: Lexington Books, 2022), 4.
59. Ochieng, "What Is African Rhetoric," 13.
60. Sabelo J. Ndlovu-Gatsheni, *Epistemic Freedom in Africa: Deprovincialization and Decolonization* (New York: Routledge, 2018), 3.
61. Daniel L. Emery, "Defending the Public: Procedural Rationality and the Limits of Actually Existing Jurisprudence," in *Rhetorical Democracy: Discursive Practices of Civic Engagement*, ed. Gerard Hauser and Amy Grim (New York: Routledge, 2004), 151.
62. Emery, "Defending the Public," 151.
63. Karen Tracy, *Challenges of Ordinary Democracy: A Case Study in Deliberation and Dissent* (University Park: Penn State University Press, Penn State Press, 2011).
64. Chirindo, "Micronations and Postnational Rhetorics," 384.
65. Twitter's name was changed to X in July 2023, but throughout this book, I refer to the social media platform as Twitter as that's what it was called during the time period under analysis.
66. "Synopsis," *An African Election: A Film by Jarreth Merz*, February 4, 2023, anafricanelection.com.
67. Bratta and Powell, "Introduction to the Special Issue."

CHAPTER 1. DELIBERATING SPEECH: COLONIAL LEGACIES AND THE PARADOXES OF POLITICAL PARTICIPATION

1. Kwaku Boahen was the Ashanti Regional Youth Organizer of the NDC. Deliberations on his case were brief and not substantive enough for an elaborate analysis in this book, and given his acquittal, his interactions with the judges are not analyzed in this chapter. Excluded here also are three others—Sammy Awuku, Hopeson Adorye, and John Owusu

Afriyie—who were all charged various sums of money as the court convicted them of contempt. Like Boahen's case, not enough deliberation in these cases exist for analysis.

2. Omedi Ochieng, "W.E.B. Du Bois and the Imagination of the Public Intellectual," *African Journal of Rhetoric* 8, no. 1 (2016): 111.
3. The phrase "god term" is invoked here in the sense in which Richard Weaver deploys it in *The Ethics of Rhetoric* to describe such words as "freedom" and "justice" that historically have contained a positive meaning and value within a culture (Richard Weaver, *The Ethics of Rhetoric* [California: Hermagoras Press, 1985], 214).
4. Gerard Hauser, "Rhetorical Democracy and Civic Engagement," in *Rhetorical Democracy: Discursive Practices of Civic Engagement*, ed. Gerard Hauser and Amy Grim (New York: Routledge, 2004), 11.
5. Craig Rood, *After Gun Violence: Deliberation and Memory in an Age of Political Gridlock* (University Park: Penn State University Press, 2019), 20.
6. Bidima, *Law and the Public Sphere in Africa*, xxvi.
7. Robert Asen, *Democracy, Deliberation, and Education* (University Park: Penn State University Press, 2015), 78.
8. The Akans are the majority ethnic group in Ghana. While there are important cultural differences across Ghana's ethnic groups, royal speech of the Akans and the institution of chieftaincy in which such speech is most quintessentially embodied have come to significantly influence institutional practices of the modern nation-state of Ghana. This reality is itself a function of postcolonial nation-building, wherein histories and sociocultural practices of majority ethnic groups, for good or ill, tend to be conflated with those of the nation-state itself.
9. Kwesi Yankah, *Speaking for the Chief: Okyeame and the Politics of Akan Royal Oratory* (Bloomington: Indiana University Press, 1995), 51.
10. Yankah, *Speaking for the Chief*, 53.
11. The sociolinguists Penelope Brown and Stephen C. Levinson use the idea of "face" to refer to "the public self-image that every member [in a conversation] wants to claim for himself." Face-threatening acts, or face-attacks, are "speech acts which threaten the positive or negative face of the addressee" (qtd. in Wardhaugh and Fuller, *Introduction to Sociolinguistics*, 7th ed. [Oxford: Wiley-Blackwell, 2015], 256–257).
12. Yankah, *Speaking for the Chief*, 54.
13. Yankah, *Speaking for the Chief*, 54–55.
14. Some of the analysis in this chapter can be viewed in terms of concepts such as decorum and civility. For a recent and persuasive treatment of these subjects, see William Keith and Robert Danisch, *Beyond Civility: The Competing Obligations of Citizenship* (University

Park: Penn State University Press, 2020). Given the cultural contingency and associated meanings emphasized in this book, I focus largely on the import of terms such as *obuo kasa* for understanding deliberation practices in Ghana's postcolonial institutions.

15. The institution of chieftaincy predated colonialism, was calcified by colonial authorities, and has survived into the postcolonial period in Ghana. While chiefs do not hold de jure executive power in Ghana, their roles as custodians of culture are recognized. With the establishment of a National House of Chiefs, the 1992 Constitution of Ghana guarantees the position of chiefs. On how chieftaincy was recreated by colonial authorities, see Benjamin Kunbuor, "Customary Law of the Dagara of Northern Ghana: Indigenous Rules or a Social Construction," *Journal of Dagaare Studies* 2, (2002): 5. For chieftaincy's promises, challenges, and characteristics within the modern state system in Ghana, particularly from the late colonial period up to the immediate postindependent era, see Richard Rathbone, *Nkrumah and the Chiefs: Politics of Chieftaincy in Ghana, 1951–1960* (Columbus: Ohio State University Press, 2000).
16. Baffour Ankomah, "Ghana's Culture of Silence," *Index on Censorship* 16, no. 10 (1987): 17–19.
17. Constitution of the Republic of Ghana, art. 21, sec. 1a, 1b.
18. Emmanuel Laryea and Kwamena Kwansah-Aidoo, "Going, Going, Gone! Implications of the Repeal of Criminal Libel and Sedition Laws in Ghana," *Ghana Studies* 8, no. 1 (2005): 129.
19. Kwesi Yankah, "Free Speech in Traditional Society: The Cultural Foundations of Communication in Contemporary Ghana," in *Reclaiming the Human Sciences and Humanities Through African Perspectives*, vol. 2, ed. Helen Lauer and Kofi Anyidoho (Accra: Sub-Saharan Publishers, 2012), 1074.
20. See, for example, Kwame Asamoah, Emmanuel Yeboah-Assiamah, and Alex Osei-Kojo, "Demons of Transitional Democracies: Politics of Insults and Acrimony in Ghana," *Journal of Social Science Studies* 1, no.1 (2014): 44–56.; Rachel Akusika Thompson and Jemima Asabea Anderson, "Interactive Programmes on Private Radio Stations in Ghana: An Avenue for Impoliteness," *Journal of African Media Studies* 10, no.1 (2018): 55–72.
21. Thompson and Anderson, "Interactive Programmes," 70.
22. Samuel Marfo, "Thinking of Peace, Democracy, and Politics of Insults in Ghana: The Paradox of Freedom and Culture of Violence," *Online Journal of African Affairs* 3 (2013): 523.
23. JoyNews, "2012 Election Petition Hearing Day 36 (2-7-13)," YouTube video, 03:17:51, July 2, 2013, www.youtube.com.
24. JoyNews, "2012 Election Petition."
25. Nancy Henaku, "Rhetoric, Power and Political Crisis: A Rhetorical Discourse Analysis of Ghana's 2012 Election Petition," *African Journal of Rhetoric* 10, no. 1 (2018): 91.
26. Gabrielle Lynch, Nic Cheeseman, and Justin Willis, "From Peace Campaigns to

Peaceocracy: Elections, Order and Authority in Africa," *African Affairs* 473 (2019): 603, 626, 607.

27. Nina M Lozano-Reich and Dana L. Cloud, "The Uncivil Tongue: Invitational Rhetoric and the Problem of Inequality," *Western Journal of Communication* 73, no. 2 (2009): 224.
28. Henaku, "Rhetoric, Power and Political Crisis," 114.
29. As would likely be apparent by this point, the expectations that undergird Atubiga's speech are far from prohibitions about speech per se, like those under the rubric of hate speech explored persuasively by Boromisza-Habashi, in *Speaking Hatefully*, for example. Instead, the expectations constitute dispositions expected toward speech in general, and formal speech more specifically.
30. See, for example, Samuel Gyasi Obeng, "Language and Politics: Indirectness in Political Discourse," *Discourse & Society* 8, no. 1 (1997): 49–83; Kofi Agyekum, "The Socio-Cultural Concept of Face in Akan Communication," *Pragmatics & Cognition* 12, no. 1, (2004): 71–92.
31. JoyNews, "2012 Election Petition."
32. Mahmood Mamdani, *Citizen and Subject: Contemporary Africa and the Legacy of Late Colonialism* (Princeton: Princeton University Press, 2018), 19.
33. Mamdani, *Citizen and Subject*, 22.
34. Bidima, *Law and the Public Sphere in Africa*, 27.
35. Patricia Roberts-Miller, *Deliberate Conflict: Argument, Political Theory, and Composition Courses* (Carbondale: Southern Illinois University Press, 2004), 154.
36. JoyNews, "2012 Election Petition."
37. JoyNews, "2012 Election Petition."
38. JoyNews, "2012 Election Petition." Emphasis added. *The Republic v. Liberty Press Ltd.* is a precedent-setting Ghanaian court case from 1968 in which it was held, among other things, that "it is contempt of court by deed or word to scandalise the courts. It is contempt of court to make statements amounting to abuse of the courts. It is contempt of court to make statements which tend to expose the courts or parties who resort thereto to the prejudice or hatred or ridicule of mankind" (cited in Kweku Ainuson, "Role of The Public and The Media in Civil Court Proceedings in Ghana," *KAS African Law Study Library* 5, no. 1 [2018]: 54–67).
39. JoyNews, "2012 Election Petition."
40. Marie Lund Klujeff, "Provocative Style: The Gaarder Debate Example," in *Rhetorical Citizenship and Public Deliberation*, ed. Christian Koch and Lisa S. Villadsen (University Park: Penn State University Park, 2012), 101.
41. Stephen Kwaku Asare, "Striking a Balance Between the Administration of Justice and

Free Speech During the Live Broadcast of a Presidential Election Petition," *African Journal of International and Comparative Law* 23, no. 2 (2015): 333.

42. Samuel Gyasi Obeng, "Grammatical Pragmatics: Language, Power and Liberty in Ghanaian Political Discourse," *Discourse & Society* 31, no.1 (2020): 100.
43. Yankah, *Speaking for the Chief*, 58.
44. Karen Tracy, "'Reasonable Hostility': Situation-Appropriate Face-Attack," *Journal of Politeness Research* 4, no. 2 (2008): 175.
45. Yankah, *Speaking for the Chief*, 64.
46. Keith Thomas, *In Pursuit of Civility: Manners and Civilization in Early Modern England* (New Haven: Yale University Press), 319.
47. Thomas, *In Pursuit of Civility*, 335.
48. Kevin Sieff, "Why African Judges Still Wearing Wigs Is a Glaring Symbol of British Colonialism," *Independent*, September 18, 2017, www. independent.co.uk.
49. Yankah, "Free Speech in Traditional Society," 1073.
50. Asare, "Striking a Balance," 317.
51. Asare, "Striking a Balance," 316.
52. Tracy, "Reasonable Hostility," 170.

CHAPTER 2. DELIBERATING GENRE: ORAL TESTIMONIES AND THE RHETORICAL WORK OF DOCUMENTARY EVIDENCE

1. Isidore Dorpenyo and Godwin Agboka, "Election Technologies, Technical Communication, and Civic Engagement," *Technical Communication* 65, no. 4 (2018): 349–352.
2. Mabel Aku Baneseh, *Pink Sheets: The Story of Ghana's Presidential Election Petition* (Accra: Graphic Communications Group Limited, 2015), 23–30.
3. Carolyn R. Miller, "Genre as Social Action," *Quarterly Journal of Speech* 70, no. 2 (1984): 159.
4. Clay Spinuzzi, *Tracing Genres Through Organizations: A Sociocultural Approach to Information Design* (Cambridge: MIT Press, 2003), 221.
5. There are several traditions of genre studies including those in literary studies, English for specific purposes, and applied linguistics. The approach emphasized in this chapter is the rhetorical genre studies tradition that highlights the rhetorical and communicative function of genres and the ways they organize activity.
6. Janet Giltrow, "Genre and the Pragmatic Concept of Background Knowledge," in *Genre*

and the New Rhetoric, ed Aviva Freedman and Peter Medway (Bristol: Taylor and Francis, 1994), 174.

7. Miller, “Genre,” 159.
8. Miller, “Genre,” 165.
9. Christa B. Teston, “A Grounded Investigation of Genred Guidelines in Cancer Care Deliberations,” *Written Communication* 26, no. 3 (2009): 331, 333, 346.
10. Anthony Paré, “Genre and Identity: Individuals, Institutions, and Ideology,” in *The Rhetoric and Ideology of Genre: Strategies for Stability and Change*, ed. Richard M. Coe, Lorelei Lingard, and Tatiana Teslenko (New York: Hampton Press, 2002), 59.
11. Paré, “Genre and Identity,” 61.
12. Natasha N. Jones and Miriam F. William, “Technologies of Disenfranchisement: Literacy Tests and Black Voters in the US from 1890 to 1965,” *Technical Communication* 65, no. 4 (2018): 371–386.
13. Charles Bazerman, “Intertextuality: How Texts Rely on Other Texts,” in *What Writing Does and How It Does It*, ed. Charles Bazerman and Paul Prior, (New York: Routledge, 2003), 84.
14. While the colors of the forms were printed blue in previous years (Baneseh, *Pink Sheets*, xii), the forms were called “pink sheet” by the general public because they were printed in pink color for Election 2012. Upon Ghana’s return to democratic rule, parliamentary and presidential elections have been held every four years since 1992.
15. Julian Pleasants, *Hanging Chads: The Inside Story of the 2000 Presidential Recount in Florida* (London: Springer, 2004).
16. There is a long tradition of scholarly debate particularly in postcolonial literary studies on the tensions between orality and literacy and writing. The tension itself is taken to be paradigmatic of postcolonial subjectivities—fractured and ambivalent. For a brief discussion, see, for example, Uzoma Esonwanne, “Orality and the Genres of African Postcolonial Writing,” in *The Cambridge History of Postcolonial Literature*, ed. Ato Quayson, vol. 1, (Cambridge: Cambridge University Press, 2012), 137–170.
17. Dorpenyo, *User Localization Strategies*, 13.
18. Dorpenyo, *User Localization Strategies*, 149.
19. JoyNews, “2012 Election Petition Hearing on Joy News (30-5-13),” YouTube video, 04:06:49, May 30, 2013, www.youtube.com.
20. Nana Addo Dankwa Akufo Addo Others v. John Dramani Mahama Others (J1 6 of 2013) [2013] GHASC 5, August 29, 2013, 71. ghanalii.org.
21. Ghana’s 275 constituencies are represented by Members of Parliament (MPs) in the country’s unicameral legislature. During elections, votes from polling stations within a constituency are collated on Collation Forms in the election of MPs and the president

and subsequently transferred to the Electoral Commission offices in Accra.

22. JoyNews, "2012 Election Petition Hearing on Joy News (30-5-13)." The phrase "You and I were not there" gained popularity in Ghanaian parlance during the election dispute deliberations when the key witness of the petitioners, Dr. Mahamudu Bawumia, used it to argue about the absence of evidence he couldn't produce.
23. The term can suggest that experience is outside the purview of "writing on paper," which it may necessarily not be. The term could also mean Africa has always been nonliterate, a claim that is not factual. Hawkins's terms are also reminiscent of Walter Ong's distinctions between orality and literacy (see Walter J. Ong and John Hartley, *Orality and Literacy* [New York: Routledge, 2013]). I set aside Ong's arguments in this discussion given that unlike Ong's major concern, the aim of this chapter is not primarily to engage the impact of literacy on thought processes nor to examine the role of cognitive capacity in the mastery of literacy. That said, I retain the terms "world of experience" and "world on paper" as used by Hawkins for their analytical utility, being cognizant that these terms are themselves limited insofar as experience may be constructed in or manifested on paper, thereby rendering the bifurcation almost a contradiction in terms.
24. The argument here is not that African societies have had no history of writing. They have. Evidence abounds of African writing systems prior to European colonial violence on the continent (e.g., there have been hieroglyphs, hieratic, and demotic scripts). The claim is rather that at the dawn of British colonialism, *this* particular society was a thoroughly oral culture and that (the technology of) writing that came with colonialism wrought a transformative effect on the society. I concur with Hawkins's view that despite earlier experiences with writing, many Africans south of the Sahara encountered writing through colonialism (Sean Hawkins, *Writing and Colonialism in Northern Ghana: The Encounter Between the LoDagaa and "The World on Paper"* [Toronto: University of Toronto Press, 2002], 15).
25. Hawkins uses the label LoDagaa. This was the term common in earlier descriptions of this ethno-linguistic group that included the Lobi people who were speakers of the Lo Dagaare variety of Dagaare. The contemporary preferred term for the group, however, is northern Dagaaba or Dagara. See Kunbuor, "Customary Law," 7; and Adams Bodomo, *The Structure of Dagaare* (Stanford: CSLI Publications), 1–3.
26. Hawkins, *Writing and Colonialism*, 4. Emphasis added.
27. Hawkins, *Writing and Colonialism*, 14.
28. Hawkins, *Writing and Colonialism*, 14.
29. On this point, see Nancy Henaku and Ruby Pappoe, "African Rhetoric as an Emergent Subfield," in *A Companion to African Rhetoric*, ed. Segun Ige, Gilbert Motsaathebe,

and Omedi Ochieng (Pennsylvania: Lexington Books, 2022), 258; Kermit E. Campbell, "Rhetoric from the Ruins of African Antiquity," *Rhetorica: A Journal of the History of Rhetoric* 24, no. 3 (2006): 255–274.

30. Johnson, "In the Midnight Hour," 161.
31. See, for example, Abby A. Knoblauch and Marie E. Moeller, ed., *Bodies of Knowledge: Embodied Rhetorics in Theory and Practice* (Denver: University Press of Colorado, 2022).
32. Kwesi Yankah, "Free Speech in Traditional Society: The Cultural Foundations of Communication in Contemporary Ghana," in *Reclaiming the Human Sciences and Humanities Through African Perspectives*, vol. 2, ed. Helen Lauer, and Kofi Anyidoho (Accra: Sub-Saharan Publishers, Ghana, 2012), 1085.
33. Bagele Chilisa, *Indigenous Research Methodologies* (New York: Sage Publications, 2019), 1–4.
34. JoyNews, "Election Petition Hearing on Joy News—Day 28 (5-6-13)," YouTube video, 02:31:30, June 5, 2013, www.youtube.com.
35. Chilisa, *Indigenous*, 2.
36. John Effah, Emmanuel Owusu-Oware, and Richard Boateng, "Biometric Identification for Socioeconomic Development in Ghana," *Information Systems Management* 37, no. 2 (2020): 136.
37. JoyNews, "Election Petition Hearing on Joy News—Day 29 (6-6-13)," YouTube video, 02:18:35, June 6, 2013, www.youtube.com.
38. Nana Akua Tweneboah-Koduah, "Is Bawumia Selling Pink Sheet Evidence on the Streets?," *Myjoyonline*, May 15, 2013, www.myjoyonline.com.
39. JoyNews, "Election Petition Hearing on Joy News—Day 29 (6-6-13)."
40. Peter Leman, "African Oral Law and the Critique of Colonial Modernity in *The Trial of Jomo Kenyatta*," *Law & Literature* 23, no. 1 (2011): 40.
41. Leman, "African Oral Law," 37.
42. Leman, "African Oral Law," 39.
43. Leman, "African Oral Law," 43.
44. Comaroff and Comaroff, *Theory from the South*, 63.
45. JoyNews, "Final Address by Counsel for 3rd Respondent Tsatsu Tsikata—2012 Election Petition Hearing (7-8-13)," YouTube video, 00:28:53, August 7, 2013, www.youtube.com.
46. JoyNews, "Final Address by Counsel for 1st Respondent Tony Lithur—Election Petition Hearing (7-8-13)," YouTube video, 00:29:48, August 7, 2013, www.youtube.com.
47. JoyNews, "Final Address by Counsel."
48. Hawkins, *Writing and Colonialism*, 31.
49. *Nana Addo Dankwa Akufo Addo Others*, 25. Emphasis added.

50. *Nana Addo Dankwa Akufo Addo Others*, 71. Emphasis added.
51. *Nana Addo Dankwa Akufo Addo Others*, 71–72.
52. *Nana Addo Dankwa Akufo Addo Others*, 79.
53. Giltrow, "Genre and the Pragmatic Concept," 174.

CHAPTER 3. DELIBERATING PARTICIPATION: DIGITAL PUBLICS AND ANALOGUE POLITICAL REALITIES

1. Robert Asen, "Public: A Network of Relationships," *Rhetoric Society Quarterly* 48, no. 3 (2018): 297.
2. Asen, "Public," 298.
3. Asen, "Public," 298, 302, 303.
4. Achille Mbembe, *On the Postcolony* (California: University of California Press, 2001), 24–26.
5. See for example, Peter P. Ekeh, "Colonialism and the Two Publics in Africa: A Theoretical Statement," *Comparative Studies in Society and History* 17, no. 1 (1975): 93; Eghosa E. Osaghae, "Colonialism and Civil Society in Africa: The Perspective of Ekeh's Two Publics," *Voluntas: International Journal of Voluntary and Nonprofit Organizations* 17, no. 3 (2006): 234; Kundai Chirindo, "Micronations and Postnational Rhetorics," *Women's Studies in Communication* 41, no. 4 (2018): 387; Helen Lauer, "Depreciating African Political Culture," *Journal of Black Studies* 38, no. 2 (2007), 299; Ochieng, "W.E.B. Du Bois and the Imagination of the Public Intellectual," *African Journal of Rhetoric* 8, no. 1 (2016): 120.
6. Ochieng, "W.E.B. Du Bois," 111.
7. Ochieng, "W.E.B. Du Bois," 111.
8. Gerard A. Hauser, *Vernacular Voices: The Rhetoric of Publics and Public Spheres* (Columbia: University of South Carolina Press, 1999), 20, xi.
9. Ralph Cintron, *Democracy as Fetish* (University Park: Penn State University Press, 2019), 9.
10. Jürgen Habermas, *The Structural Transformation of the Public Sphere: An Inquiry Into a Category of Bourgeois Society* (Cambridge: MIT Press, 1991).
11. See, for example, Kyle R. Larson and George F. McHendry Jr., "Parasitic Publics," *Rhetoric Society Quarterly* 49, no. 5 (2019): 517–541; Catherine Knight Steele, "Black Bloggers and Their Varied Publics: The Everyday Politics of Black Discourse Online," *Television & New Media* 19, no. 2 (2018): 112–127.
12. Byron Hawk, "Curating Ecologies, Circulating Musics: From the Public Sphere to Sphere Publics," *Ecology, Writing Theory, and New Media*, ed. Sidney I. Dobrin (New York: Routledge, 2011), 165.

13. Hawk "Curating Ecologies," 161.
14. I use physical and material interchangeably in this chapter in the sense in which Byron Hawk uses them to signal realms other than the digital that involve people and places, as well as social, historical, and ideological contexts. As Hawk does note, however, there is an overlap between physical and digital (Hawk, "Curating Ecologies").
15. Hawk, "Curating Ecologies," 175, 176.
16. Cintron, *Democracy as Fetish*, 9. My sense of a physical-digital dynamic for the study of democratic deliberation conforms loosely with recent research by scholars, such as Christa Olson, who have argued, in relation to the Americas, that democracy should be conceived in a telluric sense, that is, in its primordial relations to the agential quality of land and topography (Christa Olson, "The Democratic Hemisphere," *Rhetorics of Democracy in the Americas*, ed. Adriana Angel, Michael L. Butterworth, and Nancy R. Gómez [University Park: Penn State University Press, 2021], 24–25). Where Olson emphasizes the agential quality of land and topography, I defer to a physical-digital dynamic that includes social and political histories and processes.
17. Pfister, *Networked Media*, 46.
18. Pfister, *Networked Media*, 45.
19. Dan Ehrenfeld, "'Sharing a World with Others': Rhetoric's Ecological Turn and the Transformation of the Networked Public Sphere," *Rhetoric Society Quarterly* 50, no. 5 (2020): 308.
20. See, for example, Karma R. Chávez, "Beyond Inclusion: Rethinking Rhetoric's Historical Narrative," *Quarterly Journal of Speech* 101, no. 1 (2015): 163; Chirindo, "Micronations," 383.
21. Chirindo, "Micronations," 384.
22. Chirindo, "Micronations," 388–389.
23. There is a rich body of scholarship on counterpublicity especially in the context of black communities in North Atlantic societies. These include such work as Catherine R. Squires, "Rethinking the Black Public Sphere: An Alternative Vocabulary for Multiple Public Spheres," *Communication Theory* 12, no. 4 (2002): 446–468; Steele, "Black Bloggers and Their Varied Publics"; and André Brock Jr., *Distributed Blackness: African American Cybercultures* (New York: New York University Press, 2020). My work expands perspectives here by centering the colonial and postcolonial contexts that shape understandings of publics.
24. I use Africa here liberally and only as a convenient label to discuss conditions such as the common experience of colonialism across the continent. Except for the ways that this experience shapes culture and politics, the analysis here cannot usefully be read as a placeholder for the continent's fifty-four countries, which, needless to say, differ

significantly in terms of history, geography, political processes, and language, to name but a few points.

25. Sharath Srinivasan, Stephanie Diepeveen, and George Karekwaivanane, "Rethinking Publics in Africa in a Digital Age," *Journal of Eastern African Studies* 13, no. 1 (2019): 5.
26. Srinivasan, Diepeveen, and Karekwaivanane, "Rethinking Publics," 7.
27. Srinivasan, Diepeveen, and Karekwaivanane, "Rethinking Publics," 7.
28. Srinivasan, Diepeveen, and Karekwaivanane, "Rethinking Publics," 9. This claim is not to suggest that the physical-digital dynamic is unidirectional. In fact, the literature on social movements suggests that organizations may emerge online and find their way to offline contexts.
29. Irene Brunotti, "From Baraza to Cyberbaraza: Interrogating Publics in the Context of the 2015 Zanzibar Electoral Impasse," *Journal of Eastern African Studies* 13, no.1 (2019): 21.
30. Brunotti, "From Baraza," 25.
31. Brunotti, "From Baraza," 26.
32. Brunotti, "From Baraza," 28.
33. Nanjala Nyabola, *Digital Democracy, Analogue Politics: How the Internet Era is Transforming Politics in Kenya* (London: Zed Books, 2018), 27–28.
34. Nyabola, *Digital Democracy*, 31.
35. @barcampkumasi.
36. As the narratives about peace show, "god terms" may presume a sort of essential or universal understanding of meaning for "citizens" or shared communities.
37. Christopher E. Miller and Mary E. King, *A Glossary of Terms and Concepts in Peace and Conflict Studies*, 2nd ed. (Costa Rica: University for Peace, 2005), 56.
38. Institute for Economics & Peace, *Global Peace Index 2021: Measuring Peace in a Complex World* (Sydney: Institute for Economics & Peace, June 2021), visionofhumanity.org.
39. *Parliamentary Debates: Official Report*. Parliament of Ghana. Fourth Series, Vol. 72, no. 39, Tuesday, March 22nd, 2011, para 3004.
40. *Parliamentary Debates*, para. 3008.
41. *Parliamentary Debates*, para. 3018.
42. Chantal Mouffe, "Which Kind of Public Space for a Democratic Habitus?," *Habitus: A Sense of Place*, 2nd ed., ed. Jean Hillier and Emma Rooksby (New York: Routledge, 2017), 115.
43. Dana Harrington, "Developing Democratic Dispositions: Eighteenth-Century Public Debating Societies and the Generative Capacity of Decorum," *Rhetoric Society Quarterly* 45, no. 4 (2015), 325.
44. *Parliamentary Debates*, para. 3030.
45. Erik Doxtader, "Making Rhetorical History in a Time of Transition: The Occasion,

Constitution, and Representation of South African Reconciliation," *Rhetoric & Public Affairs* 4, no. 2 (2001): 226.

46. Doxtader, "Making Rhetorical History," 226.
47. Some examples of rhetorical studies on humor and its connection to politics include Kenneth Burke, *Attitudes Toward History* (Los Altos: Hermes Publications, 1959), 43–44; Jane Fife, "Peeling *The Onion*: Satire and the Complexity of Audience Response," *Rhetoric Review* 35, no. 4 (2016): 322–334.
48. Elizabeth Benacka, *Rhetoric, Humor, and the Public Sphere: From Socrates to Stephen Colbert* (Lanham: Rowman & Littlefield, 2016), 2.
49. Hauser, *Vernacular Voices*, xi.
50. Sass and Dryzek, "Deliberative Cultures," 21.
51. Sass and Dryzek, "Deliberative Cultures," 8.
52. Stephanie Newell and Okome Onookome, *Popular Culture in Africa: The Episteme of the Everyday* (New York: Routledge, 2013), 3.
53. Newell and Okome, *Popular Culture*, 4, 16.
54. Ebenezer Obadare, "The Uses of Ridicule: Humour, 'Infrapolitics' and Civil Society in Nigeria," *African Affairs* 108, no. 431 (2009): 245.
55. Benacka, *Rhetoric, Humor, and the Public Sphere*, 18.
56. Constitution of the Republic of Ghana, art. 21, sec. 1a, 1b.
57. Virgil Henry Storr, "The Market as a Social Space: On the Meaningful Extraeconomic Conversations That Can Occur in Markets," *Review of Austrian Economics* 21, no. 2–3 (2008): 144.
58. Jesse Weaver Shipley, "Transnational Circulation and Digital Fatigue in Ghana's Azonto Dance Craze," *American Ethnologist* 40, no. 2 (2013): 362.
59. Shipley, "Transnational Circulation," 363.
60. Henry Brefo, "Azonto—A Dance of Defiance," *What's On Africa*, November 21, 2013,whatsonafrica.org.
61. Given its popularity among Ghanaian youth, *azonto* has been repurposed for ends beyond entertainment. For example, to promote youth interest in HIV/AIDS testing, the Ghana AIDS Commission created and circulated a campaign in which a young person named Azonto encourages his peers to emulate his example and get tested for HIV to reduce the spread of the disease ("Ghana AIDS Commission Azonto Advert," ghanaids.gov.gh).
62. Okeja, *Deliberative Agency*, 4.
63. Admire Mare, "Popular Communication in Africa: An Empirical and Theoretical Exposition," *Annals of the International Communication Association* 44, no. 1 (2020), 88.

64. James Yeku, *Cultural Netizenship: Social Media, Popular Culture, and Performance in Nigeria* (Bloomington: Indiana University Press, 2022), 22.
65. Robert Asen, "A Discourse Theory of Citizenship," *Quarterly Journal of Speech* 90, no. 2 (2004): 201.
66. @osarpong.
67. @jabdulai.
68. @AntiRhyth.
69. Sarah J. Jackson, Moya Bailey, and Brooke Foucault Welles, *#HashtagActivism: Networks of Race and Gender Justice* (Cambridge: MIT Press, 2020), xxviii–xxix.
70. Louis M. Maraj, *Black or Right: Anti/Racist Campus Rhetorics* (Denver: University Press of Colorado, 2020), 49.
71. Maraj, *Black or Right*, 47.
72. Gerard A. Hauser and Chantal Benoit-Barne, "Reflections on Rhetoric, Deliberative Democracy, Civil Society, and Trust," *Rhetoric & Public Affairs* 5, no. 2 (2002): 262.
73. Josh M, "The Ghana Decides SC Verdict Hangout," YouTube, August 30, 2013, www.youtube.com.
74. Newell and Okome claim that electronic media may collapse the popular-elite bifurcation that may have existed in traditional discussions of popular cultural forms. I concur with this position. The panelists in this Google Hangout may include lawyers and professors, but removed from the levers of governmental power, they see their role primarily as bloggers and "people who are plugged into Ghanaian issues." There are multiple positionalities at play, regardless.
75. Josh M, "The Ghana Decides SC Verdict Hangout."
76. Ebenezer Obadare, "Civil Society in Sub-Saharan Africa," *The Oxford Handbook of Civil Society*, ed. Michael Edwards (Oxford: Oxford University Press, 2011), 189.
77. Obadare, "Civil Society," 184.
78. Wendy Willems, "'The Politics of Things': Digital Media, Urban Space, and the Materiality of Publics," *Media, Culture & Society* 41, no. 8 (2019): 1193.
79. The discussion here about the paradoxes of free speech is not dissimilar to arguments about the First Amendment in the United States, which are themselves articulated in the vernacular. The crucial distinction here is that I follow lines traced in such work as David Boromisza-Habashi's *Speaking Hatefully: Culture, Communication, and Political Action in Hungary* (University Park: Penn State University Press, 2012) that ground analyses of terms like (hate) speech on a culturally contingent footing.
80. @Kwabena.
81. Emmanuel Laryea and Kwamena Kwansah-Aidoo, "Going, Going, Gone! Implications of the

Repeal of Criminal Libel and Sedition Laws in Ghana," *Ghana Studies* 8, no. 1 (2005): 129.

82. For a historical account on Ghana's military dictatorships, see Audrey Gadzekpo, "Communication Policies in Civilian and Military Regimes: The Case of Ghana," *Africa Media Review* 11, no. 2 (1997): 31–50.
83. V. Y. Mudimbe, *The Idea of Africa* (Bloomington: Indiana University Press, 1994), 29.
84. Mbembe, *On the Postcolony*, 2.
85. Kwame Nkrumah, "Independence Speech," in *The Ghana Reader: History, Culture, Politics*, ed. Kwasi Konadu and Clifford C. Campbell (Durham: Duke University Press, 2016), 302.
86. In Western media, negative reportage of other countries in general and Africa in particular is so entrenched a practice as to be undeniable. Satirical publications such as Joshua Keating's *Slate* series "If It Happened There" (slate.com) and Karen Attiah's 2020 *Washington Post* opinion article "How Western Media Would Cover the U.S. Election If It Happened in Another Country" (*Washington Post*, November 14, 2020, washingtonpost.com) demonstrate the persistence of negative tropes in American media reportage on other countries, including the African continent.
87. See, for example, Oluseyi Adegbola, Jacqueline Skarda-Mitchell, and Sherice Gearhart, "Everything's Negative about Nigeria: A Study of US Media Reporting on Nigeria," *Global Media and Communication* 14, no. 1 (2018): 47–63.
88. Phil Bratta and Malea Powell, "Introduction to the Special Issue: Entering the Cultural Rhetorics Conversations," *Enculturation: A Journal of Rhetoric, Writing, and Culture* 21 (2016).
89. Hawk, "Curating Ecologies," 175.
90. Bratta and Powell, "Introduction to the Special Issue."

CHAPTER 4. DELIBERATING MEMORY: CONTESTED REMEMBERING, NATIONAL IDENTITY, AND THE RE/PRODUCTION OF POSTCOLONIAL HISTORIES

1. The National Reconciliation Commission Act, Act 611, 2002, Ghana.
2. Abena Ampofoa Asare, *Truth without Reconciliation: A Human Rights History of Ghana* (Philadelphia: University of Pennsylvania Press, 2018), 4.
3. Pierre Nora, "Between Memory and History: Les Lieux de Mémoire," *Representations* 26 (1989): 8.
4. John Bodnar, *Remaking America: Public Memory, Commemoration, and Patriotism in the Twentieth Century* (Princeton: Princeton University Press, 1992), 14.

5. Marouf Hasian Jr. and Robert E. Frank, "Rhetoric, History, and Collective Memory: Decoding the Goldhagen Debates," *Western Journal of Communication* 63, no. 1 (1999): 97.
6. David Glassberg, "Public History and the Study of Memory," *Public Historian* 18, no. 2 (1996): 7.
7. Nathan S. Atkinson, "Celluloid Circulation: The Dual Temporality of Nonfiction Film and Its Publics," *Rhetoric and Public Affairs* 15, no. 4 (2012): 675.
8. There was wide publicity in the Ghanaian media, and individuals were offered free tickets to the documentary premiere. Following the premiere, the documentary was also screened on the producers' popular current affairs political show, *Good Evening Ghana*, and on their social media channels.
9. Thomas W. Benson and Brian J. Snee, "New Political Documentary, Rhetoric, Propaganda, and the Civic Prospect," in *The Rhetoric of the New Political Documentary*, ed. Thomas W. Benson, and Brian J. Snee (Carbondale: Southern Illinois University Press, 2008), 4.
10. Atkinson, "Celluloid Circulation," 677.
11. Benson and Snee, "New Political Documentary," 2, 14.
12. Benson and Snee, "New Political Documentary," 14.
13. Given limitations of space and duration, what materials a documentarian decides to select for depiction are crucial. In her study of the memory-making practices of an American organization dedicated to the heritage of the Confederate States, Amy Lynn Heyse found that oversimplification was an effective rhetorical strategy used to graph the past onto the present. Selection of materials is therefore consequential. As Heyse explains, "Uncomplicated past events could be evoked more easily than elaborate ones and perhaps more readily understood by their readers" (Amy Lynn Heyse, "The Rhetoric of Memory-Making: Lessons from the UDC's Catechisms for Children," *Rhetoric Society Quarterly* 38, no. 4 [2008]: 416).
14. I speak here of pedagogical value in terms of the capacity of televisions' (and documentaries,' in this case) logics of spectacle to inform and educate. See, for example, Kristy Maddux's discussion of television shows' capacity for public pedagogies of deliberation: Kristy Maddux, "*View*ing Deliberation: Daytime Television's Public Pedagogy of Inclusion," *Argumentation and Advocacy* 58, no. 1 (2022): 1–21.
15. Hasian and Frank, "Rhetoric," 102.
16. *The Election Petition* follows somewhat in the tradition of *An African Election*, which has adopted a circulatory approach it calls a "political safari" to screen the documentary to electorates in several places as a voter education initiative ("The Tour," A Political Safari: An African Adventure in Democracy Building, July 30, 2024, politicalsafari.org). Adom-Otchere's program constitutes a public insofar as it circulates and cocreates memories

with fellow citizens (Michael Warner, *Publics and Counterpublics* [New York: Zone Books, 2002]). *The Election Petition*'s reach and institutional backing provide it the credibility to engender public memories of the election dispute.

17. "Synopsis," *An African Election: A Film by Jarreth Merz*, February 4, 2023, anafricanelection.com.
18. "2012 Election Petition Documentary Premieres January 24th," *Modern Ghana*, January 22, 2018, www.modernghana.com.
19. Recent work in the tradition of political communication and linguistic discourse studies discusses electoral politics in Ghana in the context of the coronavirus pandemic of 2020, highlighting issues including voter disenfranchisement, propaganda, and vigilantism. In this work, the editors examine transnational influences on elections and politics in Africa. See Nancy Henaku, Mark Nartey, Ruby Pappoe, G. Edzordzi Agbozo, and Eliasu Mumuni, "Election Discourse in Africa: Some Critical Considerations," in *Communication and Electoral Politics in Ghana: Interrogating Transnational Technology, Discourse, and Multimodalities*, ed. Eliasu Mumuni, Mark Nartey, Ruby Pappoe, Nancy Henaku, G. Edzordzi Agbozo (London: Springer, 2024), 4.
20. Jarreth Merz and Kevin Merz, *An African Election*, Apple TV, November 25, 2011, tv.apple.com/us.
21. Sabelo J. Ndlovu-Gatsheni, *Epistemic Freedom in Africa: Deprovincialization and Decolonization* (New York: Routledge, 2018), 6.
22. Manouchka Kelly Labouba, "An African Election directed by Jarreth Merz," *African Studies Review* 57, no. 2 (2014): 233.
23. Michael Dunaway, "Jarreth Merz: Bringing an African Election Home," *Paste*, February 27, 2012, pastemagazine.com.
24. Drawing on French sociologist Maurice Halbwachs, Kendall R. Phillips posits a difference between memory and history as ways of remembering the past. For him, "History, with its apparent claims to accuracy and objectivity, is—or at least had been—viewed as implying a singular and authentic account of the past. Memory, on the other hand, is conceived in terms of multiple, diverse, mutable, and competing accounts of past events" (Kendall R. Phillips, introduction to *Framing Public Memory*, ed. Kendall R. Philips [Tuscaloosa: University of Alabama Press, 2004], 2.) The distinguishing character here is the multiplicity and sense of objectivity that characterizes both modes of recalling the past. In relation to the election dispute case, I depart from this bifurcation, following instead Marouf Hasian and Robert E. Frank's formulation that collapses the distinction and unites them to account for their rhetorical dimensions (Hasian and Frank, "Rhetoric," 97–98).

25. Jeffrey K. Olick, *States of Memory: Continuities, Conflicts, and Transformations in National Retrospection* (Durham: Duke University Press, 2003), 1.
26. Samuel Adu-Gyamfi and Eugenia Anderson, "History Education in Ghana: A Pragmatic Tradition of Change and Continuity," *Historical Encounters* 8, no. 2 (2021): 18–33.
27. Jon Olav Hove and Kofi Baku, "Conservativism in Gold Coast Politics: From Ku-Hee (New Party) to the National Democratic Party, 1943–51," *Transactions of the Historical Society of Ghana* 17 (2015): 28.
28. Kwame A. Ninson, "The Nkrumah Government and Its Opposition," in *The Ghana Reader: History, Culture, Politics*, ed. Kwasi Konadu and Clifford C. Campbell (Durham: Duke University Press, 2016), 303–304.
29. Ninson, "The Nkrumah Government," 305–306.
30. Samuel Adu-Gyamfi and Eugenia Anderson, "History Education in Ghana: A Pragmatic Tradition of Change and Continuity," *Historical Encounters* 8, no. 2 (2021): 28.
31. Adu-Gyamfi and Anderson, "History Education," 29.
32. Some have contended, however, that Kwame Nkrumah's one-party state system and his ideals such as Nkrumahism and Pan-Africanism were geared toward this very sense of nationalism. For a thorough treatment of this subject, see Harcourt Fuller, *Building the Ghanaian Nation-State: Kwame Nkrumah's Symbolic Nationalism* (London: Springer, 2014), 133–148.
33. Joseph K. Adjaye, "Perspectives on Fifty Years of Ghanaian Historiography," *History in Africa* 35 (2008): 14.
34. For instance, while local histories on the Akan, and specifically the Asante ethnic group, are vast, recent scholarship demonstrates that relatively little has historically circulated in national discourses on the history of many ethnic groups such as those in northern Ghana. The conflation of the nation-state and larger ethnic groups partly results in the marginalization of other ethno-linguistic groups. See, for example, Moses Diyaane Awinsong, "The Making of a Nation: The Northern Territories and the Colonial Discourse of Nationhood in the Gold Coast, 1897–1950," *African Historical Review* [2022]:1–30).
35. Edem Adotey, "A Matter of Apostrophe? Founder's Day, Founders' Day, and Holiday Politics in Contemporary Ghana," *Journal of West African History* 5, no. 2 (2019): 131.
36. When the NPP government took office in 2017, one of its first noticeable acts of national memorializing was the replacement of the portraits of Nkrumah on Ghana's paper currencies with those of members of "The Big Six": the men, including Nkrumah, believed historically to have precipitated political independence after World War II.
37. Jennifer R. Mercieca, "Dangerous Demagogues and Weaponized Communication," *Rhetoric Society Quarterly* 49, no. 3 (2019): 268.

38. Bodnar, *Remaking America*, 14.
39. Bradford Vivian, "A Timeless Now: Memory and Repetition," in *Framing Public Memory*, ed. Kendall R. Phillips (Tuscaloosa: The University of Alabama Press, 2004), 190.
40. Vivian, "A Timeless Now," 190.
41. Vivian, *Public Forgetting*, 10.
42. Vivian, *Public Forgetting*, 14.
43. Vivian, *Public Forgetting*, 14.
44. See also John Oddo's discussion of recontextualization as a rhetorical strategy that may elide key details of an event: *Intertextuality and the 24-Hour News Cycle: A Day in the Rhetorical Life of Colin Powell's UN Address* (East Lansing: Michigan State University Press, 2014).
45. "'Election Petition' Premiers at AICC This Wednesday," *Myjoyonline*, January 23, 2018, www.myjoyonline.com.
46. Achille Mbembe, *Out of the Dark Night: Essays on Decolonization* (Columbia: Columbia University Press, 2021), 53. See also Franz Fanon, *Black Skin, White Masks*, trans. Charles Lam Markmann (London: Pluto, 1986).
47. Paul Adom-Otchere, "The Screening of Election Petition Documentary Film by Paul Adom-Otchere," YouTube video, 01:01:22, January 25, 2018. www.youtube.com.
48. The historical formation of the two main political parties in Ghana is complicated. The NDC developed from the Provisional National Defense Council (PNDC) that ruled Ghana as a military government. When multiparty democracy was reintroduced in the early 1990s, the NDC drew its membership from Nkrumahists, but it also drew supporters from parties historically connected to the Danquah-Busia tradition that has today crystalized into the NPP. Thus, although the NDC somewhat appropriated Nkrumah's political party ideologies and legacies, there's not a linear or direct connection with Nkrumah's Convention People's Party (CPP) that led Ghana to independence. Take two examples. First, there is the PNDC member and later speaker of the First Parliament of Ghana's Fourth Republic, Daniel F. Annan, whose father, V. B. Annan, was a leading member of the UGCC. The younger Annan crossed carpets to join the PNDC much to the surprise and anger of Danquah-Busia stalwarts. Second, Harry Sawyerr was a member of Kofi Busia's Ghana Congress Party of the Second Republic and contested elections in 1969 on the party's platform. Later in the 1990s, Sawyerr joined the NDC. (On Sawyerr, see Obed Yao Asamoah, *The Political History of Ghana (1950–2013): The Experience of a Non-Conformist*, [Bloomington: AuthorHouse, 2014], 431.)
49. Adotey, "Matter of Apostrophe?," 131.
50. Nkrumah is arguably the mostly widely known and studied of all African presidents for

his consequential role, both home and abroad, in postindependent African politics.

51. Richard Werbner, *Memory and the Postcolony: African Anthropology and the Critique of Power*, ed. Richard Werbner (New York, Zed Books, 1998), 73.
52. Werbner, *Memory*, 7.
53. Nancy Henaku, "Discourse, Women and Politics in the Postcolony: On Nana Konadu Agyeman-Rawlings, Ghana's First Female Presidential Candidate" (PhD diss. Michigan Technological University, 2020), 11.
54. Henaku, "Discourse," 10.
55. Jean Allman, "The Disappearing of Hannah Kudjoe: Nationalism, Feminism, and the Tyrannies of History," *Journal of Women's History* 21, no. 3 (2009), 31.
56. Asamoah, *The Political History of Ghana*, 443.
57. Adom-Otchere, "The Screening of Election."
58. Adom-Otchere, "The Screening of Election."
59. Adjaye, "Perspectives," 11.
60. Asare, *Truth Without Reconciliation*, 7.
61. Michael Rothberg, "Remembering Back: Cultural Memory, Colonial Legacies, and Postcolonial Studies," in *The Oxford Handbook of Postcolonial Studies*, ed. Graham Huggan (Oxford: Oxford University Press, 2012), 364.
62. Mbembe, *Out of the Dark Night*, 141.
63. Asare, *Truth Without Reconciliation*, 4.
64. Some Ghanaians perceive the narrator, Paul Adom-Otchere, as biased toward the government of Akufo-Addo. This bias is reflected in Adom-Otchere's political appointment by the president to the National Communications Authority and later as Chairperson of the Board of the Ghana Airports Company Limited ("Paul Adom-Otchere Appointed NCA Board Member," *GhanaWeb*, July 7, 2017, www.ghanaweb.com; "Prez Akufo-Addo Appoints Paul Adom-Otchere Ghana Airports Chair," *GraphicOnline*, September 8, 2021, www.graphic.com.). Some scholars see this political appointment of a journalist as reflective of the phenomenon of the "rented press" engaged in propaganda peddling (see Joseph Yaw Asomah, "Democracy, the Public Sphere, and Power Elites: Examining the Ghanaian Private Media's Role in Political Corruption," *Critical Studies in Media Communication* 37, no. 3 [2020], 230).
65. In a postscreening studio conversation with Ghanaian youth from across the political spectrum, Adom-Otchere hints at some of the editorial decisions the production team made in the documentary. He noted that Akufo-Addo was the "star of the documentary" because he initiated the election dispute case at the Supreme Court and put in the initial request to publicly broadcast the case. Adom-Otchere also indicated he included issues

that have "an organic link" to the case. For further information on these decisions and citizens' perspectives on them, see Paul Adom-Otchere, "Young People Analyse Election Petition Film," Facebook, January 30, 2018, www.Facebook.com.

66. Adom-Otchere, "The Screening of Election."
67. Adom-Otchere, "The Screening of Election."
68. Adom-Otchere, "The Screening of Election."
69. Ekaterina Haskins, "Between Archive and Participation: Public Memory in a Digital Age," *Rhetoric Society Quarterly* 37, no. 4 (2007): 402.
70. Vivian, "Timeless Now," 203.
71. Sakiru Adebayo, "Memory, Crisis and Democracy in Africa," *Memory Studies* 14, no. 6 (2021): 1385.
72. Werbner, *Memory*, 75.
73. Merilee S. Grindle, "Introduction: Democracies in the Shadow of Memory," in *Reflections on Memory and Democracy*, ed. Merilee S. Grindle and Erin E. Goodman (Cambridge: Harvard University Press, 2016), 19.
74. Grindle, "Introduction," 19.
75. Bradford Vivian, "Memory: Ars Memoriae, Collective Memory, and the Fortunes of Rhetoric," *Rhetoric Society Quarterly* 48, no. 3 (2018): 287.
76. Akpeko Agbevade and Desmond Tweneboah-Koduah, "Presidential Election Petitions in Ghana: A Catalyst for Democratic Maturity," *African Journal of Political Science and International Relations* 16, no. 2 (2022), 37–39.

CONCLUSION

1. Karen Tracy, "'Reasonable Hostility': Situation-Appropriate Face-Attack," *Journal of Politeness Research* 4, no. 2 (2008): 170.
2. Jean Comaroff and John L. Comaroff, *Theory from the South: Or, How Euro-America Is Evolving Toward Africa* (Boulder: Paradigm Publishers, 2012), 9.
3. Ralph Cintron, *Democracy as Fetish* (University Park: Penn State University Press, 2019), 4.
4. Christa J. Olson, *Constitutive Visions: Indigeneity and Commonplaces of National Identity in Republican Ecuador* (University Park: Penn State University Press, 2014).
5. Romeo García and Damián Baca, "Introduction: Hopes and Visions; The Possibility of Decolonial Options," in *Rhetorics Elsewhere and Otherwise: Contested Modernities, Decolonial Futures*, ed. Romeo García and Damián Baca (Urbana: National Council of Teachers of English, 2019), 3.

6. García and Baca, "Introduction," 4.
7. Nancy Fraser, "Rethinking the Public Sphere: A Contribution to the Critique of Actually Existing Democracy," *Social Text* 25/26 (1990): 56–80.
8. García and Baca, "Introduction," 14.

APPENDIX

1. StatCounter 2021, "Social Media Stats Ghana Apr–Aug 2013." StatCounter: Global Stats. https://gs.statcounter.com.
2. Yomi Kazeem, "Politics and Activism Are Driving Africa's Twitter Conversations to New Highs," *Quartz Africa*, April 6, 2016, available on qz.com.
3. Michael L. Best and Amanda Meng, "Twitter Democracy: Policy versus Identity Politics in Three Emerging African Democracies," *Proceedings of the Seventh International Conference on Information and Communication Technologies and Development* (2015): 6, 7, 8.
4. Cheryl Geisler and Jason Swarts, *Coding Streams of Language: Techniques for the Systematic Coding of Text, Talk, and Other Verbal Data* (Colorado: WAC Clearinghouse, 2019), 68, 69.
5. Geisler and Swarts, *Coding*, 73.
6. Geisler and Swarts, *Coding*, 73.
7. Geisler and Swarts, *Coding*, 86.
8. Geisler and Swarts, *Coding*, 124.
9. Johnny Saldaña, *The Coding Manual for Qualitative Researchers*, 2nd ed. (New York: Sage, 2013), 88.
10. Saldaña, *The Coding Manual*, 210.

Bibliography

Adebayo, Sakiru. "Memory, Crisis and Democracy in Africa." *Memory Studies* 14, no. 6 (2021): 1382–1387.

Adegbola, Oluseyi, Jacqueline Skarda-Mitchell, and Sherice Gearhart. "Everything's Negative about Nigeria: A Study of US Media Reporting on Nigeria." *Global Media and Communication* 14, no. 1 (2018): 47–63.

Adjaye, Joseph K. "Perspectives on Fifty Years of Ghanaian Historiography." *History in Africa* 35 (2008): 1–24.

Adotey, Edem. "A Matter of Apostrophe? Founder's Day, Founders' Day, and Holiday Politics in Contemporary Ghana." *Journal of West African History* 5, no. 2 (2019): 113–139.

Adu-Gyamfi, Samuel, and Eugenia Anderson. "History Education in Ghana: A Pragmatic Tradition of Change and Continuity." *Historical Encounters* 8, no. 2 (2021): 18–33.

Agbevade, Akpeko, and Desmond Tweneboah-Koduah. "Presidential Election Petitions in Ghana: A Catalyst for Democratic Maturity." *African Journal of Political Science and International Relations* 16, no. 2 (2022): 33–42.

Agyekum, Kofi. "The Socio-Cultural Concept of Face in Akan Communication." *Pragmatics & Cognition* 12, no. 1 (2004): 71–92.

Ahmed, Yunana. "Toward an Understanding of African Rhetoric: A Decolonial Approach." In

A Companion to African Rhetoric, edited by Segun Ige, Gilbert Motsaathebe, and Omedi Ochieng, 17–31. Pennsylvania: Lexington Books, 2022.

Ainuson, Kweku. "Role of the Public and the Media in Civil Court Proceedings in Ghana." *KAS African Law Study Library* 5, no. 1 (2018): 54–67.

Allman, Jean. "The Disappearing of Hannah Kudjoe: Nationalism, Feminism, and the Tyrannies of History." *Journal of Women's History* 21, no. 3 (2009): 13–35.

Anderson, Benedict. *Imagined Communities: Reflections on the Origin and Spread of Nationalism*. Rev. ed. New York: Verso, 2016.

Ankomah, Baffour. "Ghana's Culture of Silence." *Index on Censorship* 16, no. 10 (1987): 17–19.

Asamoah, Kwame, Emmanuel Yeboah-Assiamah, and Alex Osei-Kojo. "Demons of Transitional Democracies: Politics of Insults and Acrimony in Ghana." *Journal of Social Science Studies* 1, no. 1 (2014): 44–56.

Asamoah, Obed Yao. *The Political History of Ghana (1950–2013): The Experience of a Non-Conformist*. Bloomington: AuthorHouse, 2014.

Asare, Abena Ampofoa. *Truth without Reconciliation: A Human Rights History of Ghana*. Philadelphia: University of Pennsylvania Press, 2018.

Asare, Stephen Kwaku. "Striking a Balance Between the Administration of Justice and Free Speech During the Live Broadcast of a Presidential Election Petition." *African Journal of International and Comparative Law* 23, no. 2 (2015): 314–338.

Asen, Robert. "A Discourse Theory of Citizenship." *Quarterly Journal of Speech* 90, no. 2 (2004): 189–211.

Asen, Robert. "Public: A Network of Relationships." *Rhetoric Society Quarterly* 48, no. 3 (2018): 297–305.

Asen, Robert. *Democracy, Deliberation, and Education*. University Park: Penn State University Press, 2015.

Asomah, Joseph Yaw. "Democracy, the Public Sphere, and Power Elites: Examining the Ghanaian Private Media's Role in Political Corruption." *Critical Studies in Media Communication* 37, no. 3 (2020): 221–237.

Atkinson, Nathan S. "Celluloid Circulation: The Dual Temporality of Nonfiction Film and Its Publics." *Rhetoric and Public Affairs* 15, no. 4 (2012): 675–684.

Attiah, Karen. "How Western Media Would Cover the U.S. Election If It Happened in Another Country." *Washington Post*, November 14, 2020. www.washingtonpost.com.

Awinsong, Moses Diyaane. "The Making of a Nation: The Northern Territories and the Colonial Discourse of Nationhood in the Gold Coast, 1897–1950." *African Historical Review* 52, no. 2 (2022): 1–30.

Baneseh, Mabel Aku. *Pink Sheets: The Story of Ghana's Presidential Election Petition*. Accra:

Graphic Communications Group Limited, 2015.

Bazerman, Charles. "Intertextuality: How Texts Rely on Other Texts." In *What Writing Does and How It Does It: An Introduction to Analyzing Texts and Textual Practices*, edited by Charles Bazerman and Paul Prior, 89–102. New York: Routledge, 2003.

Benacka, Elizabeth. *Rhetoric, Humor, and the Public Sphere: From Socrates to Stephen Colbert.* Lanham: Rowman & Littlefield, 2016.

Benson, Thomas W., and Brian J. Snee. "New Political Documentary Rhetoric, Propaganda, and the Civic Prospect." In *The Rhetoric of the New Political Documentary*, edited by Thomas W. Benson, and Brian J. Snee, 1–23. Carbondale: Southern Illinois University Press, 2008.

Best, Michael L., and Amanda Meng. "Twitter Democracy: Policy versus Identity Politics in Three Emerging African Democracies." *Proceedings of the Seventh International Conference on Information and Communication Technologies and Development*, Singapore, May 15–18, 2015, 1–10.

Bidima, Jean Godefroy. *Law and the Public Sphere in Africa: La Palabre and Other Writings.* Bloomington: Indiana University Press, 2013.

Bodnar, John. *Remaking America: Public Memory, Commemoration, and Patriotism in the Twentieth Century.* Princeton: Princeton University Press, 1992.

Bodomo, Adams. *The Structure of Dagaare.* Stanford: CSLI Publications, 1997.

Boromisza-Habashi, David. *Speaking Hatefully: Culture, Communication, and Political Action in Hungary.* University Park: Penn State University Press, 2012.

Bratta, Phil, and Malea Powell. "Introduction to the Special Issue: Entering the Cultural Rhetorics Conversations." *Enculturation: A Journal of Rhetoric, Writing, and Culture* 21 (2016).

Brefo, Henry. "Azonto—A Dance of Defiance." *What's on Africa*, November 21, 2013. https://whatsonafrica.org.

Brock, André, Jr. *Distributed Blackness: African American Cybercultures.* New York: New York University Press, 2020.

Brunotti, Irene. "From Baraza to Cyberbaraza: Interrogating Publics in the Context of the 2015 Zanzibar Electoral Impasse." *Journal of Eastern African Studies* 13, no. 1 (2019): 18–34.

Burke, Kenneth. *Attitudes Toward History.* Los Altos: Hermes Publications, 1959.

Campbell, Kermit E. "Rhetoric from the Ruins of African Antiquity." *Rhetorica* 24, no. 3 (2006): 255–274.

Chávez, Karma R. "Beyond Inclusion: Rethinking Rhetoric's Historical Narrative." *Quarterly Journal of Speech* 101, no. 1 (2015): 162–172.

Chilisa, Bagele. *Indigenous Research Methodologies.* London: Sage Publications, 2019.

Chirindo, Kundai. "Micronations and Postnational Rhetorics." *Women's Studies in*

Communication 41, no. 4 (2018): 383–393.

Cintron, Ralph. *Democracy as Fetish*. University Park: Penn State University Press, 2019.

Cobos, Casie, Gabriela Raquel Ríos, Donnie Johnson Sackey, Jennifer Sano-Franchini, and Angela M. Haas. "Interfacing Cultural Rhetorics: A History and a Call." *Rhetoric Review* 37, no. 2 (2018): 139–154.

Comaroff, Jean, and John L. Comaroff. *Theory from the South: Or, How Euro-America Is Evolving Toward Africa*. Boulder: Paradigm Publishers, 2012.

Cornelius Castoriadis, *The Imaginary Institution of Society*. Translated by Kathleen Blamey. Cambridge: Polity Press, 1987.

Cortez, José M. "Of Exterior and Exception: Latin American Rhetoric, Subalternity, and the Politics of Cultural Difference." *Philosophy & Rhetoric* 51, no. 2 (2018): 124–150.

Dorpenyo, Isidore Kafui. *User Localization Strategies in the Face of Technological Breakdown: Biometric in Ghana's Elections*. London: Springer Nature, 2019.

Dorpenyo, Isidore, and Godwin Agboka. "Election Technologies, Technical Communication, and Civic Engagement." *Technical Communication* 65, no. 4 (2018): 349–352.

Doxtader, Erik. "Making Rhetorical History in a Time of Transition: The Occasion, Constitution, and Representation of South African Reconciliation." *Rhetoric & Public Affairs* 4, no. 2 (2001): 223–260.

Dunaway, Michael. "Jarreth Merz: Bringing an African Election Home." *Paste*, February 27, 2012, pastemagazine.com.

Effah, John, and Emmanuel Debrah. "Biometric Technology for Voter Identification: The Experience in Ghana." *Information Society* 34, no. 2 (2018): 104–113.

Effah, John, Emmanuel Owusu-Oware, and Richard Boateng. "Biometric Identification for Socioeconomic Development in Ghana." *Information Systems Management* 37, no. 2 (2020): 136–149.

Ehrenfeld, Dan. "'Sharing a World with Others': Rhetoric's Ecological Turn and the Transformation of the Networked Public Sphere." *Rhetoric Society Quarterly* 50, no. 5 (2020): 305–320.

EISA. "Election Observers Interim Report On 2012 Elections." *GhanaWeb*, December 9, 2012. www.ghanaweb.com.

Ekeh, Peter P. "Colonialism and the Two Publics in Africa: A Theoretical Statement." *Comparative Studies in Society and History* 17, no. 1 (1975): 91–112.

"'Election Petition' Premiers at AICC This Wednesday." *Myjoyonline*, January 23, 2018. www.myjoyonline.com.

Emery, Daniel L. "Defending the Public: Procedural Rationality and the Limits of Actually Existing Jurisprudence." In *Rhetorical Democracy: Discursive Practices of Civic*

Engagement, edited by Gerard Hauser and Amy Grim, 151–158. New York: Routledge, 2004.

Esonwanne, Uzoma. "Orality and the Genres of African Postcolonial Writing." In *The Cambridge History of Postcolonial Literature*, vol. 1, edited by Ato Quayson, 137–170. Cambridge: Cambridge University Press, 2012.

Fanon, Franz. *Black Skin, White Masks*. Translated by Charles Lam Markmann. London: Pluto, 1986.

Fife, Jane. "Peeling *The Onion*: Satire and the Complexity of Audience Response." *Rhetoric Review* 35, no. 4 (2016): 322–334.

Foucault, Michel. *Discipline and Punish: Birth of the Prison*. Translated by Alan Sheridan. New York: Vintage Books, 1977.

Fraser, Nancy. "Rethinking the Public Sphere: A Contribution to the Critique of Actually Existing Democracy." *Social Text* 25/26 (1990): 56–80.

Fuller, Harcourt. *Building the Ghanaian Nation-State: Kwame Nkrumah's Symbolic Nationalism*. London: Springer, 2014.

Gadzekpo, Audrey. "Communication Policies in Civilian and Military Regimes: The Case of Ghana." *Africa Media Review* 11, no. 2 (1997): 31–50.

Gaonkar, Dilip Parameshwar. "Toward New Imaginaries: An Introduction." *Public Culture* 14, no. 1 (2002): 1–19.

Gaonkar, Dilip Parameshwar. "On Cultures of Democracy." In *Cultures of Democracy*, edited by Dilip Parameshwar Gaonkar, 1–22. Durham: Duke University Press, 2007.

García, Romeo, and Damián Baca. "Introduction: Hopes and Visions; The Possibility of Decolonial Options." In *Rhetorics Elsewhere and Otherwise: Contested Modernities, Decolonial Futures*, edited by Romeo García and Damián Baca, 1–48. Urbana: National Council of Teachers of English, 2019.

Geisler, Cheryl, and Jason Swarts. *Coding Streams of Language: Techniques for the Systematic Coding of Text, Talk, and other Verbal Data*. Fort Collins: WAC Clearinghouse; Denver: University Press of Colorado, 2019.

Ghana AIDS Commission. "Ghana AIDS Commission Azonto Advert." YouTube video, 00:01:05, August 9, 2018. www.youtube.com.

Giltrow, Janet. "Genre and the Pragmatic Concept of Background Knowledge." In *Genre and the New Rhetoric*, edited by Aviva Freedman and Peter Medway, 155–178. Bristol: Taylor and Francis, 1994.

Glassberg, David. "Public History and the Study of Memory." *Public Historian* 18, no. 2 (1996): 7–23.

Grindle, Merilee S. "Introduction: Democracies in the Shadow of Memory." In *Reflections on Memory and Democracy*, edited by Merilee S. Grindle and Erin E. Goodman, 1–23. Cambridge: Harvard University Press, 2016.

Gyekye, Kwame. *Tradition and Modernity: Philosophical Reflections on the African Experience*. Oxford: Oxford University Press, 1997.

Habermas, Jürgen. *The Structural Transformation of the Public Sphere: An Inquiry into a Category of Bourgeois Society*. Cambridge: MIT Press, 1991.

Harrington, Dana. "Developing Democratic Dispositions: Eighteenth-Century Public Debating Societies and the Generative Capacity of Decorum." *Rhetoric Society Quarterly* 45, no. 4 (2015): 324–345.

Hasian, Marouf, Jr., and Robert E. Frank. "Rhetoric, History, and Collective Memory: Decoding the Goldhagen Debates." *Western Journal of Communication* 63, no. 1 (1999): 95–114.

Haskins, Ekaterina. "Between Archive and Participation: Public Memory in a Digital Age." *Rhetoric Society Quarterly* 37, no. 4 (2007): 401–422.

Hauser, Gerard A. *Vernacular Voices: The Rhetoric of Publics and Public Spheres*. Columbia: University of South Carolina Press, 1999.

Hauser, Gerard A., and Chantal Benoit-Barne. "Reflections on Rhetoric, Deliberative Democracy, Civil Society, and Trust." *Rhetoric & Public Affairs* 5, no. 2 (2002): 261–275.

Hauser, Gerard. "Rhetorical Democracy and Civic Engagement." In *Rhetorical Democracy: Discursive Practices of Civic Engagement*, edited by Gerard Hauser and Amy Grim, 1–14. New York: Routledge, 2004.

Hawk, Byron. "Curating Ecologies, Circulating Musics: From the Public Sphere to Sphere Publics." In *Ecology, Writing Theory, and New Media*, edited by Sidney I. Dobrin, 160–179. New York: Routledge, 2011.

Hawkins, Sean. *Writing and Colonialism in Northern Ghana: The Encounter Between the LoDagaa and "The World on Paper."* Toronto: University of Toronto Press, 2002.

Hengehold, Laura. "Introduction: Speech, Belief, Power." In *Law and the Public Sphere in Africa: La Palabre and Other Writings*, 1–12. Bloomington: Indiana University Press, 2013.

Henaku, Nancy, Mark Nartey, Ruby Pappoe, G. Edzordzi Agbozo, and Eliasu Mumuni. "Election Discourse in Africa: Some Critical Considerations." In *Communication and Electoral Politics in Ghana: Interrogating Transnational Technology, Discourse, and Multimodalities*, edited by Eliasu Mumuni, Mark Nartey, Ruby Pappoe, Nancy Henaku, G. Edzordzi Agbozo, 1–12. London: Springer, 2024.

Henaku, Nancy. "Rhetoric, Power and Political Crisis: A Rhetorical Discourse Analysis of Ghana's 2012 Election Petition." *African Journal of Rhetoric* 10, no. 1 (2018): 89–121.

Henaku, Nancy. "Discourse, Women and Politics in the Postcolony: On Nana Konadu Agyeman-Rawlings, Ghana's First Female Presidential Candidate." PhD diss., Michigan

Technological University, 2020.

Henaku, Nancy, and Ruby Pappoe. "African Rhetoric as an Emergent Subfield." In *A Companion to African Rhetoric*, edited by Segun Ige, Gilbert Motsaathebe, and Omedi Ochieng, 171–194. Pennsylvania: Lexington Books, 2022.

Heyse, Amy Lynn. "The Rhetoric of Memory-making: Lessons from the UDC's Catechisms for Children." *Rhetoric Society Quarterly* 38, no. 4 (2008): 408–432.

Hove, Jon Olav, and Kofi Baku. "Conservativism in Gold Coast Politics: From Ku-Hee (New Party) to the National Democratic Party, 1943–51." *Transactions of the Historical Society of Ghana*, n.s., no. 17 (2015): 27–62.

Hum, Sue, and Arabella Lyon. "Recent Advances in Comparative Rhetoric." In *The Sage Handbook of Rhetorical Studies*, edited by Andrea A. Lunsford, Kirt H. Nelson, and Rosa A. Eberly, 153–165. New York: Sage Publications, 2009.

Ige, Segun, Gilbert Motsaathebe, and Omedi Ochieng, eds. *A Companion to African Rhetoric*. Pennsylvania: Lexington Books, 2022.

Institute for Economics & Peace. *Global Peace Index 2021: Measuring Peace in a Complex World*. Sydney: Institute for Economics & Peace, 2021. www.visionofhumanity.org.

Jackson, Sarah J., Moya Bailey, and Brooke Foucault Welles. *#HashtagActivism: Networks of Race and Gender Justice*. Cambridge: MIT Press, 2020.

Johnson, Erik. "In the Midnight Hour: Anticolonial Rhetoric and Postcolonial Statecraft in Ghana." *Review of Communication* 22, no. 1 (2022): 60–75.

Jones, Natasha N., and Miriam F. Williams. "Technologies of Disenfranchisement: Literacy Tests and Black Voters in the US from 1890 to 1965." *Technical Communication* 65, no. 4 (2018): 371–386.

Kazeem, Yomi. "Politics and Activism Are Driving Africa's Twitter Conversations to New Highs." *Quartz Africa*, April 6, 2016. https://qz.com.

Keating, Joshua. "If It Happened There." *Slate*. Last updated October 24, 2018. slate.com.

Keating, Christine. *Decolonizing Democracy: Transforming the Social Contract in India*. University Park: Penn State University Press, 2011.

Keith, William, and Robert Danisch. *Beyond Civility: The Competing Obligations of Citizenship*. University Park: Penn State University Press, 2020.

Klujeff, Marie Lund. "Provocative Style: The Gaarder Debate Example." In *Rhetorical Citizenship and Public Deliberation*, edited by Christian Koch and Lisa S. Villadsen, 101–114. University Park: Penn State University Press, 2012.

Knoblauch, Abby A., and Marie E. Moeller, eds. *Bodies of Knowledge: Embodied Rhetorics in Theory and Practice*. Denver: University Press of Colorado, 2022.

Kølvraa, Christoffer, and Bernhard Forchtner. "Cultural Imaginaries of the Extreme Right: An

Introduction." *Patterns of Prejudice* 53, no. 3 (2019): 227–235.

Kunbuor, Benjamin. "Customary Law of the Dagara of Northern Ghana: Indigenous Rules or a Social Construction." *Journal of Dagaare Studies* 2 (2002): 1–18.

Labouba, Manouchka Kelly. "An African Election directed by Jarreth Merz." *African Studies Review* 57, no. 2 (2014): 232–234.

Larson, Kyle R., and George F. McHendry Jr. "Parasitic Publics." *Rhetoric Society Quarterly* 49, no. 5 (2019): 517–541.

Laryea, Emmanuel, and Kwamena Kwansah-Aidoo. "Going, Going, Gone! Implications of the Repeal of Criminal Libel and Sedition Laws in Ghana." *Ghana Studies* 8, no. 1 (2005): 127–168.

Lauer, Helen. "Depreciating African Political Culture." *Journal of Black Studies* 38, no. 2 (2007): 288–307.

Leman, Peter. "African Oral Law and the Critique of Colonial Modernity in *The Trial of Jomo Kenyatta*." *Law & Literature* 23, no. 1 (2011): 26–47.

Lozano-Reich, Nina M., and Dana L. Cloud. "The Uncivil Tongue: Invitational Rhetoric and the Problem of Inequality." *Western Journal of Communication* 73, no. 2 (2009): 220–226.

Lynch, Gabrielle, Nic Cheeseman, and Justin Willis. "From Peace Campaigns to Peaceocracy: Elections, Order and Authority in Africa." *African Affairs* 118, no. 473 (2019): 603–627.

Lyon, Arabella. *Deliberative Acts: Democracy, Rhetoric, and Rights*. University Park: Penn State University Press, 2015.

Maddux, Kristy. "*View*ing Deliberation: Daytime Television's Public Pedagogy of Inclusion." *Argumentation and Advocacy* 58, no. 1 (2022): 1–21.

Mamdani, Mahmood. *Citizen and Subject: Contemporary Africa and the Legacy of Late Colonialism*. Princeton: Princeton University Press, 2018.

Mao, LuMing. "Thinking beyond Aristotle: The Turn to How in Comparative Rhetoric." *PMLA* 129, no. 3 (2014): 448–455.

Maraj, Louis M. *Black or Right: Anti/racist Campus Rhetorics*. Denver: University Press of Colorado, 2020.

Mare, Admire. "Popular Communication in Africa: An Empirical and Theoretical Exposition." *Annals of the International Communication Association* 44, no. 1 (2020): 81–99.

Marfo, Samuel. "Thinking of Peace, Democracy, and Politics of Insults in Ghana: The Paradox of Freedom and Culture of Violence." *Online Journal of African Affairs* 3 (2013): 522–530.

Mbembe, Achille. *On the Postcolony*. California: University of California Press, 2001.

Mbembe, Achille. *Out of the Dark Night: Essays on Decolonization*. Columbia: Columbia University Press, 2021.

Mercieca, Jennifer R. "Dangerous Demagogues and Weaponized Communication." *Rhetoric*

Society Quarterly 49, no. 3 (2019): 264–279.

Miller, Carolyn R. "Genre as Social Action." *Quarterly Journal of Speech* 70, no. 2 (1984): 151–167.

Miller, Christopher Allan, and Mary E. King. *A Glossary of Terms and Concepts in Peace and Conflict Studies*. San Jose, Costa Rica: University for Peace, 2005.

Mouffe, Chantal. "Which Kind of Public Space for a Democratic Habitus?" In *Habitus: A Sense of Place*, 2nd ed., edited by Jean Hillier and Emma Rooksby, 109–116. New York: Routledge, 2017.

Mudimbe, V. Y. *The Idea of Africa*. Bloomington: Indiana University Press, 1994.

Nana Addo Dankwa Akufo Addo Others v. John Dramani Mahama Others (J1 6 of 2013) [2013] GHASC 5, August 29, 2013, 71. ghanalii.org.

Ndlovu-Gatsheni, Sabelo J. *Epistemic Freedom in Africa: Deprovincialization and Decolonization*. New York: Routledge, 2018.

Newell, Stephanie, and Onookome Okome, eds. *Popular Culture in Africa: The Episteme of the Everyday*. New York: Routledge, 2013.

Ninson, Kwame A. "The Nkrumah Government and Its Opposition." In *The Ghana Reader: History, Culture, Politics*, edited by Kwasi Konadu and Clifford C. Campbell, 303–306. Durham: Duke University Press, 2016.

Nkrumah, Kwame. "Independence Speech." In *The Ghana Reader: History, Culture, Politics*, edited by Kwasi Konadu and Clifford C. Campbell, 301–302. Durham: Duke University Press, 2016.

Nora, Pierre. "Between Memory and History: Les Lieux de Mémoire." *Representations* 26 (1989): 7–24.

Nyabola, Nanjala. *Digital Democracy, Analogue Politics: How the Internet Era is Transforming Politics in Kenya*. London: Zed Books, 2018.

Obadare, Ebenezer. "The Uses of Ridicule: Humour, 'Infrapolitics' and Civil Society in Nigeria." *African Affairs* 108, no. 431 (2009): 241–261.

Obadare, Ebenezer. "Civil Society in Sub-Saharan Africa." In *The Oxford Handbook of Civil Society*, edited by Michael Edwards, 183–194. Oxford: Oxford University Press, 2011.

Obeng, Samuel Gyasi. "Grammatical Pragmatics: Language, Power and Liberty in Ghanaian Political Discourse." *Discourse & Society* 31, no. 1 (2020): 85–105.

Obeng, Samuel Gyasi. "Language and Politics: Indirectness in Political Discourse." *Discourse & Society* 8, no. 1 (1997): 49–83.

Ochieng, Omedi. "W.E.B. Du Bois and the Imagination of the Public Intellectual." *African Journal of Rhetoric* 8, no. 1 (2016): 107–124.

Ochieng, Omedi. *Groundwork for the Practice of the Good Life: Politics and Ethics at the Intersection of North Atlantic and African Philosophy*. London: Routledge, 2017.

Ochieng, Omedi. "What Is African Rhetoric: The Constitutive Imagination in Olaudah Equiano's *The Interesting Narrative and Other Writings*." In *A Companion to African Rhetoric*, edited by Segun Ige, Gilbert Motsaathebe, and Omedi Ochieng, 3–15. Pennsylvania: Lexington Books, 2022.

Oddo, John. *Intertextuality and the 24-Hour News Cycle: A Day in the Rhetorical Life of Colin Powell's UN Address*. East Lansing: Michigan State University Press, 2014.

Okeja, Uchenna. *Deliberative Agency: A Study in Modern African Political Philosophy*. Bloomington: Indiana University Press, 2022.

Olick, Jeffrey K. *States of Memory: Continuities, Conflicts, and Transformations in National Retrospection*. Durham: Duke University Press, 2003.

Olson, Christa J. *Constitutive Visions: Indigeneity and Commonplaces of National Identity in Republican Ecuador*. University Park: Penn State University Press, 2014.

Olson, Christa. "The Democratic Hemisphere." In *Rhetorics of Democracy in the Americas*, edited by Adriana Angel, Michael L. Butterworth, and Nancy R. Gómez, 23–38. University Park: Penn State University Press, 2021.

Ong, Walter J., and John Hartley. *Orality and Literacy*. New York: Routledge, 2013.

Osaghae, Eghosa E. "Colonialism and Civil Society in Africa: The Perspective of Ekeh's Two Publics." *Voluntas: International Journal of Voluntary and Nonprofit Organizations* 17, no. 3 (2006): 233–245.

Paley, Julia. "Toward an Anthropology of Democracy." *Annual Review of Anthropology* 31, no. 1 (2002): 469–496.

Paller, Jeffrey W. *Democracy in Ghana: Everyday Politics in Urban Africa*. Cambridge: Cambridge University Press, 2019.

Paré, Anthony. "Genre and Identity: Individuals, Institutions, and Ideology." In *The Rhetoric and Ideology of Genre: Strategies for Stability and Change*, edited by Richard M. Coe, Lorelei Lingard, and Tatiana Teslenko, 57–71. New York: Hampton Press, 2002.

"Paul Adom-Otchere Appointed NCA Board Member." *GhanaWeb*, July 7, 2017. www.ghanaweb.com.

Pfister, Damien Smith. *Networked Media, Networked Rhetorics: Attention and Deliberation in the Early Blogosphere*. University Park: Penn State University Press, 2015.

Phillips, Kendall R. Introduction to *Framing Public Memory*, edited by Kendall R. Phillips, 1–16. Tuscaloosa: University of Alabama Press, 2004.

Pleasants, Julian. *Hanging Chads: The Inside Story of the 2000 Presidential Recount in Florida*. London: Springer, 2004.

"The Tour." A Political Safari: An African Adventure in Democracy Building. July 30, 2024. www.politicalsafari.org.

"Prez Akufo-Addo Appoints Paul Adom-Otchere Ghana Airports Chair." *GraphicOnline*, September 8, 2021. www.graphic.com.

Quayson, Ato. *Tragedy and Postcolonial Literature*. Cambridge: Cambridge University Press, 2021.

Rai, Candice. *Democracy's Lot: Rhetoric, Publics, and the Places of Invention*. Tuscaloosa: University of Alabama Press, 2016.

Rathbone, Richard. *Nkrumah & the Chiefs: The Politics of Chieftaincy in Ghana, 1951–60*. Columbus: Ohio State University Press, 2000.

Roberts-Miller, Patricia. *Deliberate Conflict: Argument, Political Theory, and Composition Courses*. Carbondale: Southern Illinois University Press, 2004.

Rood, Craig. *After Gun Violence: Deliberation and Memory in an Age of Political Gridlock*. University Park: Penn State University Press, 2019.

Rothberg, Michael. "Remembering Back: Cultural Memory, Colonial Legacies, and Postcolonial Studies." In *The Oxford Handbook of Postcolonial Studies*, edited by Graham Huggan, 359–379. Oxford: Oxford University Press, 2012.

Saldaña, Johnny. *The Coding Manual for Qualitative Researchers*. 2nd ed. London: Sage, 2013.

Sass, Jensen, and John S. Dryzek. "Deliberative Cultures." *Political Theory* 42, no. 1 (2014): 3–25.

Shipley, Jesse Weaver. "Transnational Circulation and Digital Fatigue in Ghana's Azonto Dance Craze." *American Ethnologist* 40, no. 2 (2013): 362–381.

Shogimen, Takashi. "On the Elusiveness of Context." *History and Theory* 55, no. 2 (2016): 233–252.

Shome, Raka, and Radha Hegde. "Culture, Communication, and the Challenge of Globalization." *Critical Studies in Media Communication* 19, no. 2 (2002): 172–189.

Sieff, Kevin. "Why African Judges Still Wearing Wigs Is a Glaring Symbol of British Colonialism." *Independent*, September 18, 2017. www.independent.co.uk.

Spinuzzi, Clay. *Tracing Genres Through Organizations: A Sociocultural Approach to Information Design*. Cambridge: MIT Press, 2003.

Srinivasan, Sharath, Stephanie Diepeveen, and George Karekwaivanane. "Rethinking Publics in Africa in a Digital Age." *Journal of Eastern African Studies* 13, no. 1 (2019): 2–17.

"Social Media Stats Ghana Apr–Aug 2013." StatCounter: Global Stats, September 14, 2020. https://gs.statcounter.com.

Steele, Catherine Knight. "Black Bloggers and Their Varied Publics: The Everyday Politics of Black Discourse Online." *Television & New Media* 19, no. 2 (2018): 112–127.

Storr, Virgil Henry. "The Market as a Social Space: On the Meaningful Extraeconomic Conversations that Can Occur in Markets." *Review of Austrian Economics* 21 (2008): 135–150.

Squires, Catherine R. "Rethinking the Black Public Sphere: An Alternative Vocabulary for Multiple Public Spheres." *Communication Theory* 12, no. 4 (2002): 446–468.

"Synopsis." *An African Election: A Film by Jarreth Merz*, February 4, 2023. anafricanelection.com.

Taylor, Charles. "Modern Social Imaginaries." *Public Culture* 14, no. 1 (2002): 91–124.

Teston, Christa B. "A Grounded Investigation of Genred Guidelines in Cancer Care Deliberations." *Written Communication* 26, no. 3 (2009): 320–348.

Thomas, Keith. *In Pursuit of Civility: Manners and Civilization in Early Modern England.* New Haven: Yale University Press, 2018.

Thompson, Rachel Akusika, and Jemima Asabea Anderson. "Interactive Programmes on Private Radio Stations in Ghana: An Avenue for Impoliteness." *Journal of African Media Studies* 10, no. 1 (2018): 55–72.

Tracy, Karen. "'Reasonable Hostility': Situation-Appropriate Face-Attack." *Journal of Politeness Research* 4, no. 2 (2008): 169–191.

Tracy, Karen. *Challenges of Ordinary Democracy: A Case Study in Deliberation and Dissent.* University Park: Penn State University Press, 2011.

Tweneboah-Koduah, Nana Akua. "Is Bawumia Selling Pink Sheet Evidence on the Streets?" *Myjoyonline*, May 15, 2013. www.myjoyonline.com.

"2012 Election Petition Documentary Premieres January 24th." *Modern Ghana*, January 22, 2018. www.modernghana.com.

Vivian, Bradford. "Memory: Ars Memoriae, Collective Memory, and the Fortunes of Rhetoric." *Rhetoric Society Quarterly* 48, no. 3 (2018): 287–296.

Vivian, Bradford. "A Timeless Now: Memory and Repetition." In *Framing Public Memory*, edited by Kendall R. Phillips, 187–211. Tuscaloosa: University of Alabama Press, 2004.

Vivian, Bradford. *Public Forgetting: The Rhetoric and Politics of Beginning Again.* University Park: Penn State University Press, 2010.

Wardhaugh, Ronald, and Janet M. Fuller. *An Introduction to Sociolinguistics*. 7th ed. Chichester, UK: John Wiley & Sons, 2015.

Warner, Michael. *Publics and Counterpublics*. New York: Zone Books, 2002.

Weaver, Richard M. *The Ethics of Rhetoric*. Davis: Hermagoras Press, 1985.

Werbner, Richard. *Memory and the Postcolony: African Anthropology and the Critique of Power*, edited by Werbner Richard. New York: Zed Books, 1998.

Willems, Wendy. "'The Politics of Things': Digital Media, Urban Space, and the Materiality of Publics." *Media, Culture & Society* 41, no. 8 (2019): 1192–1209.

Yankah, Kwesi. "Free Speech in Traditional Society: The Cultural Foundations of Communication in Contemporary Ghana." In *Reclaiming the Human Sciences and Humanities Through African Perspectives*, vol. 2, edited by Helen Lauer, and Kofi

Anyidoho. Accra: Sub-Saharan Publishers, Ghana, 2012.

Yankah, Kwesi. *Speaking for the Chief: Okyeame and the Politics of Akan Royal Oratory*. Bloomington: Indiana University Press, 1995.

Yar, Majid. *The Cultural Imaginary of the Internet: Virtual Utopias and Dystopias*. London: Springer Nature, 2014.

Yeku, James. *Cultural Netizenship: Social Media, Popular Culture, and Performance in Nigeria*. Bloomington: Indiana University Press, 2022.

You, Xiaoye. *Genre Networks and Empire: Rhetoric in Early Imperial China*. Carbondale: Southern Illinois University Press, 2023.

Index

A

accessibility, 41
Accra, 2, 11, 77, 106
Addison, Philip, 45–46, 48–50, 117
Adebayo, Sakiru, 120–121
Adjaye, Joseph, 102–103, 112
Adom-Otchere, Paul, 106–107, 119, 161 (n. 64), 161–162 (n. 65)
Adu, Kajsah, 83–84
Adu Boahen, Albert, 110
Adu-Gyamfi, Samuel, 101–102
Afari-Djan, Kwadwo, 40–51, 117
African Election, An (documentary), 97–101, 105–106, 108–110
African rhetoric, xxvi–xxvii, 30, 44, 131
African writing systems, 43–44, 149 (n. 24)
Afromodernity, 129
Agboka, Godwin, 34
agency, xxii, xxv–xxvi, 37, 38, 75; colonialism and, 102; deliberative, 127; documentary's depiction of, 100–101; exercise of, 80, 90; political, 112
Agyeman-Rawlings, Nana Konadu, 112
Ahmed, Yunana, xxvi, xxvii
Akans, 4, 6, 8, 29, 46, 103, 144 (n. 8). See also *obuo kasa*
Akufo-Addo, Nana Addo Dankwa, xiv, xv, xvi, 11, 97–100, 106, 111–120
Allman, Jean, 112
Amoaning, Moses Foh, 117
analog politics, 63, 64, 68–69, 71, 75, 80, 91
Anderson, Benedict, xix
Anderson, Eugenia, 101–102
Anderson, Jemima, 10

Ankomah, Baffour, 9
Ankuma, Phelix Appiah, 120
Ansah, Julius, 42, 57
apologetic speech forms, 3, 7, 11–22, 25–27, 30
Asare, Abena Ampofoa, 94
Asempa FM, 2, 11
Asen, Robert, 6, 61–62, 64, 81
Atkinson, Nathan, 95–96
Atta Akyea, Samuel, 23, 26–27
Atta Mills, John Evans, xiv, 108
Atubiga, Stephen, 2, 8, 11–22, 25–30, 85, 126
Atuguba, William, 56–57, 87
azonto dance, 78–81, 154 (n. 61)

B

Bakhtin, Mikhail, xxii
"Battle of the Apostrophe," 103, 109
Bawumia, Mahamadu, 49, 53–54, 117–118
Bee, Sammy, 119
Benson, Thomas, 96
Best, Michael L., 134
Bidima, Jean Godefroy, xxv
biometric verification devices (BVDs), xiv, 35, 40–42, 45–49, 122
"Black Star of Africa," Ghana as, xiii, 72, 139 (n. 1)
Blogging Ghana (BloGh), 81–85
Boafo, William O., 74
Boahen, Kwaku, 2, 143–144 (n. 1)
Bratta, Phil, xxi
British colonialism, 9, 43–44, 50, 56, 72, 88, 102; Ghana's independence from, xiii, 72, 88, 102, 109; judicial infrastructure's roots in, xxvii, 3, 4, 8, 16–18, 27–32, 56, 125; Kenya and, 50. *See also* colonialism
Brunotti, Irene, 68, 91
Burkina Faso, 73

C

Captured Voter Information Form, 38, 41, 48
Castoriadis, Cornelius, xix, 140 (n. 15)
celluloid circulation, 95
Cheeseman, Nic, 14
Chilisa, Bagele, 45
Chirindo, Kundai, 66–67
Christian, Phillis Maria, 116
chronotope, xxii
chronotopia, xxii
chronotype, xxiv
Cintron, Ralph, xxii, 66
circulation, xxx, 64–65, 89, 94; celluloid, 95; of Constitution resources, 82; of historical events and memory, 100, 102–104, 108, 122, 123, 132; of marginalized perspectives, 84; of music and dance, 64–65, 78–81, 78; of peace narratives, 71, 85, 118
citizen commentary, 23
citizens and subjects: democratic aspiration and, 70–75; democratic practice and, 61–77, 81–92, 126–129; digital publics and, 64–70; enfranchisement of, 41, 55; justice system and, 26, 117–119; political engagement and, 134; public pedagogy of citizenship, xxxi, 96–97, 104, 108–110, 113–114, 120, 122–123, 131
civility, 7–8, 14, 20, 29, 31, 126, 144–145 (n. 14)
clarifications, 15, 18, 24–26, 40
Coat of Arms of Ghana, 38
Collation Forms, 38, 42–43, 48, 57
colonialism: court as legacy of, xxvii, 3, 4,

8, 16–18, 27–32, 56, 125; deliberative norms and, 11, 27–32; digital publics and, 63, 66–69, 88–92; neoliberalism and, 62; writing and, 40, 43–44, 48–59, 127. *See also* British colonialism
colonial legacies, xxix, 29, 31–32, 44, 50, 62, 125–128
"colonial library," 88–90
Comaroff, Jean, xvii, 53, 128–129
Comaroff, John, xvii, 53, 128–129
Constitution of Ghana, 9, 16, 19, 27, 47, 77, 82, 117; freedom of speech, 10, 16; "Fundamental Human Rights and Freedoms," 9
contempt of court, 2, 4, 8, 11, 28, 77, 85, 146 (n. 38)
Convention People's Party (CPP), 102, 108–109
Cortez, José, xxiv
Côte d'Ivoire, 14, 73
coups d'état, 9, 24, 99, 109, 121, 131
courtroom deliberations, 2–3, 6, 13, 25, 79–80, 128
Criminal Libel and Seditious Laws, 9, 86, 113
critical communication studies, xx–xxi
cultural iconoclasm, 79
cultural imaginaries, xvii, xx, xxii–xxiii, xxvi, xxvii–xxxi, 125; digital publics and, 64, 66, 68, 70, 73, 78, 81, 85, 91, 128; documentary evidence and, 39, 40, 43, 59; free speech and, 132; memory and, 115, 131; speech and, 3–5, 12, 17, 19–20, 22, 25, 30, 31, 32
cultural imprints, 38–40
cultural netizenship, 80
cultural rhetorics, xx–xxii, 5, 20, 24–25, 30, 95
culture of silence, 2, 9, 86, 87
cyberbaraza, 68, 75, 91

D

Dagaaba, 43–44, 56, 149 (n. 25)
Daily Searchlight (newspaper), 2, 22
Dame, Godfred, 114
Danquah, Joseph Boakye, 102, 109, 112
decoloniality, xxvi–xxvii, xxxi, 45, 51, 91, 107–108, 128–132
decorum, 3, 7, 29, 30, 144–145 (n. 14)
deliberative norms, 3, 5–8, 11–12, 14, 16, 19–22, 26–32, 126
democracy, xvi–xx, xxii, xxii–xxv, xxvii, xxix, xxxi; courts and, xv; deliberation and, xxiv–xxviii, xxv; election and, xxiii; globalization and, xxiv–xxv
democratic aspiration, 70–75
democratic participation, 64–70
democratic practice, humor in, 75–81
diaspora, 69, 113
Diepeveen, Stephanie, 67–68
digital democracy, 69, 75, 91
digitality, 68, 128
digital publics, 61–64; blogging and bloggers, 81–85; citizenship and, 64–70; colonialism and, 63, 66–69, 88–92; cultural imaginaries and, 64, 66, 68, 70, 73, 78, 81, 85, 91; *cyberbaraza*, 68, 75, 91; democratic participation and, 64–70; free speech and, 85–88; humor and, 76–81; peace narratives and, 70–75; postcolonial election library and, 88–90. *See also* hashtags
discomforts of deliberation, 14, 20, 26, 30, 72
disenfranchisement, 37, 41–42

documentaries: *An African Election*, 97–101, 105–106, 108–110; *The Election Petition*, 94–99, 101, 103–116, 119–120, 122–124
documentary evidence: cultural imprints, 38–40; genre and, 36–38; in the postcolony, 52–56; Supreme Court and, 56–58. *See also* Statement of Poll and Declaration of Results
Dorpenyo, Isidore, 34
Doxtader, Erik, 74
Dryzek, John S., xxiii, 76

E

Economic Community of West African States (ECOWAS), xiv, 99–100
education: historical production and, 101–102; policy, 134; voter and democratic education; 34, 81–84; Western education, 18–20
Ehrenfeld, Dan, 66
Election 2008, 99, 101, 106, 110
Election 2012, xiii–xvii, 1, 38–40, 81–82, 108, 110, 122
Election 2016, 118–119, 122
Election 2020, 122, 123
Election Petition, The (documentary), 94–99, 101, 103–116, 119–120, 122–124
election technologies, 34
Electoral Commission (EC), xiv, xv, 34–35, 38–42, 45, 48, 54–55, 98–99, 107, 117–118, 122
Electoral Institute for Sustainable Democracy in Africa (EISA), xiv–xv
Emery, Daniel, xxvii
empty container, 129
epistemology, xxvii–xxviii, xxi, xxv–xxvii, 76, 83, 88–89, 130–132
essentialization, xxi, 89, 100
ethnic groups, 103, 144 (n. 8), 159 (n. 34)
Eurocentrism, xxi, xxiii, xxxi, 130, 140 (n. 15)

F

face-only verification, 41–42
Fanon, Frantz, 107–108
female political agency, 112
fetishism, 48, 58, 129
fingerprint verification, 40, 41, 46
forgetting, 95, 98, 104–105, 112–117, 123–124
formal speech, 3, 5–8, 12, 15, 16, 28
Foucault, Michel, xxv
Founder's vs. Founders' Day, 103
"founding father" trope, 103–104
Frank, Robert E., 94, 97
Fraser, Nancy, 130

G

Gadzekpo, Audrey, 117
Gaonkar, Dilip, xxii, xxiii
"Gateway to Africa," Ghana as, xiii, 135, 139 (n. 1)
Geisler, Cheryl, 135
genres, 58–59, 122, 127, 130–131; communicative, 68, 80; as cultural inheritance, xxix; defining, 36; documentary, 96, 111, 113; pink sheet as, 34, 36–38. *See also* Captured Voter Information Form; Collation Forms; documentaries; Statement of Poll and Declaration of Results; Voters' Register
genre studies, xxix, 35, 148 (n. 5)
Ghana Decides, 81–82
globalization, xx, xxi, xxiv–xxv

Global North, xxi
Global Peace Index Report, 73
Global South, xvii, xxi
"god term," 14, 132; freedom of speech as, 4, 32, 132; peace as, 71; use of the term, 144 (n. 3)
golden jubilee, Ghana's, 112–113
Goodman, Erin E., 121
Google Hangout, 83, 84, 85
Grindle, Merilee S., 121
guardians of democracy, 14, 27, 77, 86
Gyekye, Kwame, xx

H

Habermas, Jürgen, 64, 90
Harrington, Dana, 74
hashtags, 63, 67, 83, 134; #ElectionPetition, 63, 71–72, 77–78, 82–83, 86–87, 89, 134; #GhanaDecides, 63, 78, 82–83, 134; #SupremeCourt, 63, 70, 71, 86–87, 134; #TheVerdict, 63, 71, 72, 77, 78, 83, 87, 89, 134
Hasian, Marouf, 94, 97
Haskins, Ekaterina, 119
Hauser, Gerard, 5, 76, 83
Hawk, Byron, 64–65, 75
Hawkins, Sean, 36, 43–44, 49, 56
Hedge, Radha, xx–xxi
hegemony, xxiv, 80, 83, 130
Henaku, Nancy, xxvi, xxvii, 13, 112
heroism, 111–117
historiographies, 102–103, 112, 114
human rights, 9–10, 93, 113
humor, 75–81

I

ideologies, xxii; colonial, xxvi, 54, 56, 58; democratic deliberation and, 55–56, 127; documentaries and, 96; genre and, 34–39; historical memory and, 94; nationalist, 67; political, 102–103, 109, 119–120, 160 (n. 48); postcolonial, xxix, 52, 59
Ige, Segun, xxvi
imagined community, xix, xvii
India, xxvii
indirection, 7, 27–28
indirectness, 16–17
inflammatory language, 19, 20, 27
irresponsible language, 12, 15, 18–19, 20–21, 25, 27

J

Johnson, Erik, 44
Jones, Natasha N., 37

K

Karekwaivanane, George, 67–68
Keating, Christina, xviii
Kenya, 14, 50–51, 67–69, 75, 99, 134
Kenyatta, Jomo, 50–51
Koo, Agya, 77
Kufuor, John Agyekum, 9, 93, 112
Kume Preko (political protest), 113
Kuranchie, Ken, 2, 16, 21–28, 30, 85, 86, 126

L

Latin America, xxiv, 121
legitimacy, 14; calls for peace and, 26; colonial legacies of, 50–52, 56; deliberative practices and, 34–36; democratic, 100,

121, 129; political, 100, 103–104, 109–111, 115; vote, 34, 38, 57; written records as arbiters of, 43, 45, 49–52, 56, 58
Leman, Peter, 50–51
Limann, Hilla, 109
literacy tests, 37
Lithur, Tony, 54–55
Lynch, Gabrielle, 14
Lyon, Arabella, xxiv–xxv, 142 (n. 40)

M

Mahama, John, xiii–xiv, xv, xvi, 2, 107, 108, 118
Mamdani, Mahmood, 18
Mare, Admire, 80
Marfo, Samuel, 10
materiality, 65, 68, 85, 128
Mau Mau liberation movement, 50–51
Mbembe, Achille, xvii, 62, 88, 107, 108, 115
memory: artifacts of, 94–95, 104; audience challenges to dominant, 119–122; history and, 94, 101–110, 130; National Reconciliation Commission (NRC), 93–94, 114–116. *See also* documentaries
Meng, Amanda, 134
Merz, Jarreth J., 98, 101, 105–106. See also *African Election, An*
military rule, xiii, 9, 93, 109, 115–116
Miller, Carolyn, 34, 36
modernity, xix, 51, 128–129
Motsaathebe, Gilbert, xxvi
Mouffe, Chantal, 74
Mudimbe, V. Y., 88
multiculturalism, xx

N

National Democratic Congress (NCD), xiii–xiv, 2, 8, 11, 98–99, 102–110, 113–119, 122, 160 (n. 48)
national identity, 95, 120, 122
nationalist history, 67, 72, 96–97, 101–103, 108, 112, 118
National Peace Council, 73–74
National Reconciliation Commission (NRC), 93–94, 114–116
nationhood, xx
nation-state, xix–xxii, xxv, xxvii, 30–31, 47, 62–67, 91, 128, 144 (n. 8)
neoliberalism, 62
Newell, Stephanie, 76, 155 (n. 74)
New Patriotic Party (NPP), xiv, 1, 8, 11, 39, 98, 102–103, 107, 109–120, 122
New Statesman (newspaper), 2, 11
Nigeria, 14, 134
Nkrumah, Kwame, 9, 72, 88–89, 102–103, 108–110, 114, 139 (n. 1)
non-Western rhetorics, xx–xxi, 91, 130–131
No Verification, No Vote policy, 42
Nyabola, Nanjala, 68–69, 75, 91

O

Obeng, Samuel Gyasi, 28
obuo kasa (polite speech), 4, 5, 7, 8, 28, 125
Ochieng, Omedi, xxii, xxiv, xxvi–xxvii, 4, 63, 81
Okeja, Uchenna, xxv, 80
Okome, Onookome, 76, 155 (n. 74)
Okudzeto, Sam, 119
okyeame (messenger between chief or king and assembly), 7, 28–29
Olick, Jeffrey, 101

Olson, Christa, 152 (n. 16)
oral testimony, 40, 43–45, 48, 50–52, 55, 57–59, 127
"ordinary democracy," xxvii

P

palabre, xxv, 5, 20, 86, 131
Paley, Julia, xxii
Paller, Jeffrey, xviii
Pan-Africanism, 72
Pappoe, Ruby, xxvi, xxvii
pardon, judicial, 19
Paré, Anthony, 37
peace fatigue, 71
peace narratives, 70–75, 76, 78, 85, 118, 136
peaceocracy, 14
performative deliberation theory, 142 (n. 40)
Pfister, Damien Smith, xix, 66
Phillips, Kendall R., 158 (n. 24)
pink sheets. *See* Statement of Poll and Declaration of Results
pluralism: cultural, xxi; media, 8, 9, 69
polite speech (*obuo kasa*), 4, 5, 7, 8, 28, 125
polling agents, 38–39, 50, 53–57
poll workers, 46
popular culture, 63, 67, 75–81, 91, 126, 131
postcolonial documentary evidence, 52–56
postcolonial election library, 88–90
"postcolonialism," use of the term, 129–130
postcolonial present, 8
Powell, Malea, xxi
prison sentences, 2, 27, 30, 126
Provisional National Defense Council (PNDC), 160 (n. 48)
Proxy List, 38, 39
public memory, 104, 105
public pedagogy, xxxi, 96–97, 104, 108–110, 113–114, 120, 122–123, 131
public sphere, xvi, xvii, xxvii–xxviii, xxx, 1, 20, 64–68, 128–130

R

racial contracts, xviii
radio, 2, 9–11, 12, 16, 135
Rai, Candice, xxiii
Rawlings, Jerry John, 99–100, 114–115
reasonable hostility, 31, 126
rhetoric, xvi–xix, xxi–xxvii, 30–31, 103, 129–132
rhetorical norms, 20–25, 30
rhetorical practices, xvi, xx–xxiv, xxx, 5, 35–36, 91, 125, 130
rhetorical strategies, 3, 6–7, 11, 76, 123, 131, 157 (n. 13)
rhetorical studies, xx, xxi–xxiv, xxvi, xxix
Roberts-Miller, Patricia, 20
Rood, Craig, 5
Rothberg, Michael, 115

S

Sackey, Phylix, 119–120
sanctioned forgetting, 107, 112–113, 117, 124
Sass, Jensen, xxiii, 76
Sawyerr, Amos, 99–100
sexual contract, xviii
Shipley, Jesse Weaver, 78–79
Shome, Raka, xx–xxi
signatures, 52–53
silence, culture of, 2, 9, 86, 87
Snee, Brian, 96
SOAS and Spurs, 105–106. See also *Election Petition, The*

social imaginaries, xix, 68
social position, 20, 31
South Africa, 74, 93
speech, freedom of, xvi, xviii, xxvi, 4, 125–128, 131–132; apologetic speech forms and, 13; constitutional protections, 9–10, 13, 16, 19–20, 23–24, 30; paradoxes of, 85–88, 91, 136
speech-without-caveats, 24, 26
sphere publics, 65
Srinivasan, Sharath, 67–68
Standard of Care document, 36, 39
Statement of Poll and Declaration of Results (pink sheets), xv, xvi, xxix, 33–35, 79, 122, 127, 129–131; arguments on evidentiary role of, 52–56; evidence concerning electoral irregularities and, 40–52; as genre, 34, 36–38; history of, 38–40; length and contents of, 38–39; in postcolonial context, 58–59; Supreme Court's verdict and, 56–58
"stolen verdict" trope, 119
subjectivities, 8, 29, 103, 111, 113, 148 (n. 16)
Sumani Abukari, Alhaji, 73
SuperLock Technologies Limited (STL), xiv, 40
Supreme Court of Ghana, xv, xxix, 1–2, 10–13, 22, 125–126, 134–135; digital publics and, 77, 80, 82, 83, 86; NPP and, 117, 125; pink sheet and, 33, 34, 35, 39, 40, 42, 56–58; summons to Kuranchie, 22
Swarts, Jason, 135

T

Tanzania, 68
Taylor, Charles, xix–xx
technologies, election, 34
temporality, 65
testimony, 36, 40, 43, 45, 50–51, 53, 59, 127–128
Teston, Christa, 36
Tetteh, Hannah, 100–101
Thomas, Keith, 29
Thompson, Rachel, 10
Togo, 73
Tracy, Karen, 28, 31, 126
transcendental point of view, xxii
Transfer Voter's List, 49–50
transnationalism, xxi, 78
transparency, 84, 117
transposition errors, 42
Tsikata, Tsatsu, 21, 53–54, 117–119
Twitter, 61–70, 75–76, 80–81, 83, 85, 89, 133–134

U

Uganda, 14
uncivil language, 3, 10
United Gold Coast Convention (UGCC), 102, 109, 112
universalizing narratives, xxiv, xxvi, 5, 66–67, 92, 141–142 (n. 39)
U.S. Capitol attack of January 6, 2021, 131
U.S. presidential election of 2000, xxvii

V

violence, 70, 72–73, 75, 89–90; of colonialism, xxviii; electoral, 20, 70, 73; political, 73, 75, 99–100; racial, 37
Vivian, Bradford, 104–105, 120, 121
Voters' Register, 38–41, 46–50

W

Warner, Michael, 64–65
Weaver, Richard, 144 (n. 3)
Werbner, Richard, 111, 121
Westphalian state system, 64, 67, 128
White supremacist ideals, 37, 132
William, Miriam F., 37
Willis, Justin, 14
"world of experience," 36, 43–50, 56, 58, 127, 149 (n. 23)
"world on paper," 36, 43–50, 53, 56–58, 127, 149 (n. 23)

Y

Yankah, Kwesi, 6–7, 28, 29
YouTube, 63, 78–80, 83, 133

Z

Zanzibar, 68
Zimbabwe, 99, 111